VICTOR WILLING

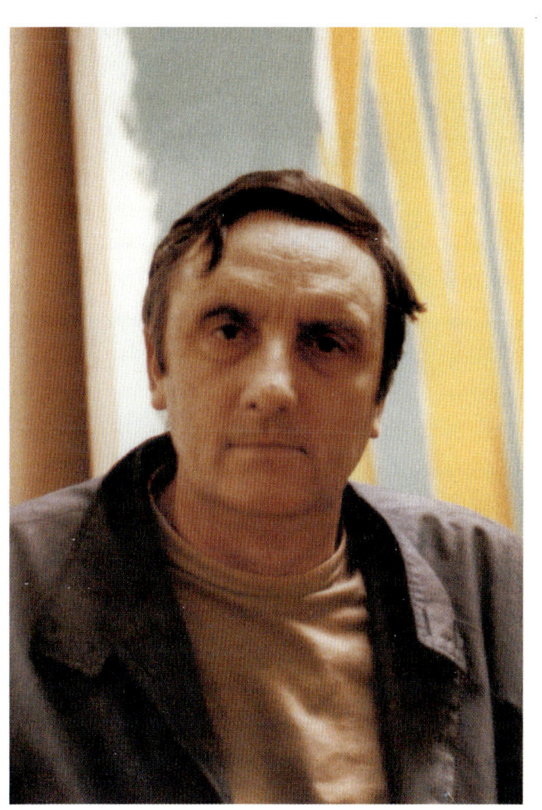

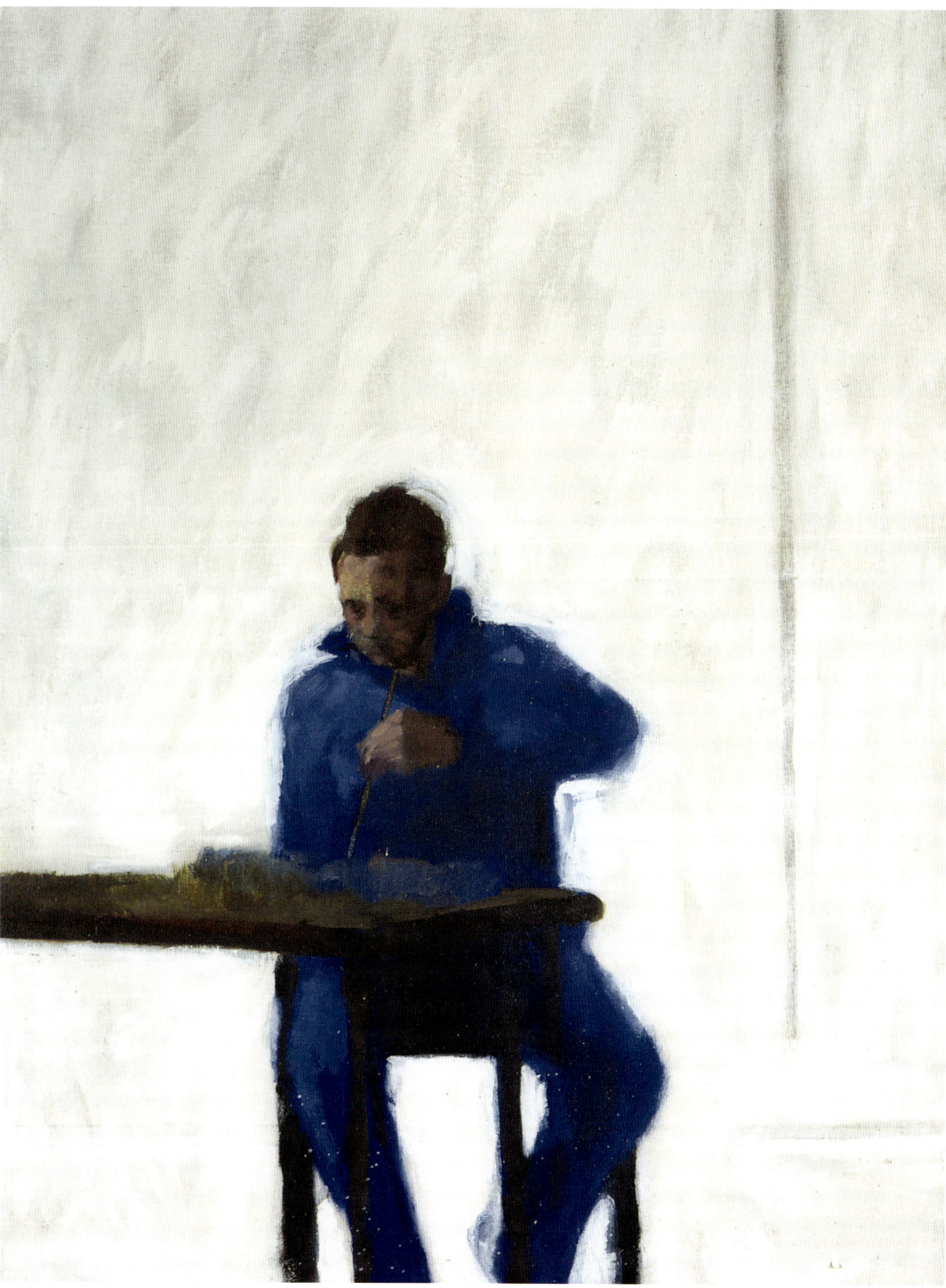

VICTOR WILLING
VISIONS

with a foreword by

Nicholas Serota

and texts by

Elizabeth Gilmore
Victoria Howarth
John McEwen

ART/BOOKS

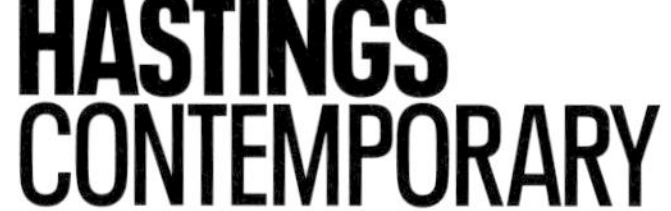

'IT'S A MEANS OF HAVING A SORT OF CONVERSATION WITH MYSELF, AN ATTEMPT TO DISCOVER MYSELF IN A WAY.... I DON'T PAINT PICTURES IN ORDER TO IMPROVE THE WORLD. I DON'T DO THEM IN A DIDACTIC OR PEDAGOGICAL SPIRIT AT ALL. I REALLY AM, I MUST CONFESS, PAINTING VERY MUCH FOR MYSELF.'

PAGE 1
Victor Willing in his
London studio, 1981

PAGE 2
Self-Portrait 1957
Oil on canvas
140 × 100 cm

First published in the United Kingdom in 2019
by Art Books Publishing Ltd in association with
Hastings Contemporary and the Estate of Victor Willing
on the occasion of the exhibition

Victor Willing: Visions

Hastings Contemporary, Hastings
19 October 2019 – 5 January 2020

Art Books Publishing Ltd
18 Shacklewell Lane
London E8 2EZ
Tel: +44 (0)20 8533 5835
info@artbookspublishing.co.uk
www.artbookspublishing.co.uk

British Library Cataloguing-in-Publication Data
A catalogue record for this book is available from
the British Library

ISBN 978-1-908970-53-4

Design, repro, and production by Art / Books
Printed and bound in Latvia by Livonia

Distributed outside North America by
Thames & Hudson
181a High Holborn
London WC1V 7QX
United Kingdom
Tel: +44 (0)20 7845 5000
Fax: +44 (0)20 7845 5055
sales@thameshudson.co.uk

Available in North America through
ARTBOOK | D.A.P.
75 Broad Street, Suite 630
New York, N.Y. 10004
www.artbook.com

FOREWORD
NICHOLAS SEROTA

'In a bright generation Victor Willing burned brighter than most' were the words I used in a catalogue note to introduce Victor to an audience that was almost entirely unfamiliar with his work. The occasion was a retrospective exhibition at the Whitechapel Art Gallery in 1986, in which were included many of the paintings, drawings, and sculptures that Willing had produced in two short periods of activity separated by an unwelcome hiatus of more than fifteen years. Then, as now, his work was little known and underappreciated.

I had seen small exhibitions of new work made after his return from Portugal in the mid-1970s. Here was an artist who seemed to spring, fully formed, from nowhere. In one exhibition at AIR Gallery in 1978, I had been struck by the psychological complexity of his haunting images in which strange conjunctions of metaphysical objects were set on a stage or contained within a room. You could feel the hot dry wind blowing through the dusty scene, or the helplessness of an abandoned sailing boat on a storm-tossed sea. I was also seduced by the beauty and intensity of his small pastel-and-charcoal drawings, isolated on the page by the thin charcoal line of a frame. It was in these fragile images that he first captured compositions that had appeared to him during the 'reverie' associated with the periods of intense pain that occurred when multiple sclerosis began to torment his body.

Of course, I soon discovered that Victor had experienced another life as a star pupil at the Slade in the early 1950s, before his development as a painter was arrested by family responsibilities in Portugal. As I learned more about his beginnings, I came across references to Victor's writing and to his friendship with Michael Andrews, another then underrated painter whom I greatly admired, and his association with a circle that included Francis Bacon and the critic David Sylvester. I began to discover striking images in much earlier paintings, including *Act of Violence*, a composition completed while still a student, and *Winter Machine*, a powerful and original painting that hovers between figuration and abstraction. The idea of making a large exhibition, bringing together early and mature work, began to grow in my mind.

Conversations with Victor ensued and I came to appreciate the depth of thought and the facility that underpinned all of his work. Here was an artist whose practice was founded on an understanding of the European tradition of figurative painting, and yet he also had a profound appreciation of postwar abstraction. His work had been enriched by the experience of a precarious life in a Mediterranean culture and a familiarity with twentieth-century European literature. His illness had obliged him to turn inwards and to explore his own subconscious as a source for narratives that have a universal meaning. Together, these ingredients gave the work a compelling strength.

In the same catalogue note for the Whitechapel exhibition, I asserted that this strength would surely be recognized and that the Slade student 'was no shooting star, but rather a fiery comet which would eventually guide us all'. This exhibition in Hastings provides another opportunity to experience the continuities of touch and composition that are present throughout his career. Willing originally enrolled at the Slade as a student of sculpture, and his early awareness of the way in which the figure occupies space eventually evolved into compositions in which objects become surrogates for the physical and mental states of human existence. His work has an enduring presence and continues to surprise and appeal in its rich complexity.

INTRODUCTION

ELIZABETH GILMORE
VICTORIA HOWARTH

Victor Willing: Visions is the first major British retrospective of work by the artist since his death in 1988. It is also the first gallery-wide exhibition of the new Hastings Contemporary. We relaunched in 2019 with an expanded and dynamic international programme of contemporary and modern art. It could not be more fitting for us, in our inaugural year, to dedicate the entire gallery space to Victor Willing, an artist who has inspired and continues to inspire generations of artists, but perhaps has still not yet received the public recognition that he deserves, following his last significant UK exhibition at the Whitechapel Art Gallery in 1986.

Victor Willing: Visions marks a new and important chapter for Hastings, drawing works from prestigious public and private collections across Europe to the South East and rightly placing Willing back into the public spotlight. The sixty-five paintings, drawings, and sculptures selected for display chart each decade of his tumultuous life and visionary artistic practice, until his untimely death from multiple sclerosis, aged just sixty. From his time at the Slade and celebrated early paintings, through works created in Portugal, where he shared a studio with his wife and fellow artist Paula Rego, to the dynamic 'vision' pictures made in the 1970s as a result of hallucinations, the exhibition offers multiple revelations.

Taking centre stage in the exhibition is the large-scale triptych *Place* (1976–8), described by Rego as 'the best thing Vic ever did'. She identifies the empty chair in the central panel as her husband and the hanging bag as belonging to him, both objects in her mind capturing the lonely abode of the artist. The elevated placement of the two smaller panels on either side of the central canvas plays with the work's elaboration of space, 'enlarging its possibilities', as Rego puts it. She, like many, admired the complexity and heightened sense of reality of *Place*, noting how its unfinished nature resembled the drawings that Willing made when having his visions. These drawings, of which twenty-four are included in the show, were core to his later practice. Their raw directness was a vital life source to his paintings.

As well as previously unseen material from the family archives, the exhibition also features contextual paintings and drawings by several of Willing's contemporaries, namely his wife Rego, Michael Andrews, and Dame Elisabeth Frink. Willing studied with Frink at Guildford School of Art and with Michael Andrews, who became his best friend, at the Slade. Between 1956 and 1974, he lived with Paula in the Rego family home in Ericeira, Portugal. A double-sided canvas features a nude portrait of Paula that Willing painted in 1958, while two years later on the reverse Rego painted her celebrated *Turkish Bath*. The couple were not in the habit of recycling canvases in this way, but it was a legacy of the proximity of their working. We are pleased to premiere as part of the exhibition a new short film about Willing's life and career by his son, the celebrated filmmaker Nick Willing.

An exhibition and publication of this scale would not have been possible without the support of so many lenders and supporters of Victor Willing. We thank Andrew Brown of Art / Books for his intelligent and thoughtful approach to the planning, design, and delivery of this book; and to Sir Nicholas Serota and John McEwen for their insightful writings.

We are very grateful to Tate, Arts Council Collection, Pallant House Gallery, the Ingram Collection, and the Dumfriesshire Educational Trust and Gracefield Arts Centre, who have made the loans of works possible. Also, our grateful thanks go to Marlborough Fine Art for their invaluable support and assistance, particularly John Erle-Drax and Frankie Rossi; to Simon Martin at Pallant House, Jo Baring at the Ingram Collection, and Marcus Harvey and Scott McCracken at Turps art school; and to all of the private lenders who have contributed works to the show.

Most importantly, we are indebted to the assistance of Victor Willing's wife, Dame Paula Rego, and children, Nick, Victoria, and Cas Willing, who collectively embraced the artistic momentum behind this show, and whose commitment, support, and creative generosity have helped make this monumental exhibition a reality.

WHEN WAS NOW?

JOHN McEWEN

'You know that I have eaten of the fruit of the subconscious.'
Jules Laforgue, 'Moralités légendaires'*

'I hope that if my paintings get to you, they do so before the sensible person has had time to draw any conclusion about them at all.'
Victor Willing

'When was now?'
Victor Willing

'People who don't know about art always think it's about being able to make things look like things. No, the difficulty is to do something exclusive to ourselves', said Victor Willing. What makes an artist? What frame of mind produces art? In an age of self-expression, we rely on words like 'being in the zone' to produce that 'soulful' apogee, when, like a lumbering aircraft, the artist, or indeed ourself in sublime moments, defies the gravity of the conscious and has lift off into the freedom of instinct.

The modern artist is confronted not only with the immense baggage train of art history, but with the subjectivity that has grown ever more dominant since the Renaissance, and, in our own era, also with an increasingly diverse perception of his or her physical and psychological being. Much modern art in consequence has searched for the liberation found in childhood. Willing pondered and articulated the ambiguities that arise from these changes, although he did not live to see the full implications of the computer-dominated world. It shows in his artistic memories of being a child. How many children today scribble or draw as a principal pastime? His generation, which was even pre-television, did so as a matter of course.

'We must all remember from childhood the magic when a drawn line "became" an object – cat, dog, horse or whatever. However bizarre the drawing, this line was an exact fit. You could taste your satisfaction as the object appeared before your eyes, first-time excitement palpable in the drawn line. Just so, for the adult, "the thought made in the mouth" determines the speed of its expression, the speed of the drawn line.' In a conversation towards the end of his life, he repeated the thought. 'All my life, I've tried to recapture the intense pleasure in painting and drawing that I had as a child, when I did battles with people going "Aaaaarrgh!"' Gurgling laughter followed the blood-curdling cry.

* A quotation from one of Victor Willing's favourite books, *The Poetics of Reverie* by Gaston Bachelard

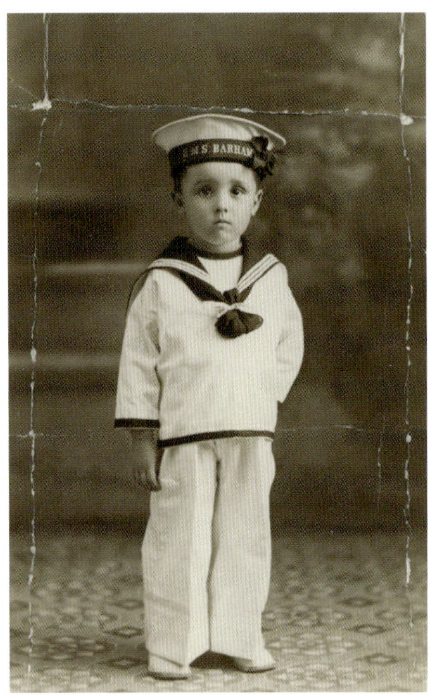

ABOVE
Willing dressed as a sailor, age three

BELOW
With his father, in the late 1930s

His father was a regular soldier, so his early life was peripatetic, including childhood years in Egypt. The camp bordered the desert. He did not remember ever wandering beyond the block-house grid of the compound, but there was a family legend that his father once rescued him from the sandy wastes where he was found 'shooing' some vultures from the carcass of a donkey.

In later years, he underwent Jungian analysis and was told he might have suffered from being a 'battered baby'. Again, he had no memory of anything so drastic, but one painful episode from childhood did stand out. It was after the return to England, a move not welcomed by his mother, who loathed the climate and blamed it for an irritating skin complaint. 'Once she was so exasperated by me that she hung me up by my braces from a hook behind a cupboard door and then shut me in, so that I was hanging in the dark. Apparently, I was so enraged and frightened I kicked out the panels of the door.'

The vital witness to these boyhood years is Willing's best friend since their first meeting at Guildford's Royal Grammar School, John Mills, later the head of the Scientific Department at the National Gallery. Mills remembered his friend's schooling being 'punctuated by moves from place to place' as his soldier father was posted around southern England. 'Vic was always aware ... that we *do* live on the edge; that the cherished, the comfortable, the familiar is indeed

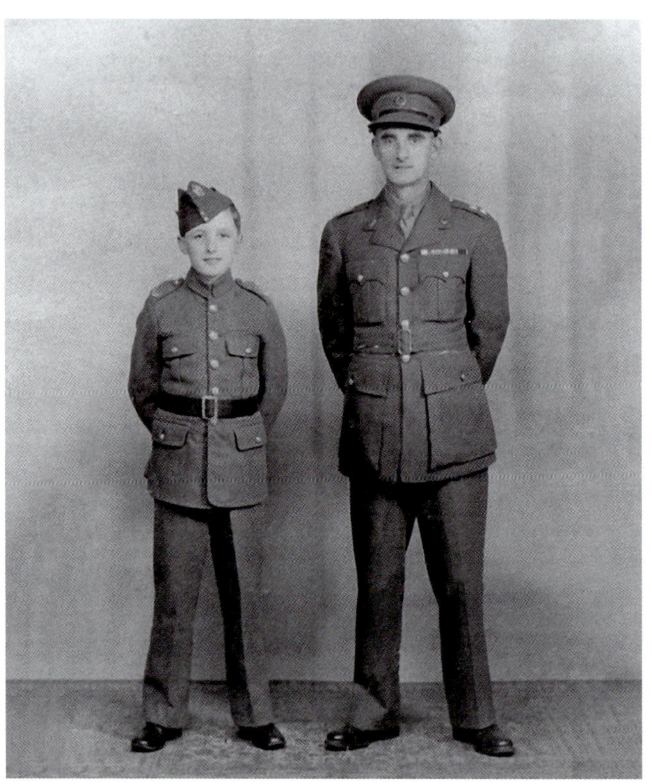

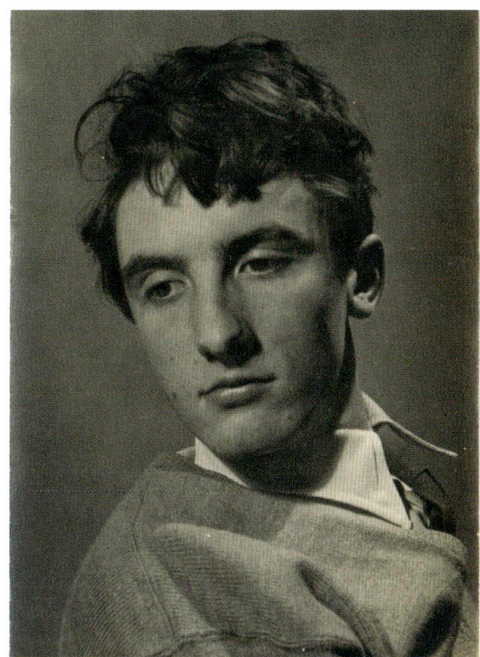

ABOVE
Willing at the age of seventeen

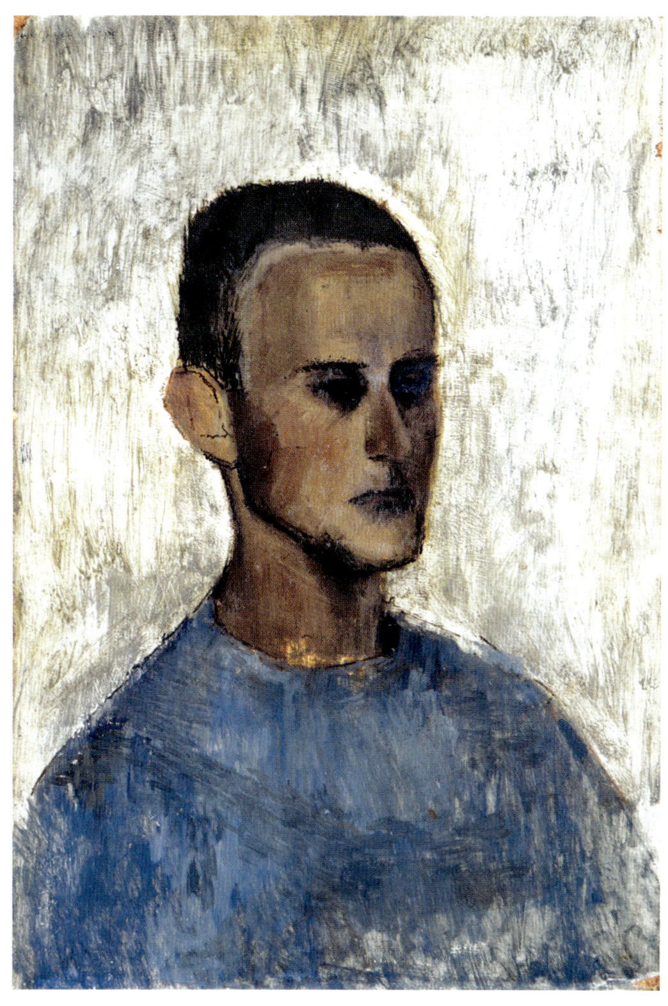

RIGHT
Portrait of John Mills 1951
Oil on board
56 × 38 cm

delicately poised and easily subverted. When mischance makes itself manifest, the only true response is the laugh (perhaps the slightly bitter laugh) of recognition ... the frequent removals of his childhood may have had much to do with this.'

The art historian Lynne Cooke in her catalogue essay 'Thought made in the mouth' for Willing's 1986 retrospective at the Whitechapel Art Gallery, the worthy climax to his career granted by Nicholas Serota to his great credit, identified three periods in his artistic evolution. The first began with his paintings done at the Slade School of Art, from which he graduated in 1954, and up to 1960. It was largely concerned with the figure, both the nude model and from the wider world of acquaintance and observation. It reflected what Professor Alfred Gerrard, his tutor in the sculpture department into which he was first enrolled, pointed out: that it is possible to recognize persons we know at a distance, as an entity. It was the following year that he had his first solo show – at Erica Brausen's prestigious Hanover Gallery, which represented Francis Bacon.

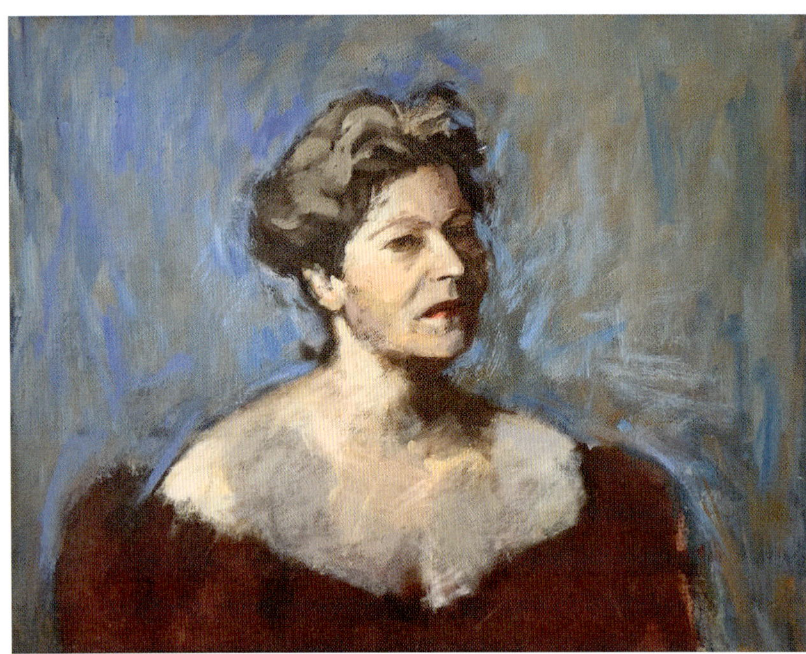

LEFT
Portrait of Tia Narcisa *c.* 1958
Oil on canvas
50 × 65 cm

BELOW
Act of Violence
(also known as Fighting Men) 1952
Oil on board
153 × 182 cm
UCL Art Museum

OPPOSITE
Standing Nude
c. 1952–3
Oil on canvas
154 × 123 cm
Tate: Purchased 1996

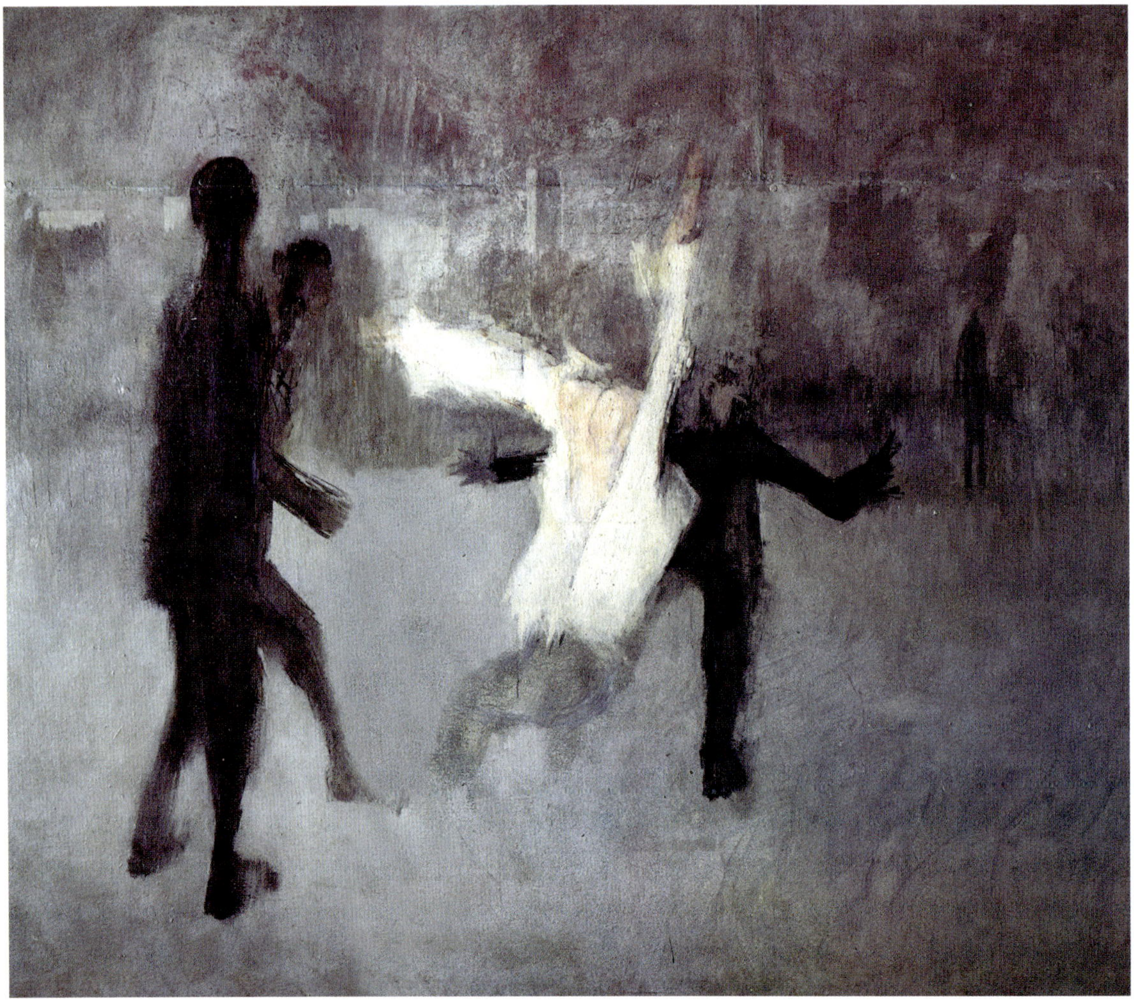

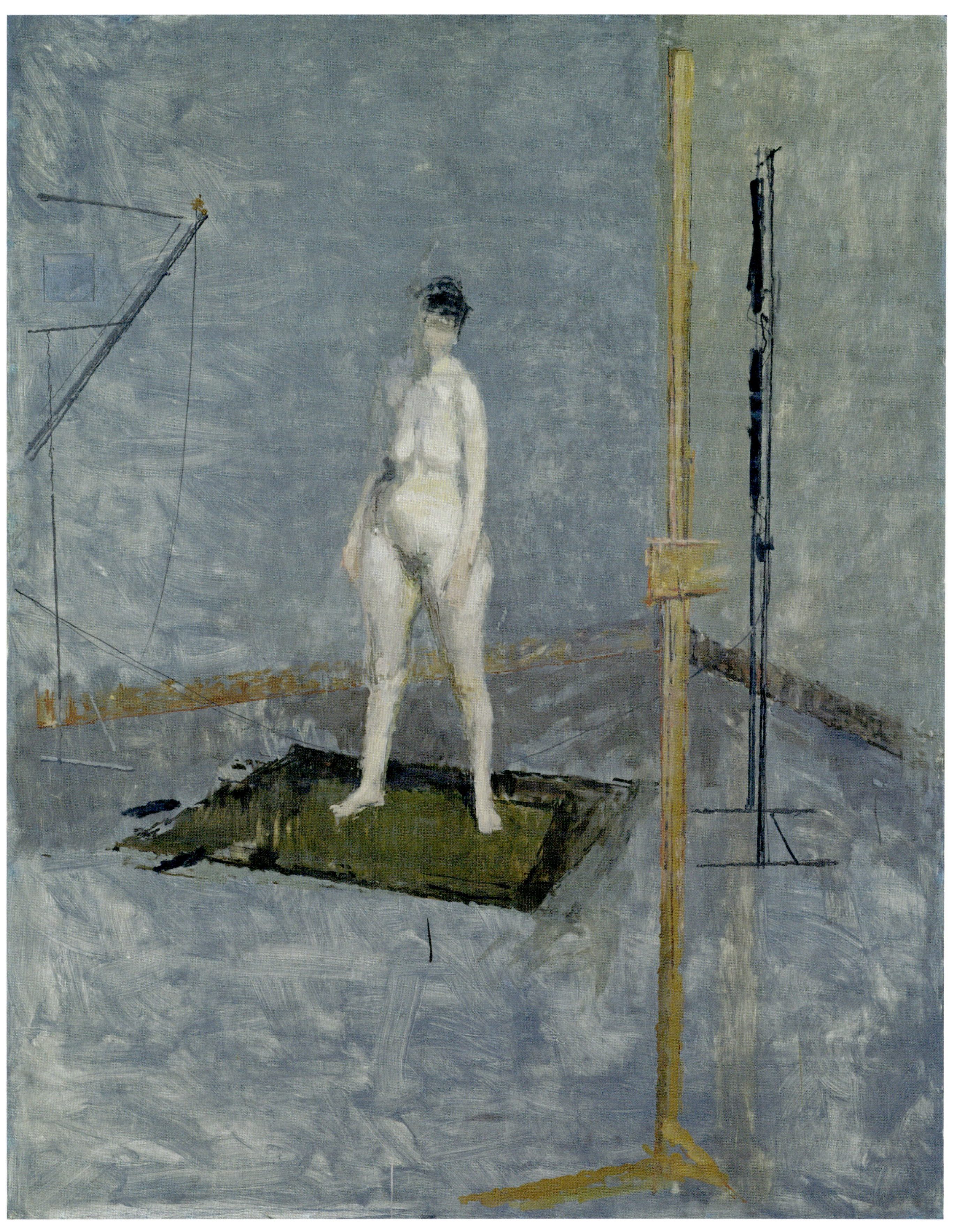

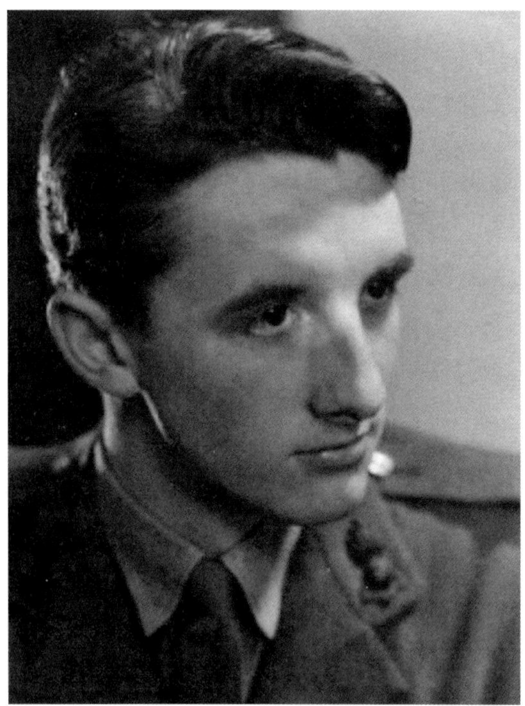

Victor Willing in his Royal Artillery uniform during his period of National Service, 1946–8

The next period that Cooke identified marks the years he resumed painting in earnest, between 1974 and 1984, after more than a decade of stasis and non-involvement spent largely in Portugal with his second wife Paula Rego and their three children, Caroline (Cas), Victoria (Vicky), and Nicholas (Nick), today respectively writer, actress, and film director. And finally to the period of the nine pastel drawings and ten paintings of humorously imagined heads that constituted his last work and were inspired by watching television coverage of Royal Ascot, with its often ludicrously competitive ladies' hats. This has become the consensus view of his development, but there is another set of surviving paintings, done in the late 1950s and early 1960s, that disrupts the progression to a dramatic climax. Canvases such as *Precarious Drag* and *Lech* from 1957 (*pp. 60–1, 62*), *No. 13* from 1959 (*p. 63*), and two untitled 1961 pictures (*pp. 31, 65*) anticipate the work for which he is best known and are discussed later.

Willing was a born artist. Mills remembered him as a schoolboy 'drawing a swallow in flight as if he were tracing the outline of an image already on the paper'. But before the Slade came National Service. 'He once explained to me how closely the army paralleled the monastic life: the abnegation of self and submission to others' will; the regularity of its discipline; the careful delineation and organisation of the soldier's living space and the disposition of his few necessary possessions. I am not wrong, I think, in finding echoes of this still in his late work.'

'"Travel light" was one of his mantras', Cas Willing recalls, 'he had a bit of the nomad about him.' Her brother Nick remembers the insistence 'to plough your own furrow'. When he was having a hard time at film school, his father advised him: 'You're only ever really good when you're too young to know or too old to care, so do your own thing while you can, you may not get another chance to take such risks for a long time.'

At the Slade, Willing was the star of a talented generation that included his particular friend Michael Andrews, as well as Peter Snow, Myles Murphy, Euan Uglow, Craigie Aitchison, and the younger prize-winning Rego, his wife-to-be. 'I was a bit of a rebel at the Slade and quite a star, as a result', Willing recalled. 'I used to scandalise my sober teachers by telling them I admired Sargent, that sort of thing.' His rebellious nature also showed in a painting of a monkey on a table, currently lost. It did not please his teachers. Slade teaching was based on drawing and the life class, legacy of a long-held reverence for Cézanne's dictum: 'Treat nature in terms of the cylinder, the sphere, the cone, everything brought into proper perspective.' Meticulous use of the plumb line and the marked and measured position of the model

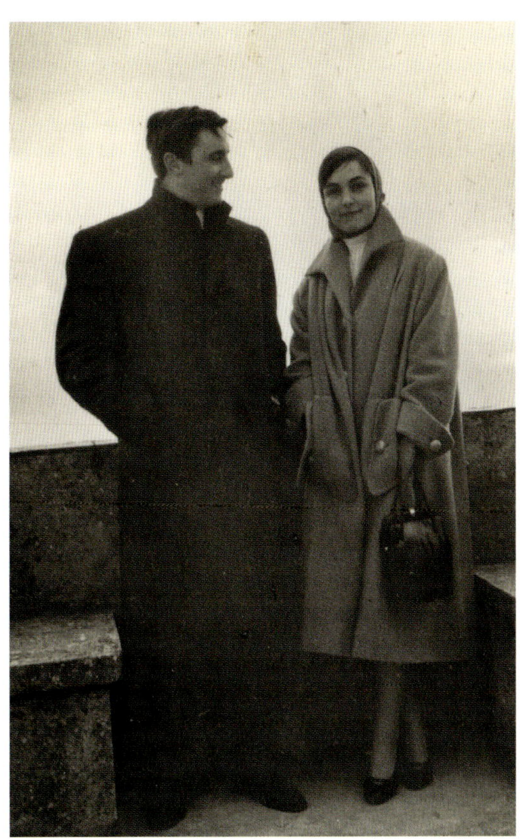

ABOVE
With Paula Rego,
early to mid-1950s

BELOW RIGHT
Head of a Girl (Paula Rego) 1954
Oil on canvas
49 × 62 cm
Dumfriesshire Educational Trust, Gracefield Arts Centre, Dumfries

to ensure exact perspectival accuracy were sacrosanct. 'Oh Cézannah!' a joshing pre-First World War retort was still applicable. Willing's monkey was considered 'outré', monkey business indeed; but the monkey, the need to be true to himself, would one day triumph. In *Judge* from 1982 (p. 44), with its makeshift 'throne' and accusatory plumb line, he seems to have taken wry revenge.

Willing invited artists to the school, most daringly Francis Bacon. 'Bacon was a hero because he was a dandy. He didn't conform to the normal idea of an artist at all.' And he persuaded David Sylvester, later Bacon's chronicler, to address the sketch club. 'That is how I got to know these glamorous, demi-mondain figures.' 'Vic was so brainy' is how Aitchison, a mature student who had qualified as a lawyer, summed up his friend.

For a short time after his graduation in 1954, Willing lodged in the same building as Bacon. Subsequent critical conclusions that he was influenced by the association earned his strong disapproval. He disliked criticism that sought to expose artistic influences. 'I admit to Bacon's influence, but I like to think it was more to do with his personality, his attitudes, than any imitation of his pictures. For instance, he introduced me to Nietzsche's book *The Birth of Tragedy*, which explains a lot about his attitude to art. Much of the theatricality in Bacon's work owes its origin to Nietzsche. Nietzsche examines the Dionysian origins of Greek tragedy, which are the excessive opposite of the Apollonian orderliness commonly associated with the art of Ancient Greece.' What image could be more Dionysian than Willing's 1982 painting *Cythère* (pp. 98–9), where the rampant plant threatens to engulf rigid geometrical order?

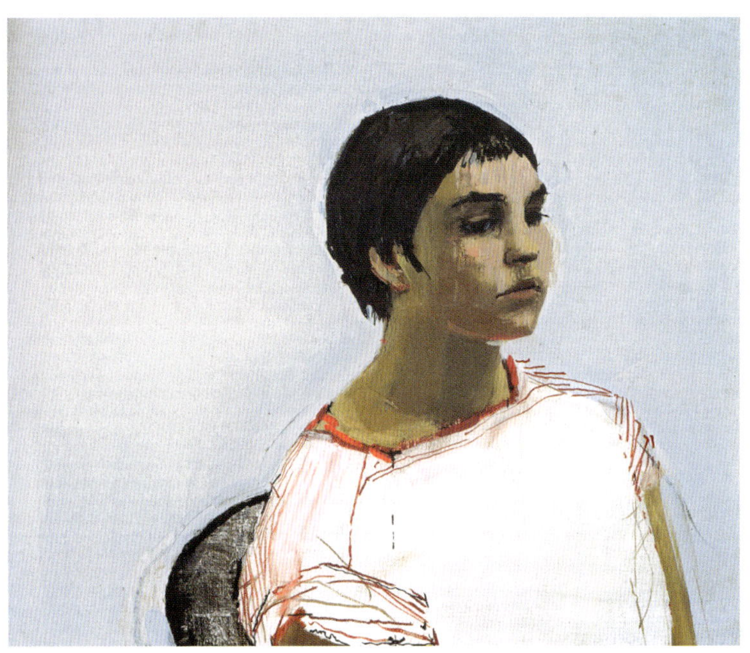

In one of his celebrated interviews with Sylvester, Bacon said: 'You see, all art has now become completely a game by which man distracts himself. And you may say it has always been like that, but now it's entirely a game. And I think that that is the way things have changed, and what is fascinating now is that it's going to become more difficult for the artist, because he must really deepen the game to be any good at all.' In conversation, Bacon joked that these interviews were more about Sylvester than him, but the above quotation has the ring of truth. He thought his best interview was one for television over lunch with Melvyn Bragg, when alcohol loosened his tongue. He told Bragg: 'I've made images that the intellect would never make. I make images of realism. The violence of life, of sensation. I believe in nothing, except the sensation of the moment. I drift.' To me, he once said: 'All I want from art is excitement.' Willing called Bacon 'the autumn rose of Romanticism'.

On graduating from the Slade, Willing's professional career began with the bang of the Hanover Gallery show in 1955. Then he abandoned his wife and fled to Portugal in the wake of Rego, who was carrying his first child. They married in due course and set up home

Michael Andrews
Quinta in Ericeira 1963
Pencil on paper
50 × 30 cm
Copyright © The Estate of Michael Andrews

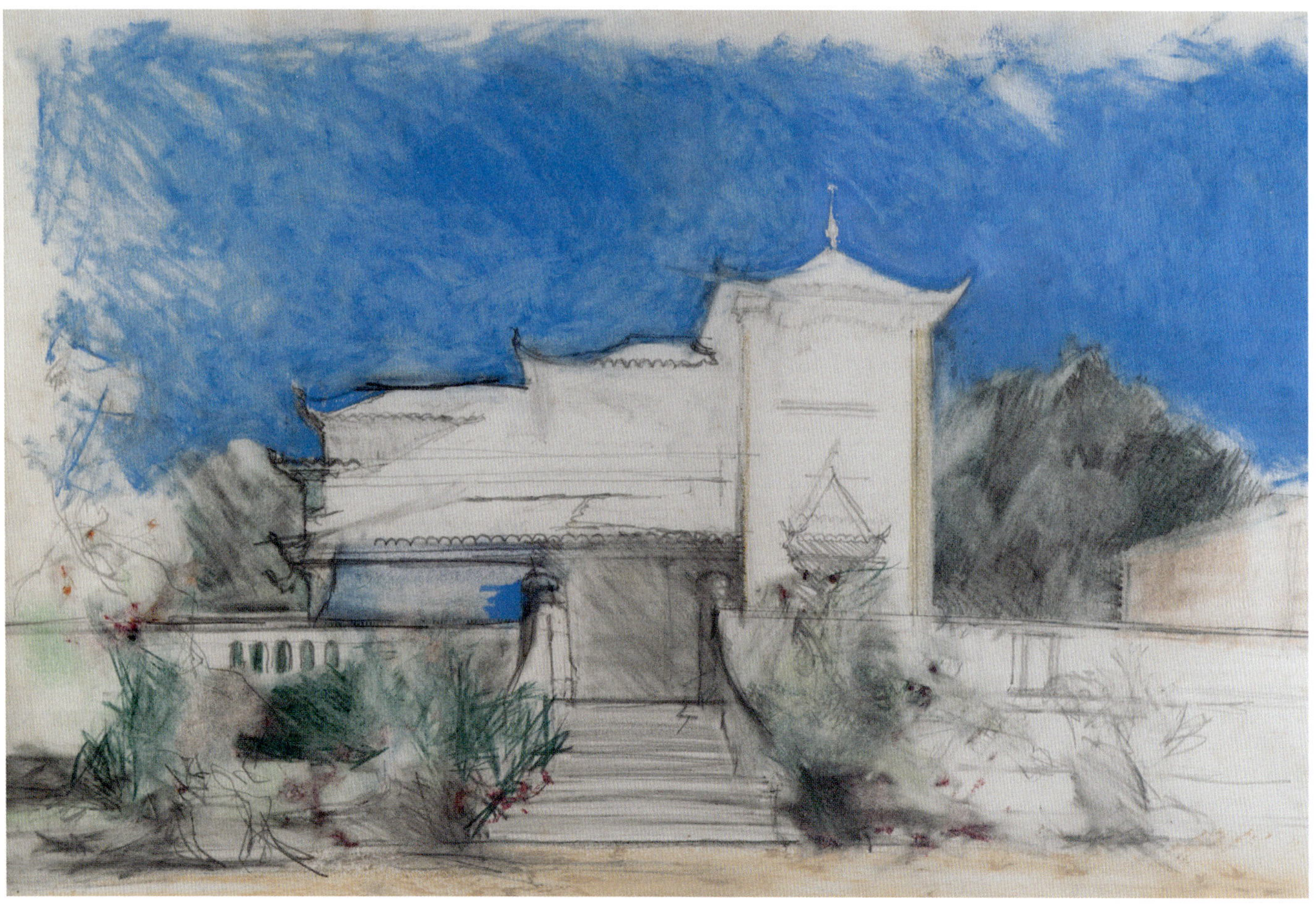

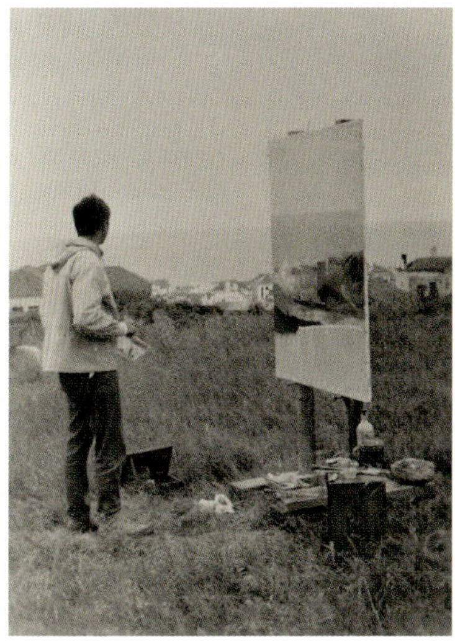

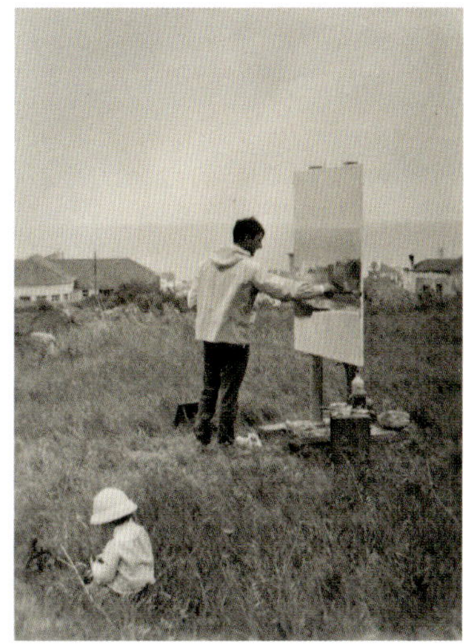

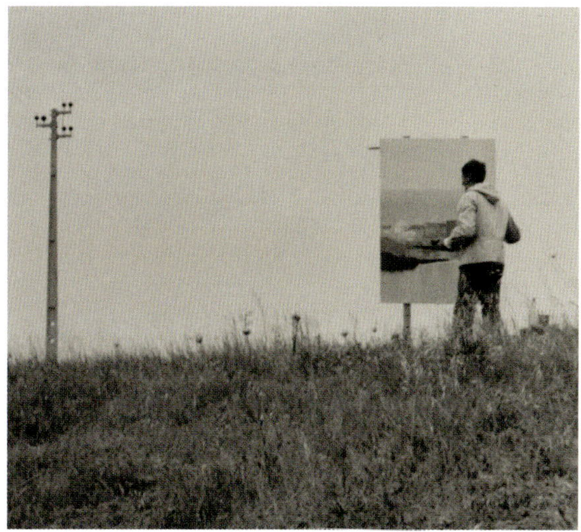

Willing painting in Ericeira, 1958

in the delightful family *quinta* outside the fishing village of Ericeira, using a barn as their shared studio. Suspended sacking divided the space. While Rego busily painted, he deliberated. 'We'd talk about art together all the time', Paula has written in an essay on the much later painting *Callot: Harridan* (p. 101). And she always says he was her best critic. They were utterly different artists, but they knew each other's art inside out. They were guardians of each other's artistic independence. Nonetheless in Portugal, while her career blossomed, his went on hold. Life should have been idyllic, but lack of English company sometimes drove them to hang out at tourist bars merely to hear the language spoken. Visiting artist friends from London – among them Peter Snow, Michael Andrews, Patrick Caulfield, and Andrew Forge – were eagerly anticipated.

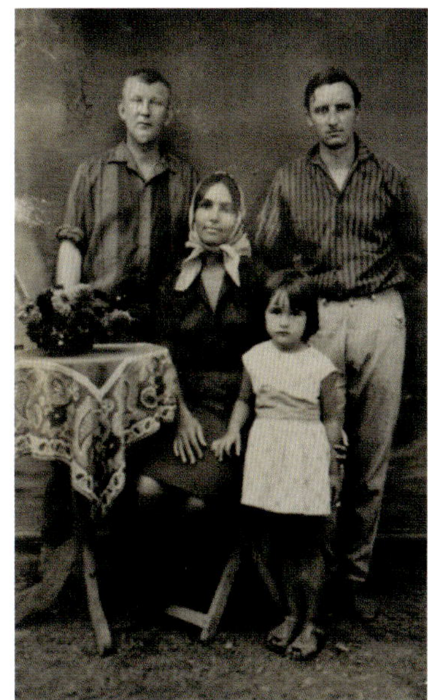

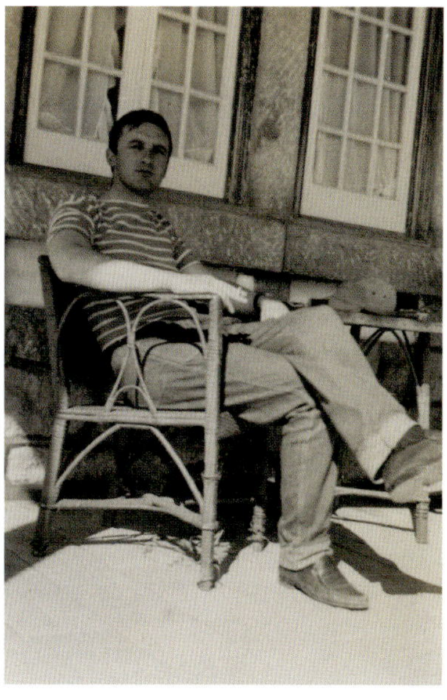

RIGHT
Willing and Rego with their daughter Caroline and Peter Snow, Ericeira, 1960

FAR RIGHT
Willing at the family *quinta* in Ericeira, late 1950s

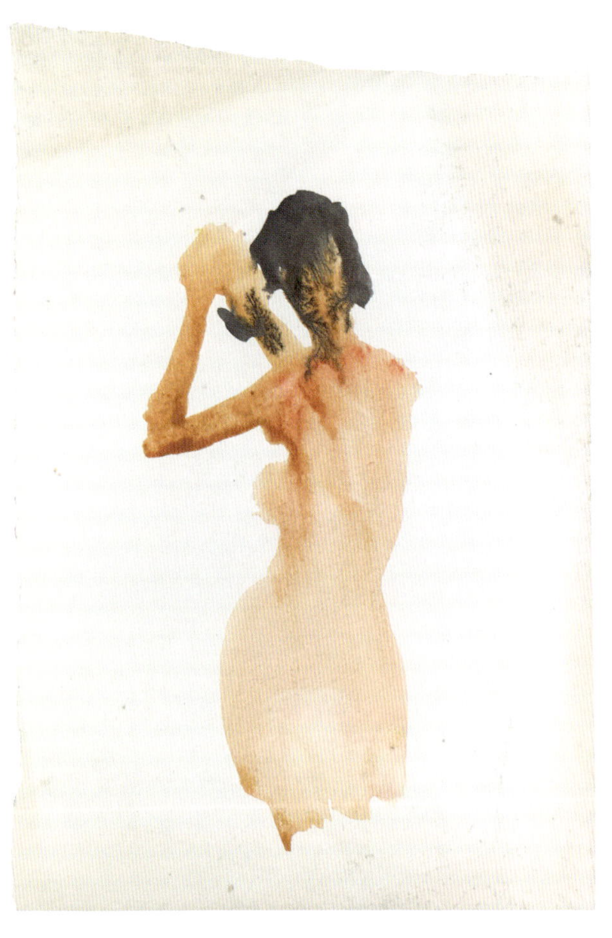
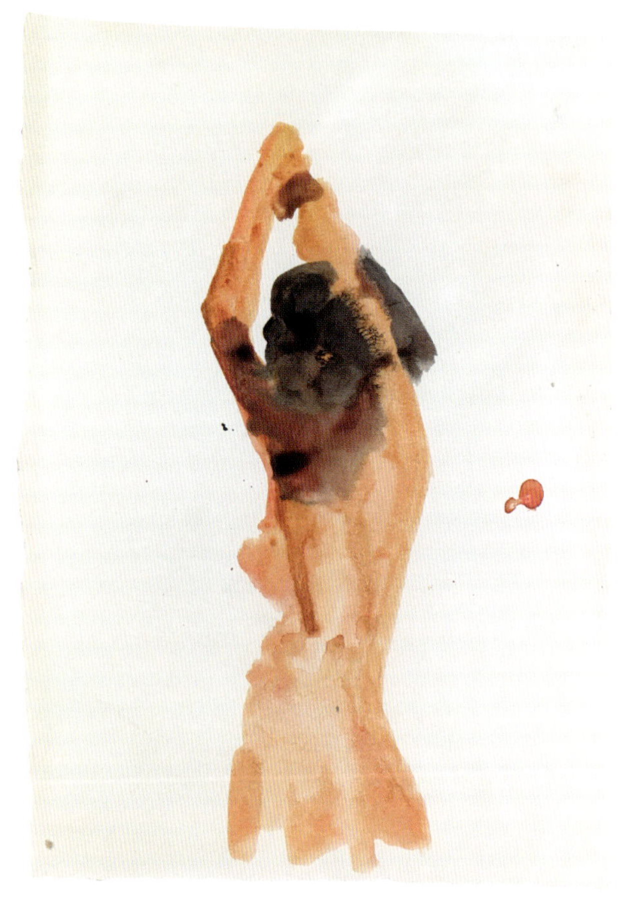
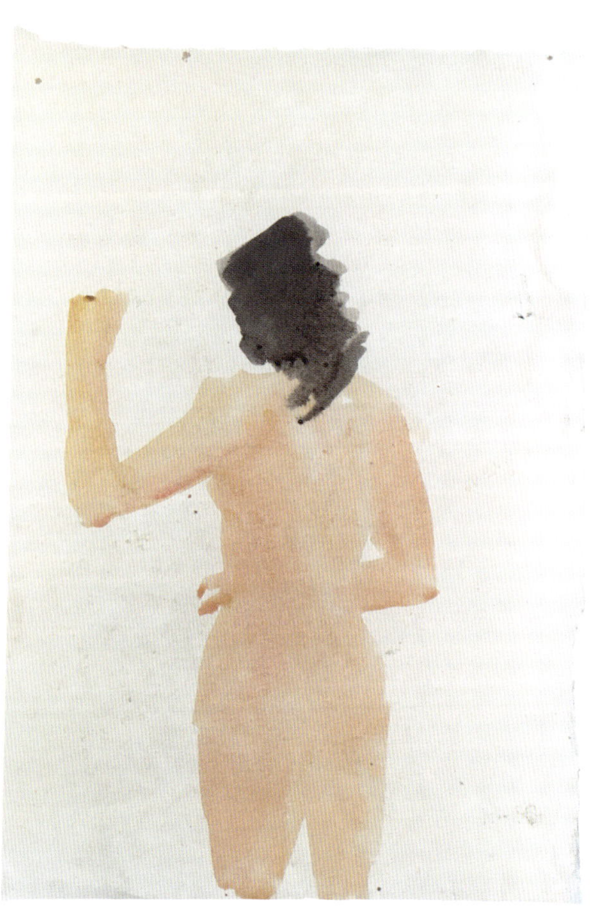
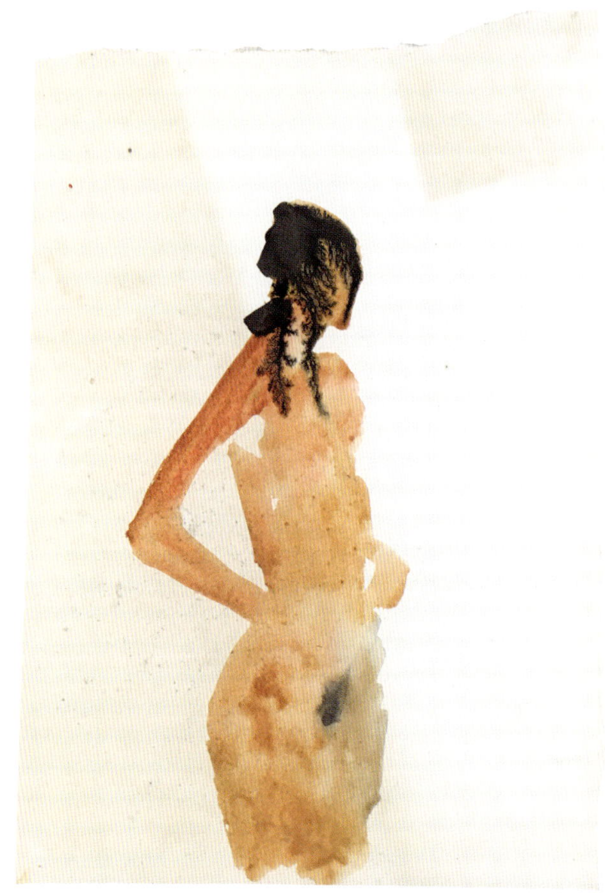

OPPOSITE
Paula nudes *c.* 1958
Watercolour on paper
each 30 × 21 cm

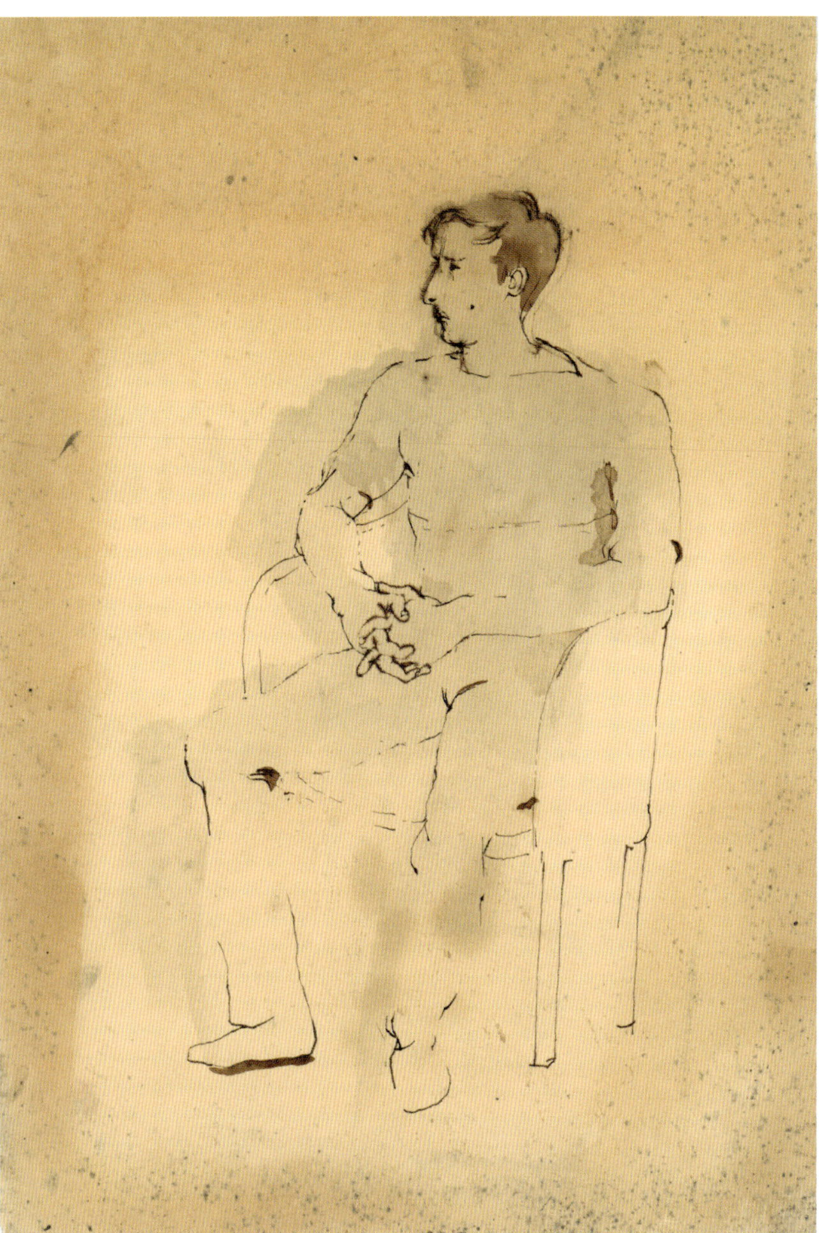

Paula Rego
Portrait of Vic 1957
Pen and ink
on paper
30.5 × 21 cm

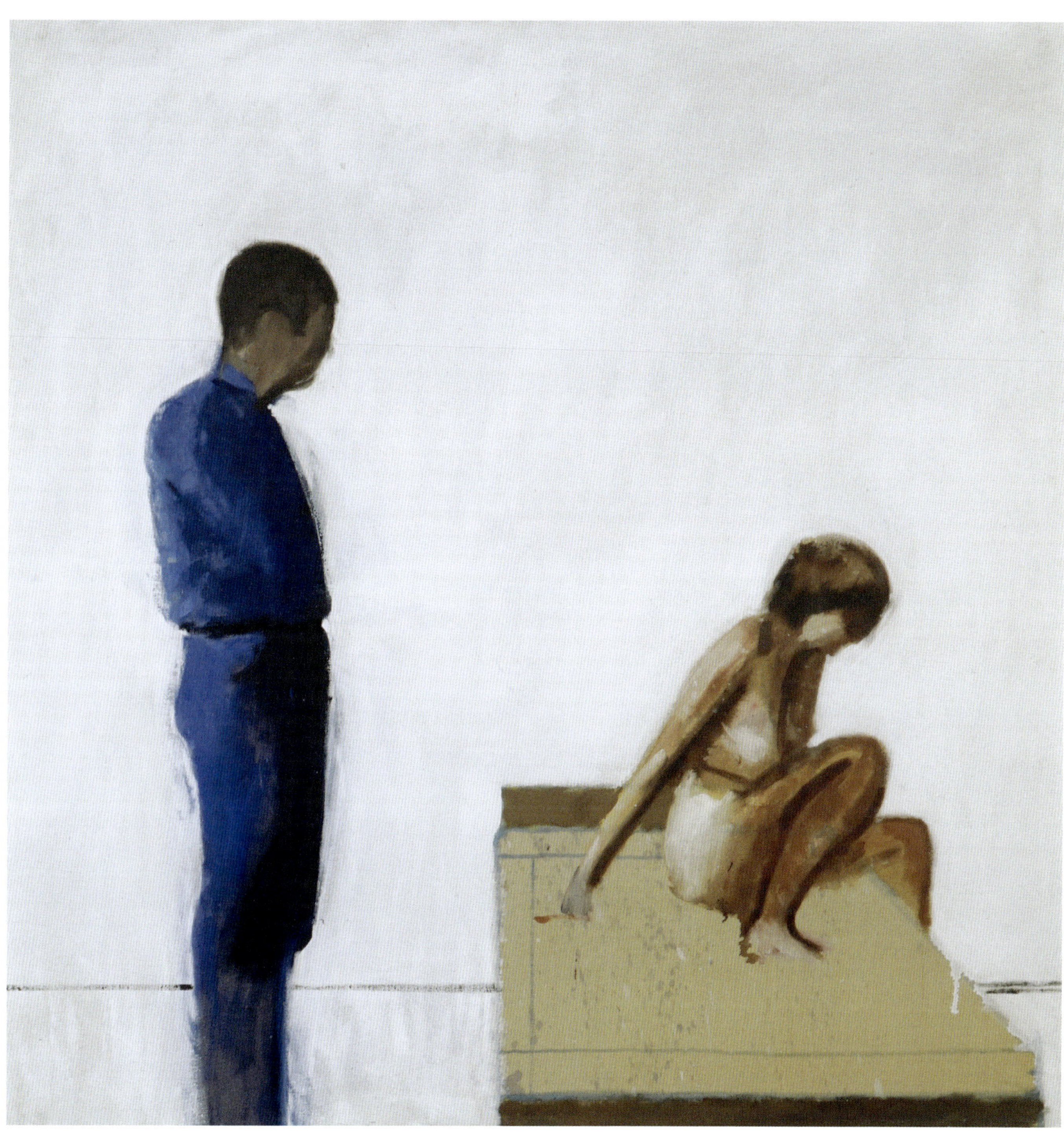

Standing Figure and Nude 1957
Oil on canvas
140 × 140 cm

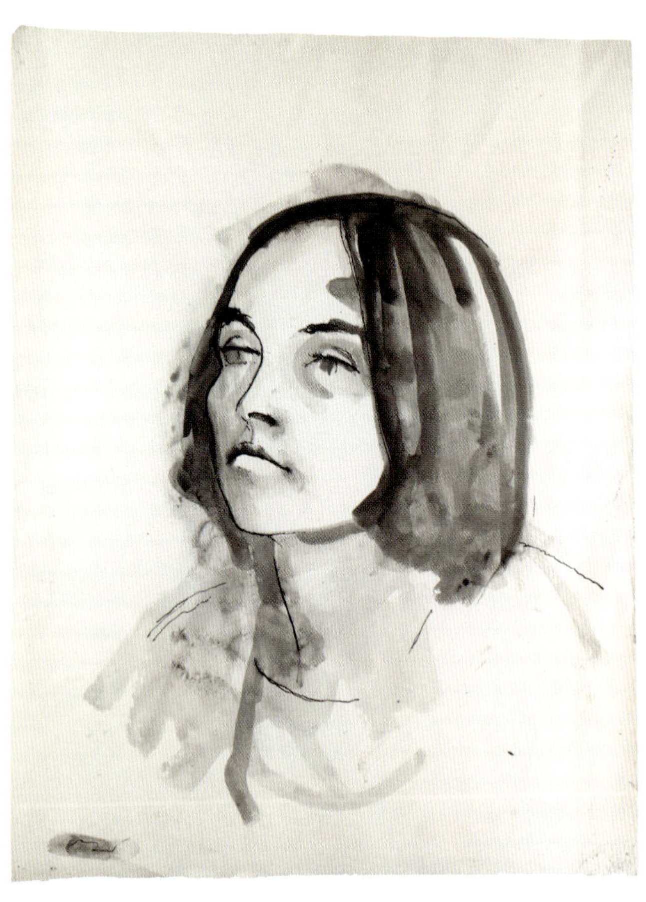

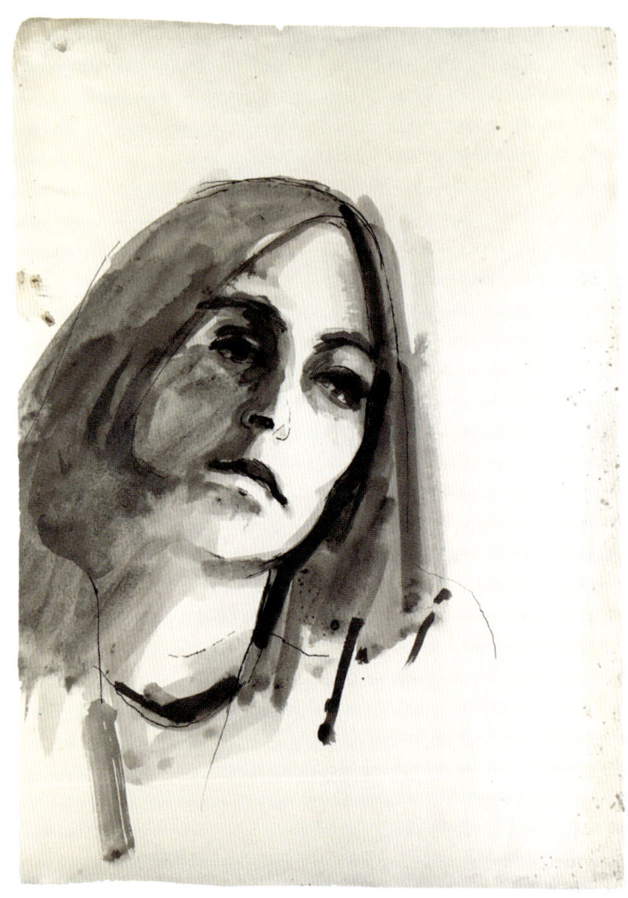

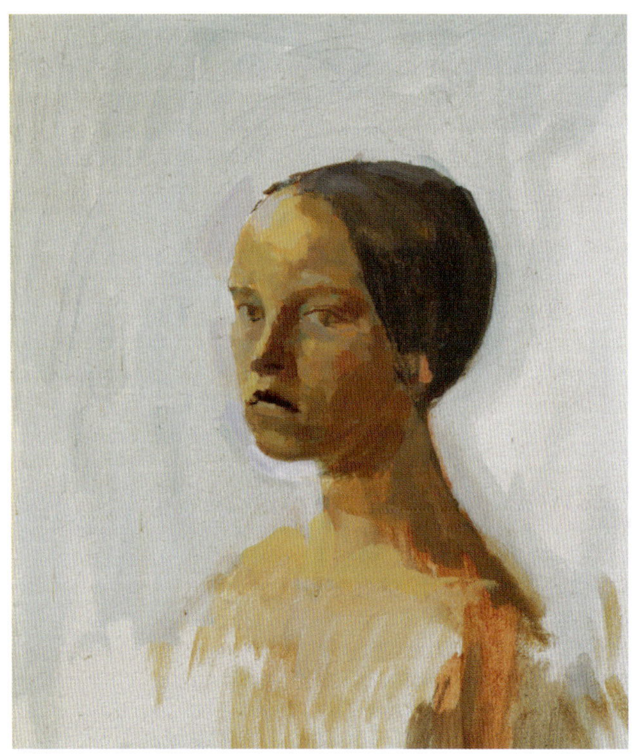

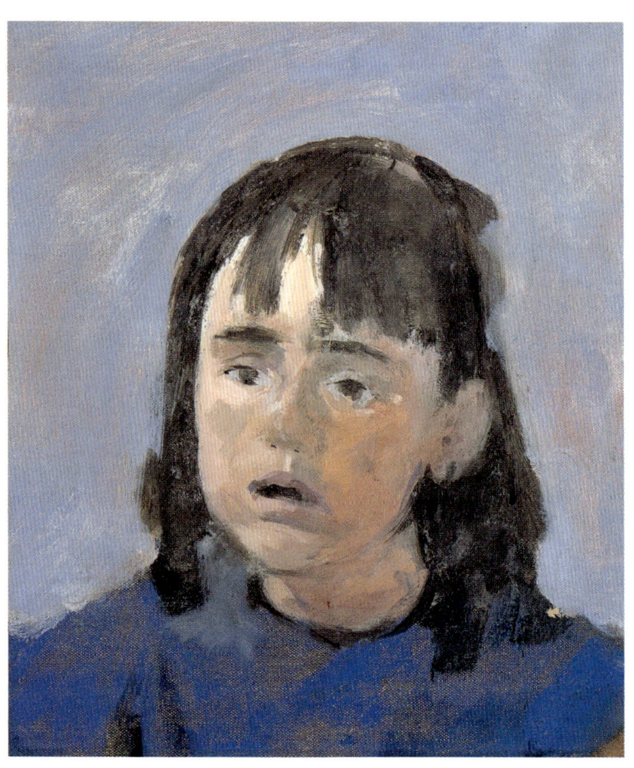

OPPOSITE, TOP
Paula 1958
Indian ink and
wash on paper
each 43 × 29 cm

OPPOSITE,
BOTTOM LEFT
Portrait of Victoria 1973
Oil on canvas
35 × 27 cm

OPPOSITE,
BOTTOM RIGHT
Portrait of Caroline 1958
Oil on canvas
32 × 29 cm

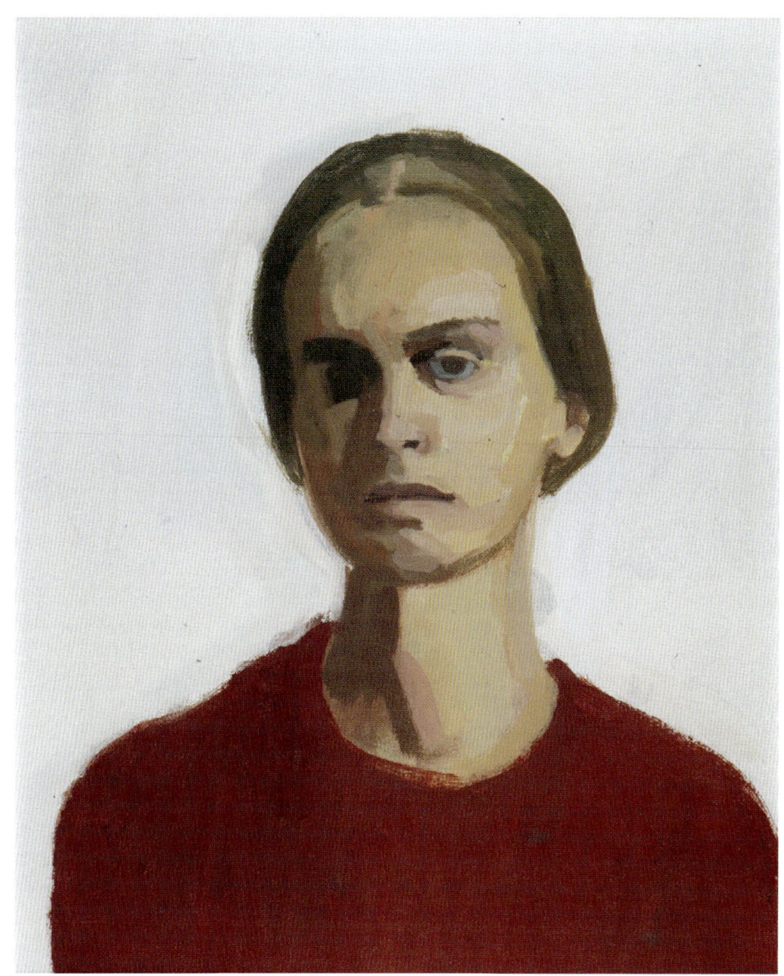

Portrait of Ana 1972
Oil on canvas
49 × 41 cm

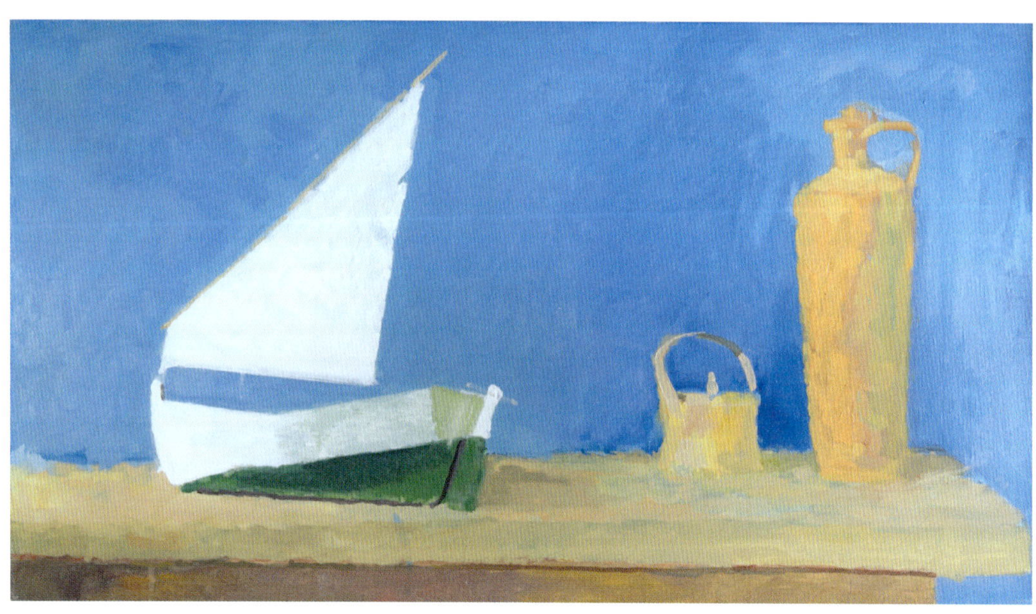

Still Life with Model Boat 1957
Oil on canvas
53 × 95 cm

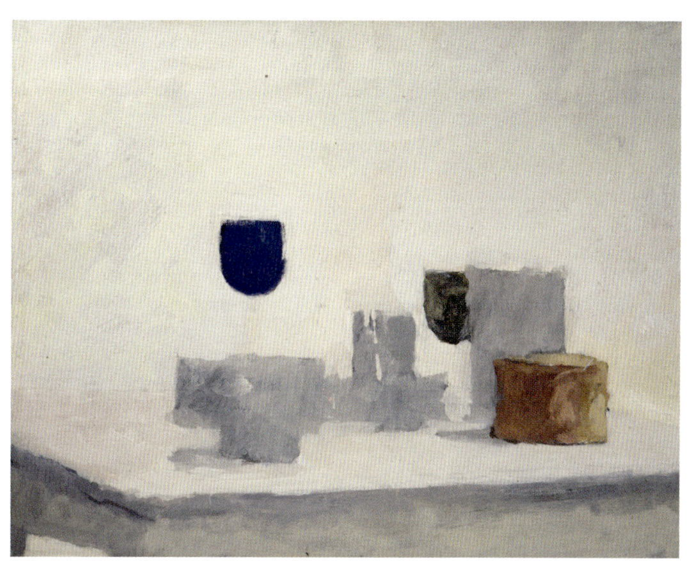

Still Life 1958
Oil on canvas
42 × 54 cm

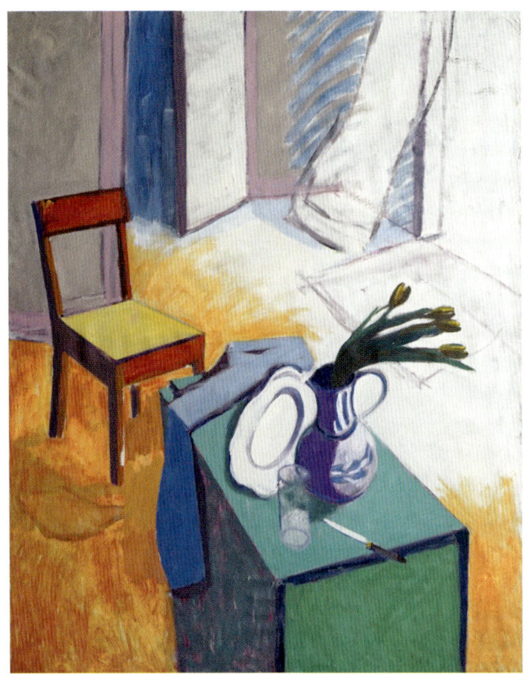

ABOVE
Matisse's Sideboard 1974
Oil on canvas
150 × 121 cm

RIGHT
Victor Willing in his studio
in Ericeira, 1957

Once, impulsively, Willing rolled up some experimental canvases, personal expressions in the spirit of the outlawed monkey of his student days, and drove to London to show them to Forge, a Slade contemporary whose opinion he respected and whose career as a teacher and radio pundit had burgeoned. But Forge remained true to Slade methodology. He told Willing that the pictures were no good and he should return to the figurative painting that had earned him his Hanover show. Willing went back to Portugal crushed. 'Dad knew about painting and he knew what he wanted to achieve', Cas has written. 'He set himself such high standards that ultimately it was his own inner critic that crippled him. Andrew Forge voiced his fears.'

The few of these paintings from the late 1950s and early 1960s that survive, among them *Precarious Drag*, *Lech*, *No. 13*, and the two untitled canvases from 1961, show that they anticipate the work of his self-discovery in the 1970s and 1980s, the art of his acclaim. There is the same sense of absence (no figures) and of suspension (hanging clothes and objects). What they lack is the clarity that was to come and is already there in the two versions of *Matisse's Sideboard*, painted in 1974, a prelude to the soon-to-be witnessed 'scenarios', when the 'monkey' of his subconscious at last ran riot.

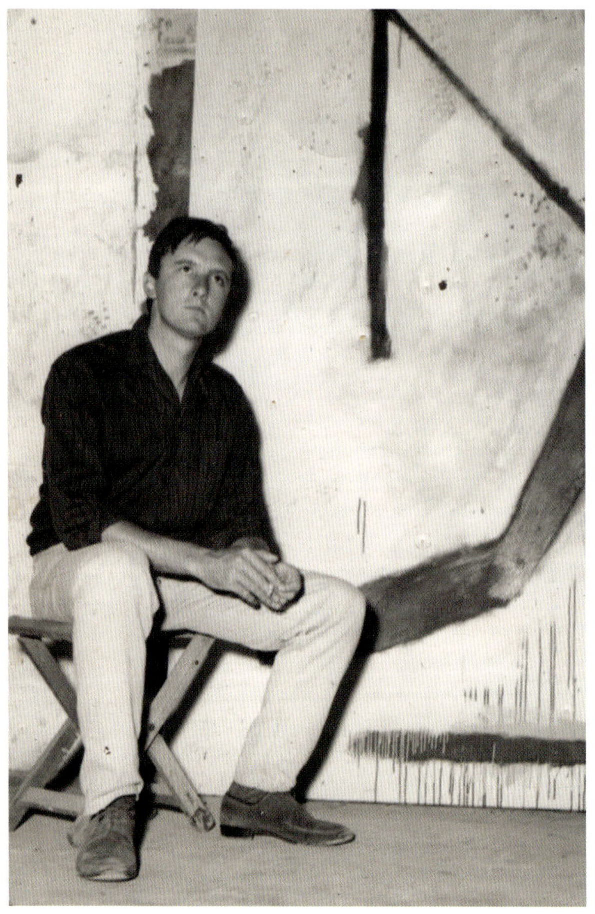

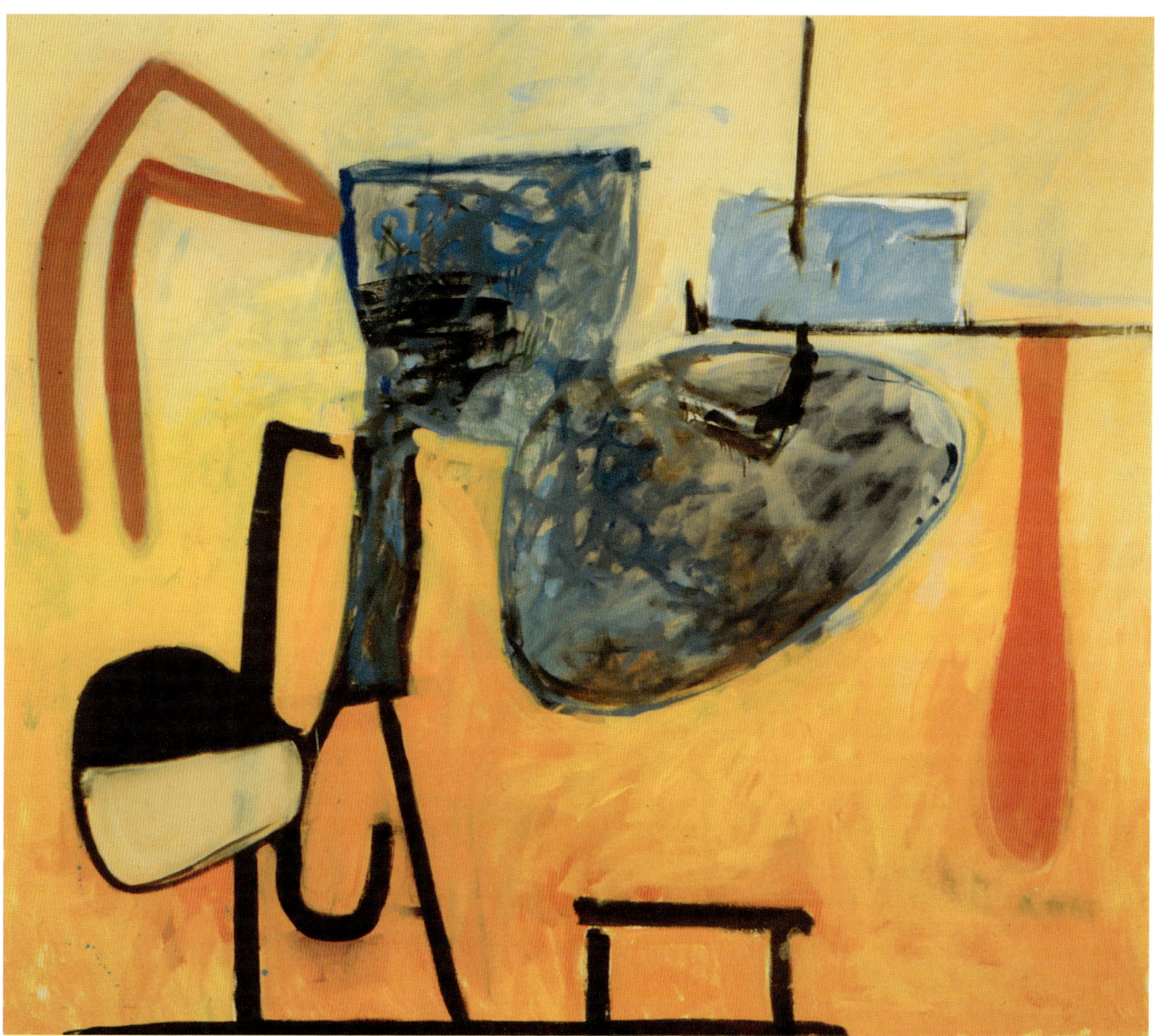

Untitled 1961
Oil on canvas
176 × 150 cm

After six years, Rego's father eased this artistic isolation. In 1962, he enabled the family to spend part of the year in London by buying them a house in Camden Town. Meanwhile, Paula's career would continue to prosper to the degree that by the end of the decade she represented Portugal at the 1969 São Paulo Bienal.

One afternoon, musing on the terrace of the *quinta* after a simple but delicious Portuguese lunch of grilled fish bought on the beach that morning, newly baked bread, and local wine, Willing thought: 'This is it, for God's sake! People work all their lives to be in my situation, and here I am, young and healthy, getting it now – yet I know there's something wrong with my life.' Not long after, he woke in darkness with earth in his mouth. He thought he had been buried alive, but he had blacked out and fallen on his face from a heart attack.

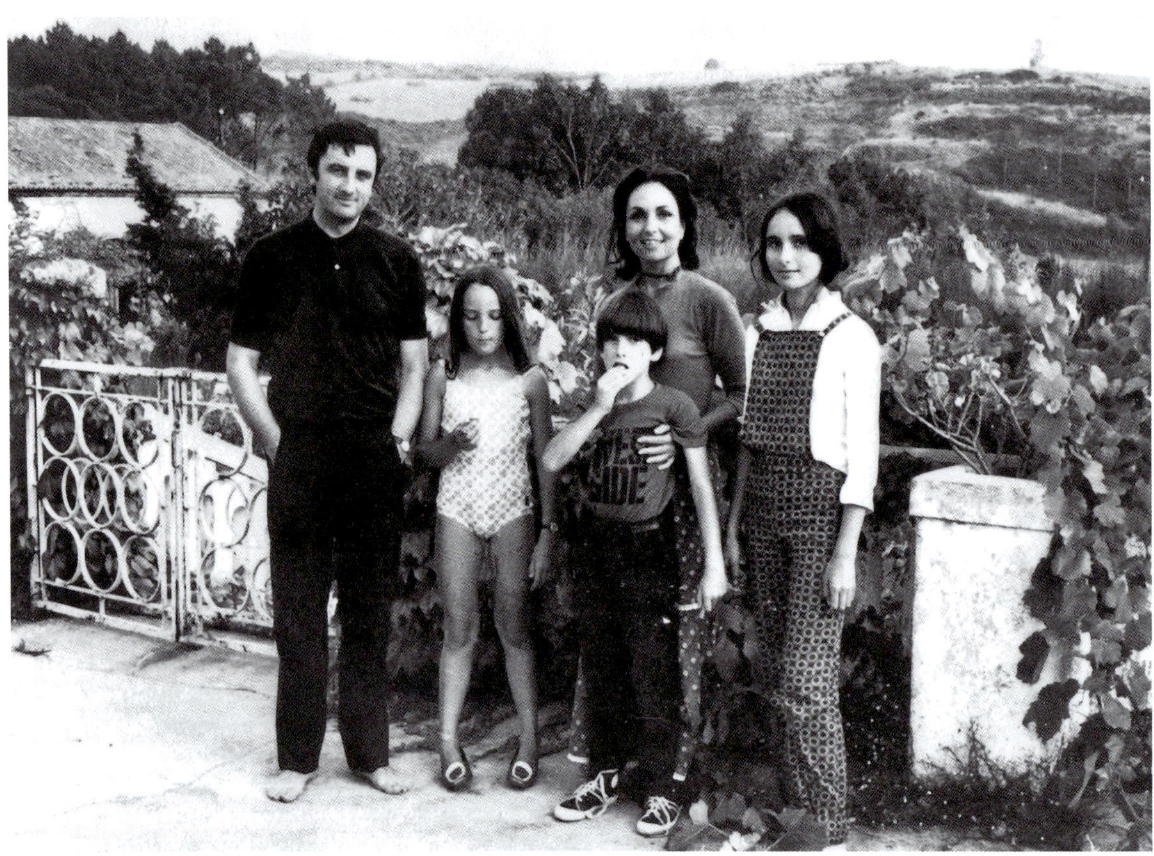

Willing and Rego with Caroline, Nicholas, and Victoria on the *quinta* terrace in 1970 (all photographs on these pages by Rego's cousin Manuela Morais)

BELOW
Vic and Paula at the *quinta*, 1960s

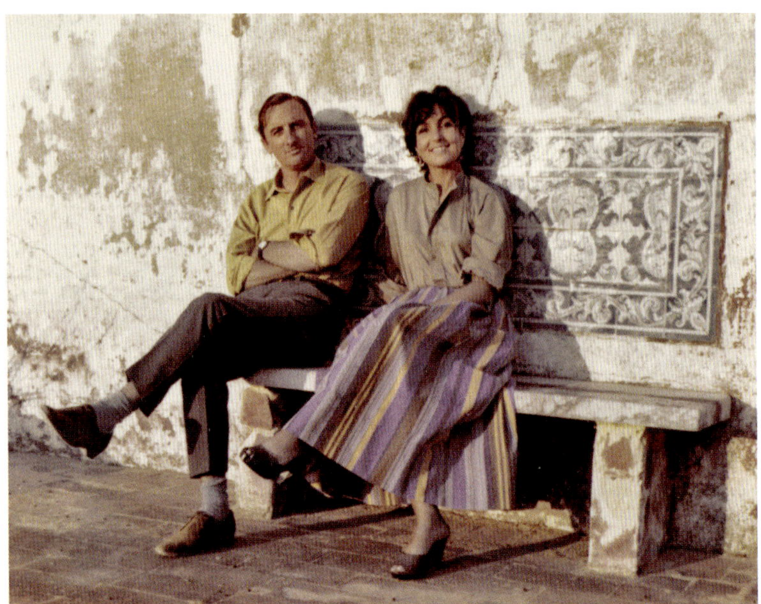

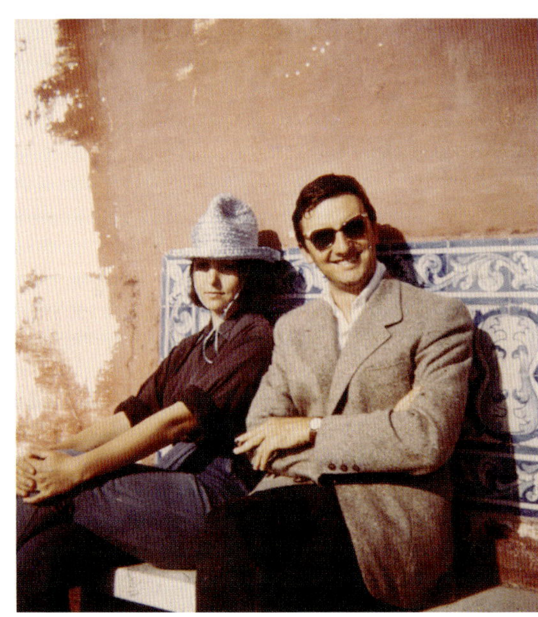

RIGHT, TOP
On the *quinta* terrace,
1960s

RIGHT, CENTRE
Vic and Paula in Granada,
1960s

RIGHT, BOTTOM
Vic and Paula at Ericeira
c. 1976

BELOW
The Willing family
in their orchard,
1972

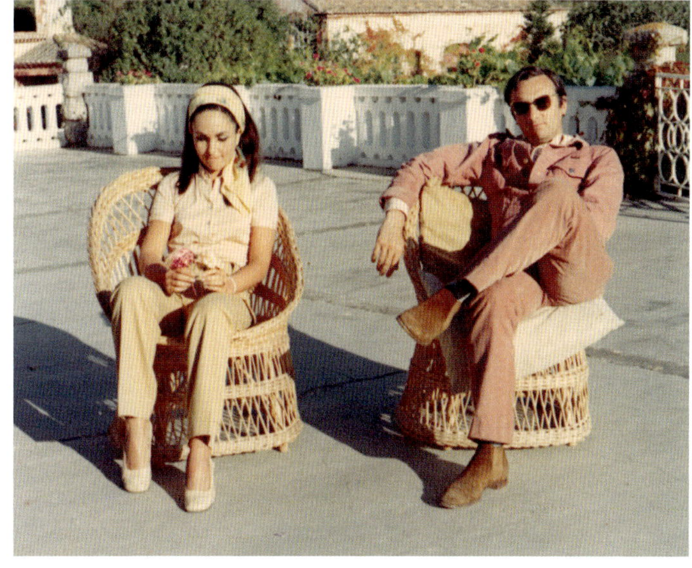

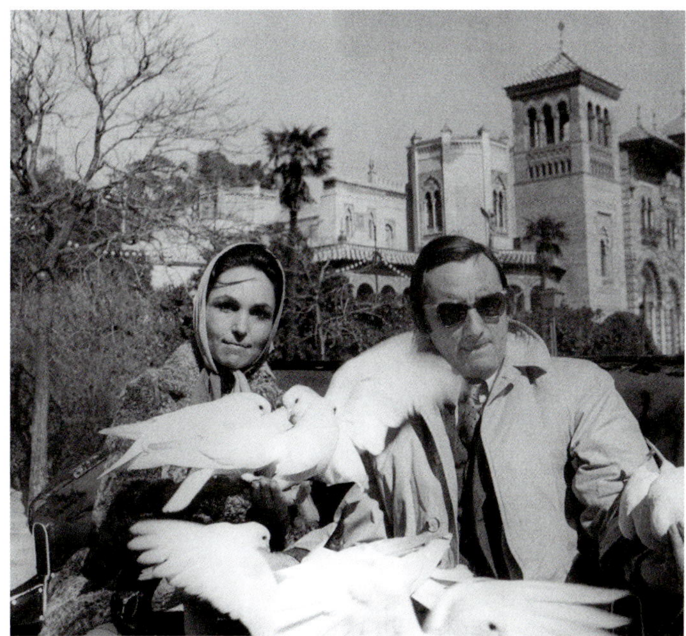

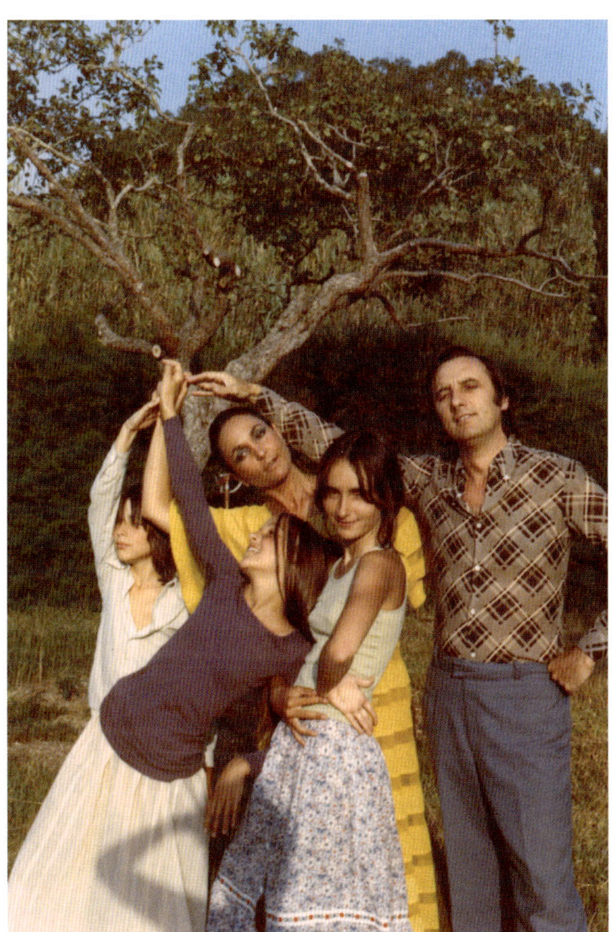

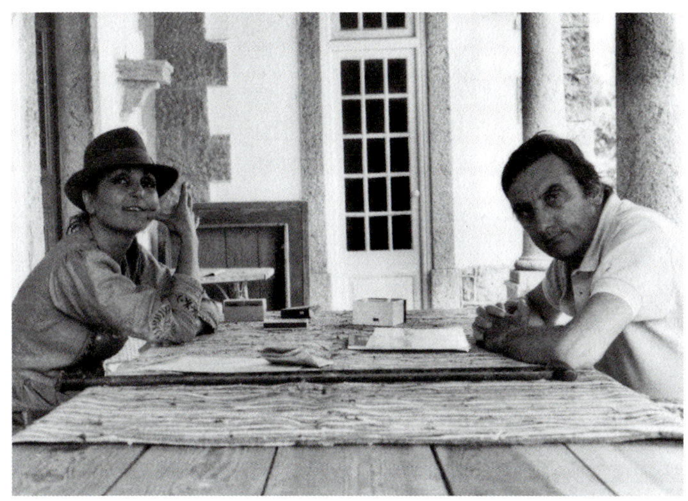

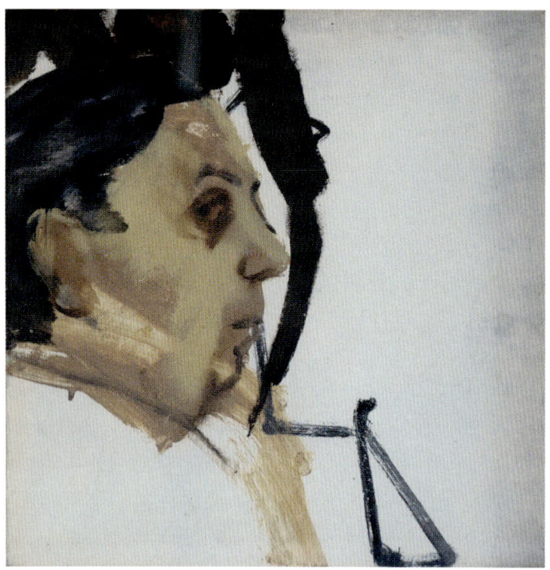

Michael Andrews
Portrait of José Figueiroa Rego 1964
Oil on board
30 × 30 cm

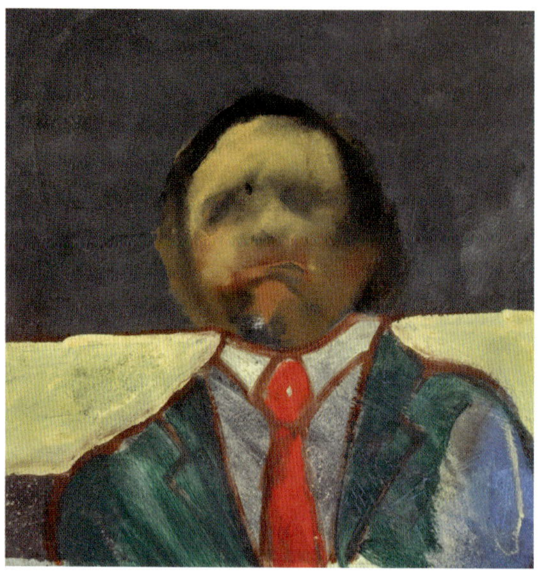

Michael Andrews
Portrait of Victor Willing at the Seaside 1967
Oil on board
23 × 23 cm

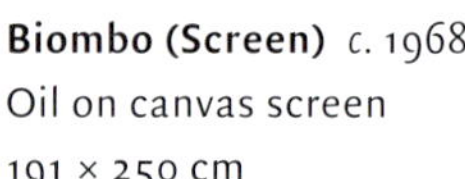

Biombo (Screen) *c.* 1968
Oil on canvas screen
191 × 250 cm

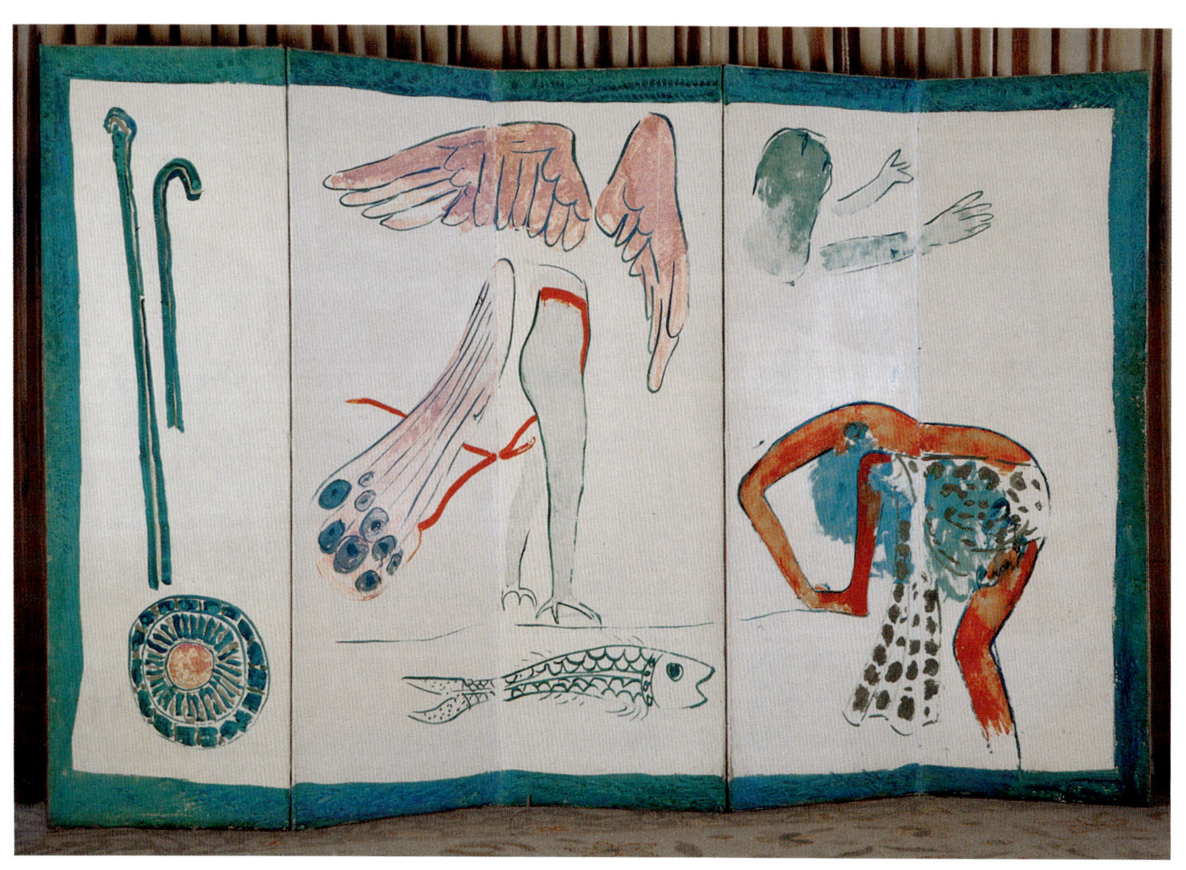

BELOW LEFT
Paula 1975
Crayon and
pastel on paper
32 × 27 cm

BELOW RIGHT
Paula 1975
Crayon and
pastel on paper
32 × 27 cm

Nineteen sixty-six proved a low point. Both his father and his benevolent father-in-law, José Figueiroa Rego, died. As can happen with the death of those dearest to us, loss can be accompanied, even assuaged, by a feeling of heady release. Willing was an excellent dancer and he and Paula went dancing as never before – 'Dance through life' he would tell his daughter Vicky on her twenty-first birthday. One morning, he complained of a blind spot in one eye. By the end of the year his feet were numb, leading strangers to assume that he was drunk. The eventual diagnosis was multiple sclerosis, a disorder of the nerve cells leading to partial or complete paralysis.

A final blow was to come. Having inherited management of his father-in-law's electronics business, virtually all was lost in the Portuguese revolution of 1974 following the dictatorial President António de Oliveira Salazar's death. Lifelong employees regarded as friends staged a lockout and took control of the factory. They called Willing, a supporter of the revolution who prided himself on being a model employer, a 'filthy fascist'. 'To be a liberal in a revolution counts for nothing', he said. 'It just results in your being hated by both sides, right and left.' The family salvaged what they could and escaped to London.

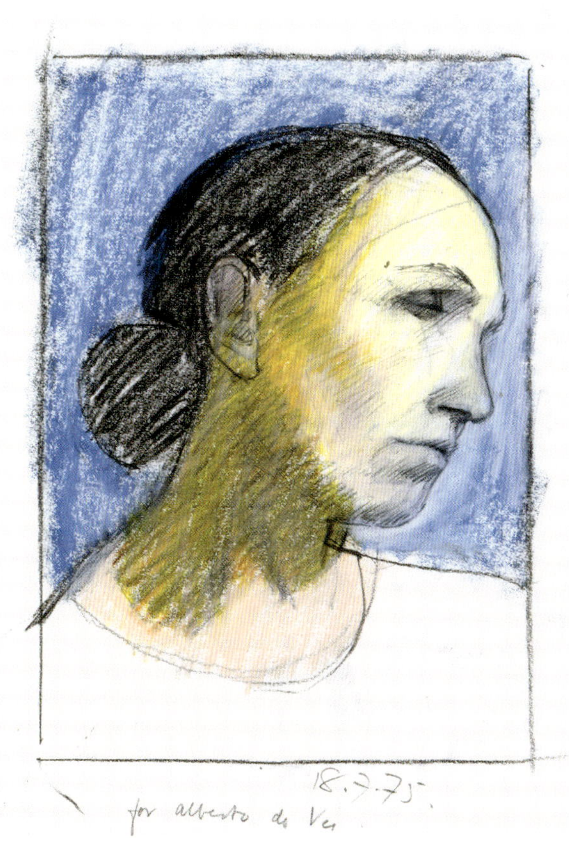

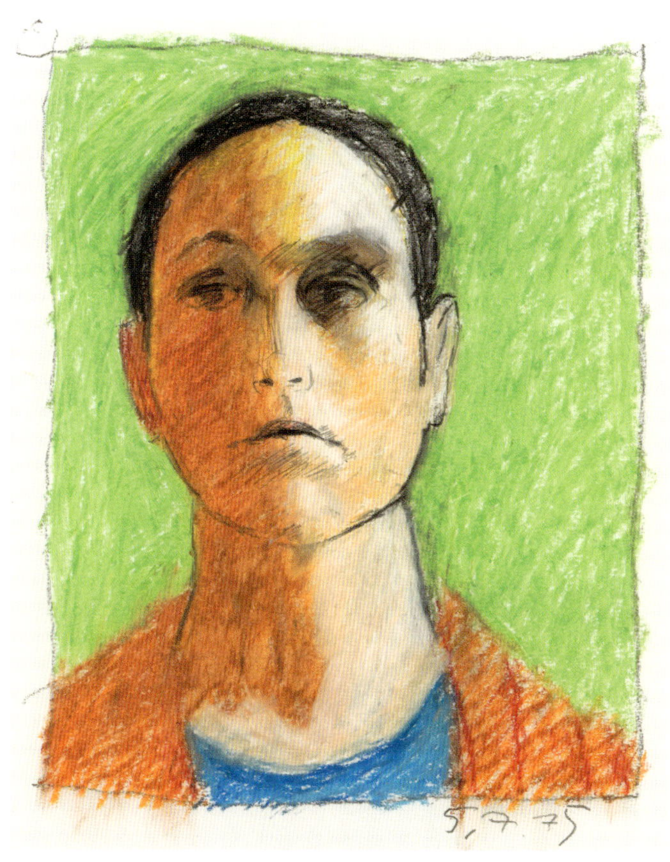

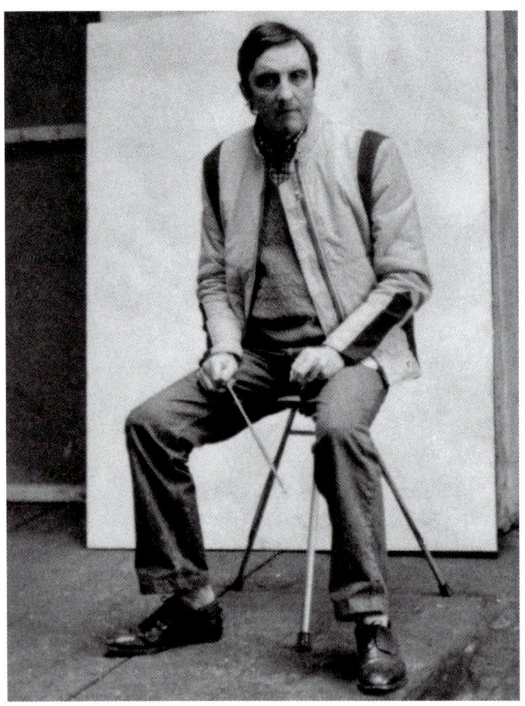

Victor Willing in his London studio, 1979

Willing returned to painting as a last resort. He took a windowless room in a condemned school building in Stepney made available for the charitable benefit of artists in want of studios. Although it was forbidden, he sometimes stayed overnight, sleeping rough. He was on steroids and could now stand only with the aid of a stick. Most of the time, he sat and stared at the wall and the blank canvas, seeking inspiration. One day in 1976, as he sat drifting in a daydream, the wall seemed to open, giving a vivid view into another space beyond – 'a scene, brightly lit, clearly defined on the other side, like a stage, spot-lit'. After a while, the wall became blank again. He sketched what he had seen on a pad as a memory aid and began to commit the first of these hallucinogenic scenes to canvas. It was to become the triptych *Place* (*below and pp. 68–9*). The central and right-hand panels was what he had seen; the left was an additional afterthought. He continued to experience these unbidden visions, what he called 'scenarios', in which something has happened or is about to happen but is not happening at the time depicted. They do indeed ask the question: 'When was now?'

The phenomenon lasted for four years. The suggestion that it was drug induced was discounted both by his psychotherapist and by his neurologist. The psychotherapist said that it was instead due to his mental state, and that he had taken steroids before the hallucinatory years (and would continue to do so afterwards). It seems that the perfect storm of tribulation blew away the overanalysis that had previously beset him. Now physically crippled, his imagination was released in apparent compensation. 'The difficulty for an artist is to do something exclusive to ourselves. I was fortunate in that I had these hallucinations. Eventually they stopped, but by then the experience had had the beneficial effect of making me much more receptive to my imagination.'

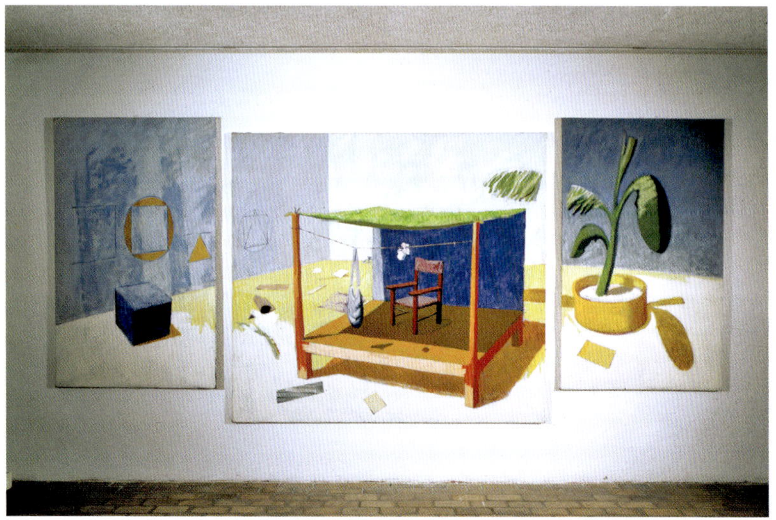

The triptych **Place** (also see pages 68–9)

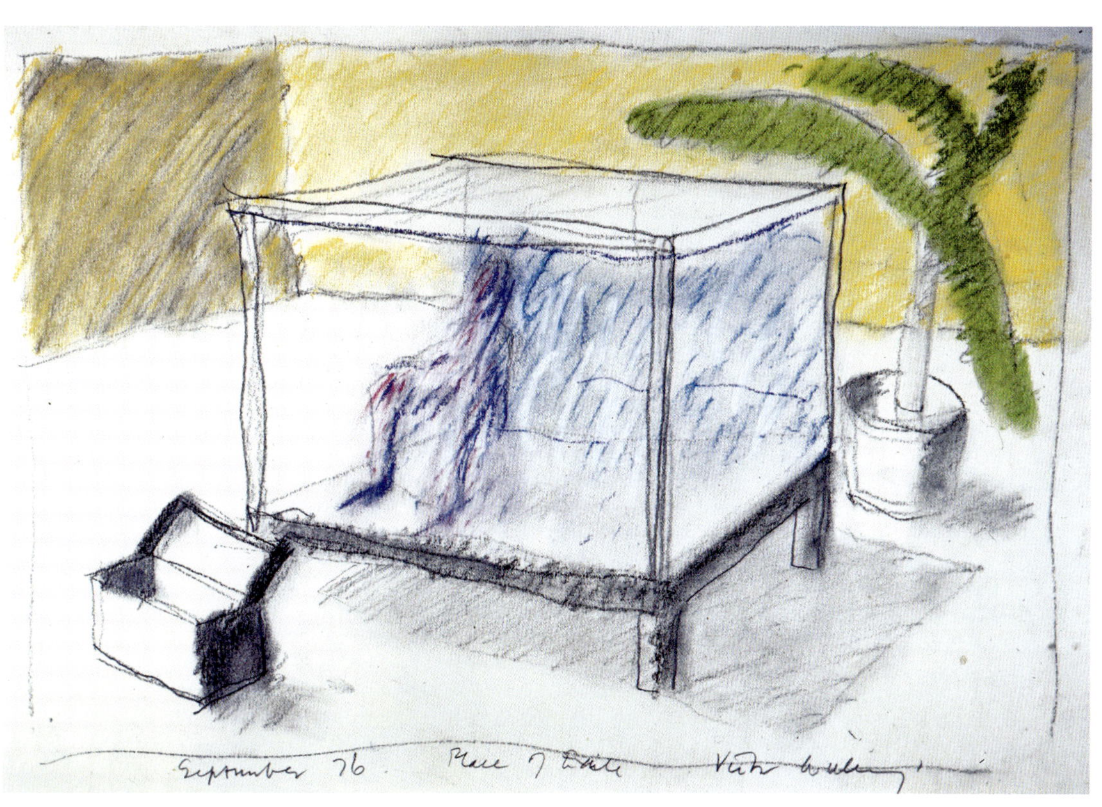

Place of Exile
(September 1976) 1976
Charcoal and
pastel on paper
33 × 50 cm

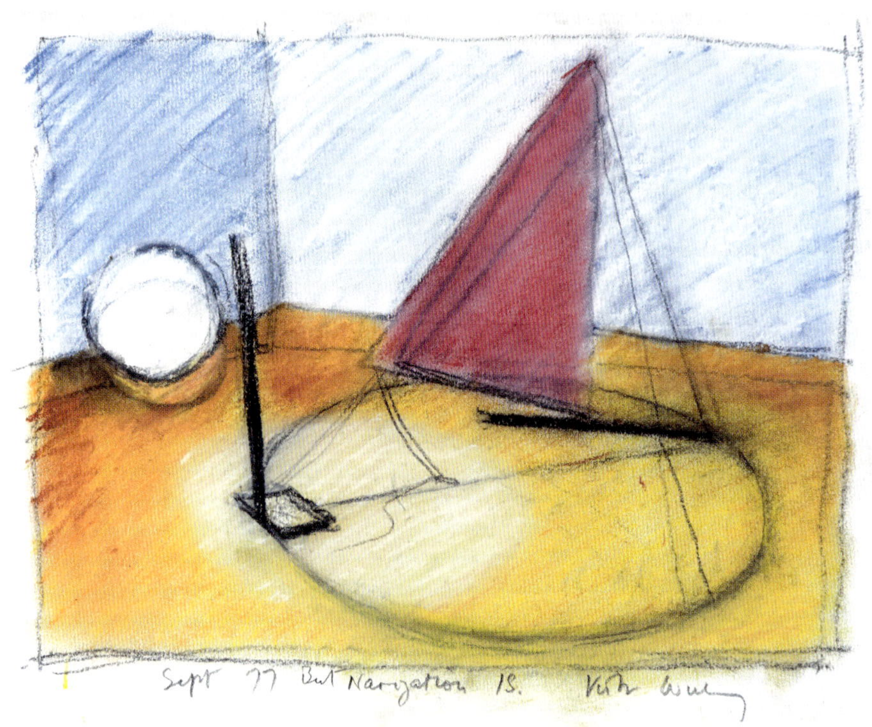

But Navigation Is
(September 1977) 1977
Charcoal and
pastel on paper
26 × 33 cm

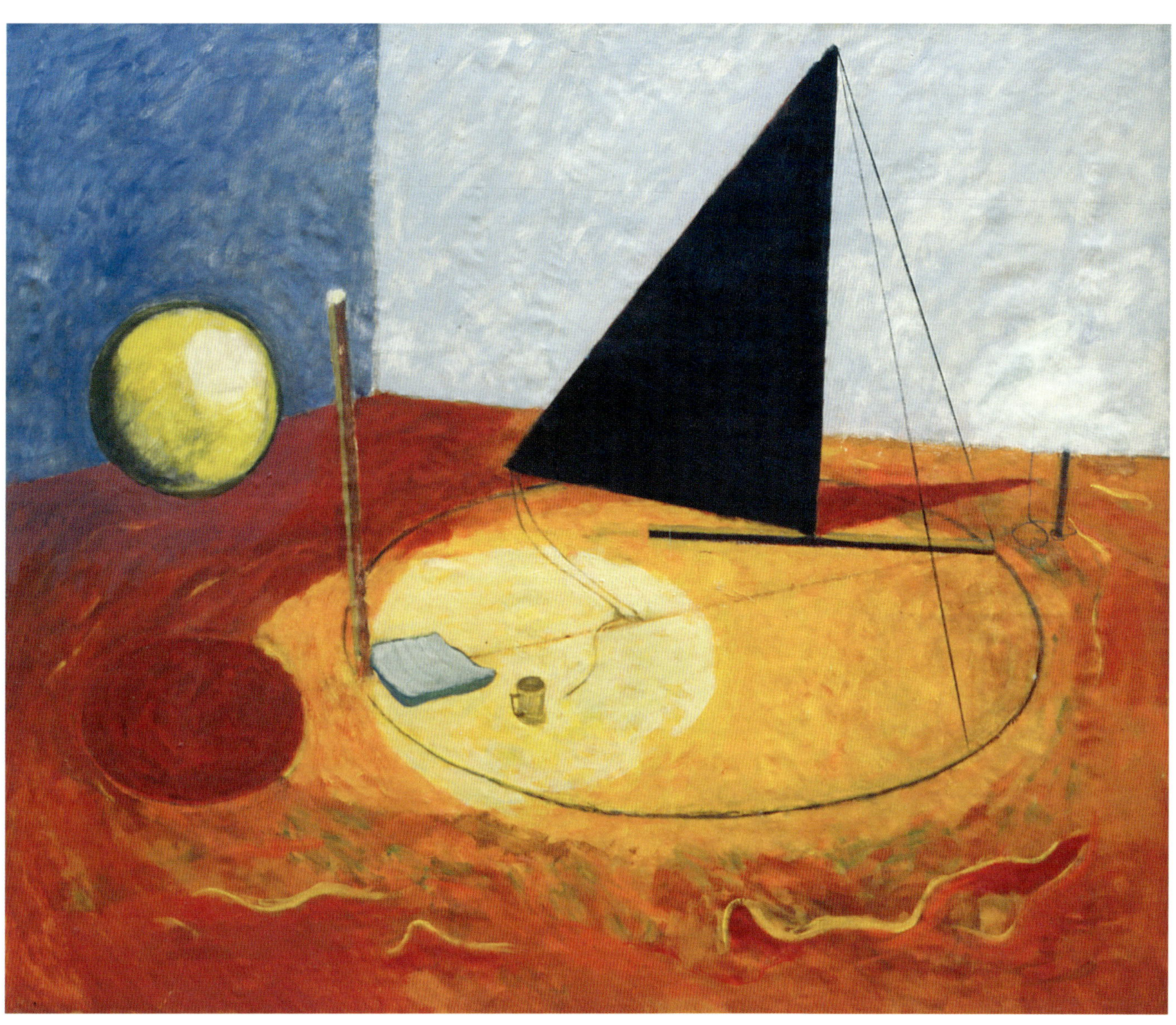

Navigation 1977
Oil on canvas
200 × 240 cm

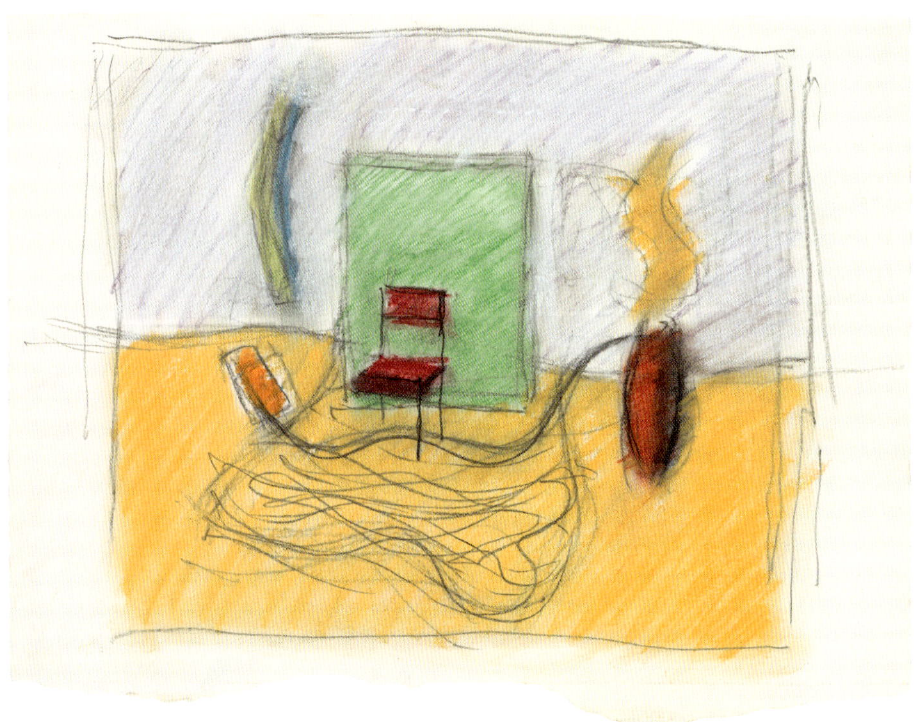

Study for Errant 1978
Charcoal and
pastel on paper
32 × 45 cm

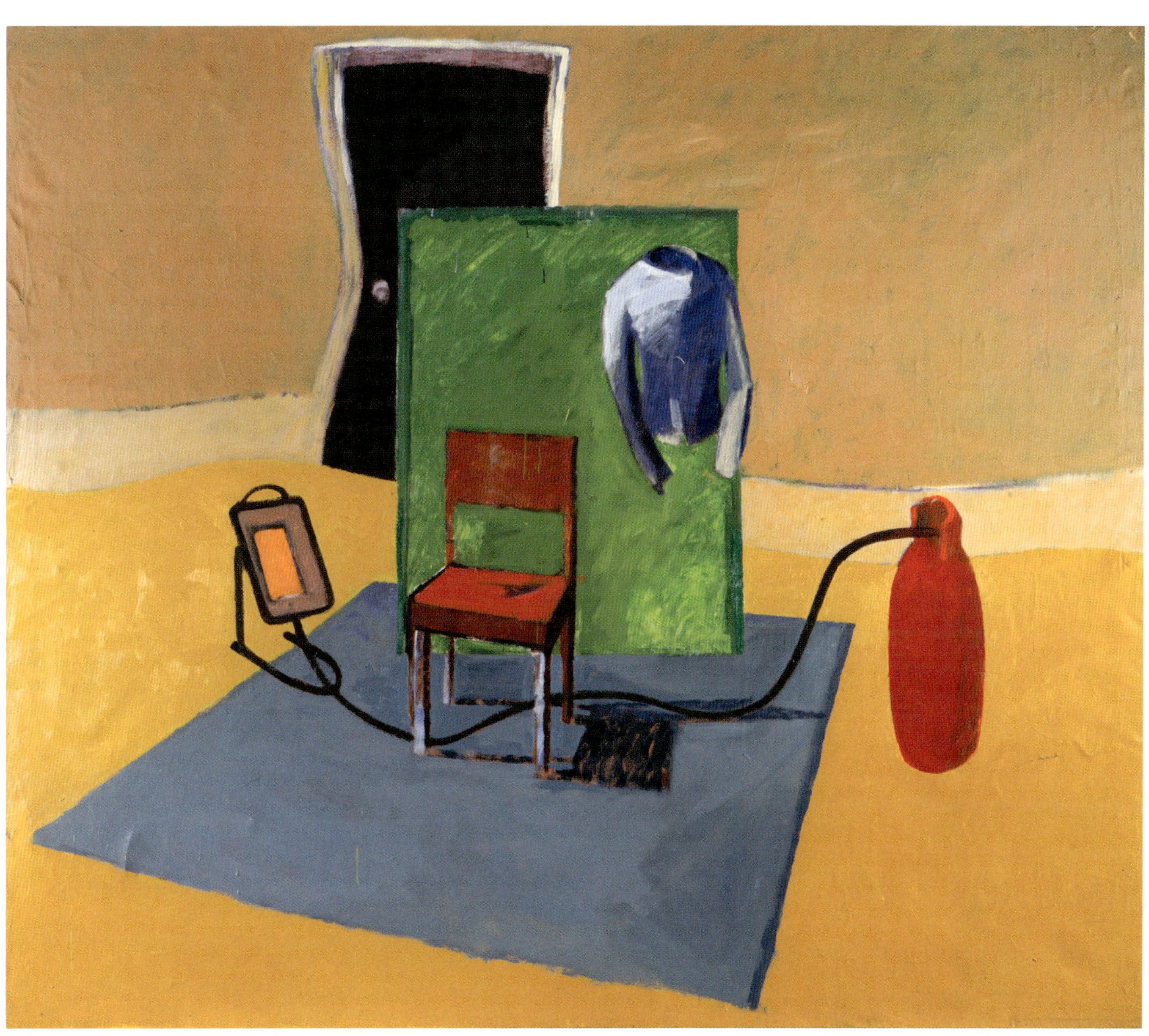

Knight Errant 1978
Oil on canvas
200 × 240 cm

RIGHT
Untitled 1979
Charcoal and pastel on paper
32 × 45 cm

BELOW
Untitled (chair and table) 1979
Charcoal on paper
32 × 45 cm

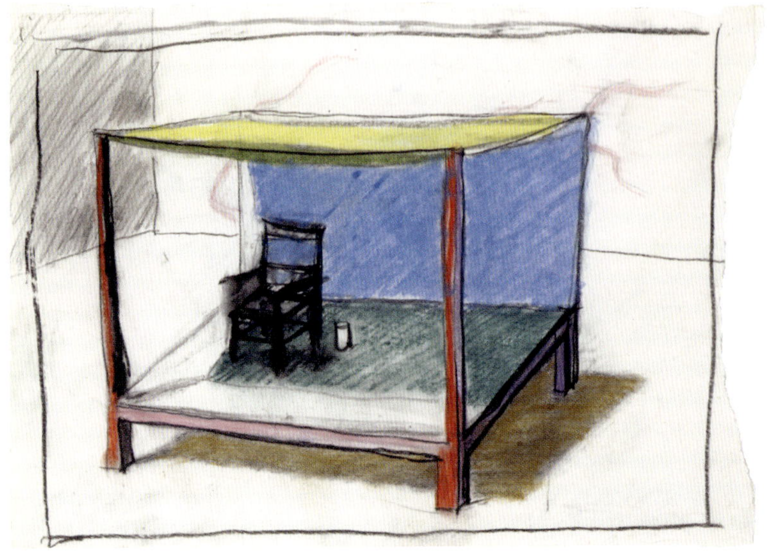

The poet Alberto de Lacerda defined the phenomenon. 'Is Willing a visionary painter? Not really: the semi-hallucination, semi-vision is a point of departure, and the drawing or painting is a point of arrival. Even the most disturbed work has a conscious tranquillity. Visionary painting – as in Blake – is a window onto another dimension, a flight into the transcendental. One of the most persistent metaphors in Willing's work is the wall, but with dramatic possibilities. The intimation of action, the virtual play – no characters, only objects – have to do with an inner reality. His paintings are powerful static presences and not products of, or inducements to, ecstasy. Blake gave form to the invisible, as with all mystics. Willing gives form, not to the invisible, but to absence.' As Willing himself said: 'In the back of my mind in Portugal was the realisation that I had run away from England and one day I'd have to return. Maybe all exiles feel like that.' De Chirico's early paintings haunted him, not least those far-off passing trains.

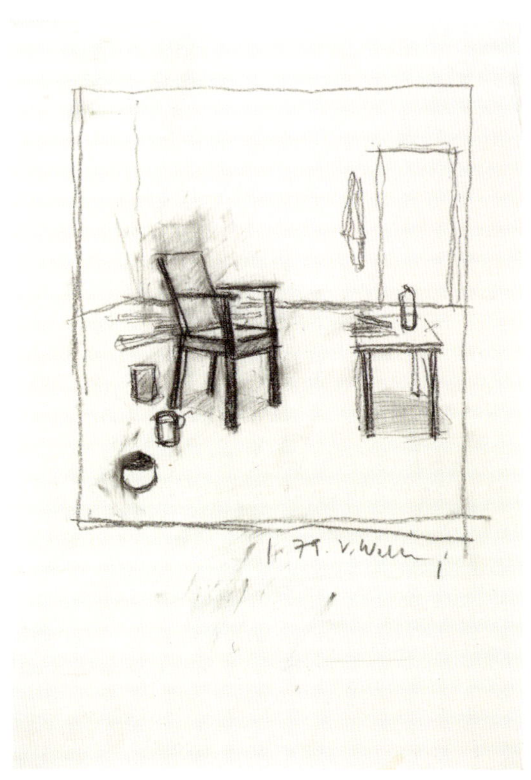

Moira Kelly showed the hallucinatory pictures at the AIR Gallery in London in the autumn of 1978. Nick Willing played truant on a school outing to visit the show: 'The pictures hit me like a punch. I was so moved that I forgave my father everything.... His pictures still have that effect on me.' Among them was *Place*, which Rego and Andrews both liked best. The left-hand panel is a conscious reflection on his Slade-induced reverence for measured 'reality'. As Willing said, 'geometric forms keep the imagination at bay'. And a propos of 'reality', his retort to Lucian Freud's claim that he, Freud, only painted 'reality' was: 'One man's "reality" is another man's "abstraction".'

The genesis of the right-hand panel casts a decidedly odd light on the subconscious. The biblical story of Jonah being swallowed and then vomited to safety by the whale was a favourite of his children. It was only much later that he read the second part of the story, which described Jonah exiling himself in the desert outside Nineveh, where he built himself a shelter:

> 'And the Lord God prepared a gourd, and made it to come up over Jonah, that it might be a shadow over his head, to deliver him from his grief. So Jonah was exceeding glad.
>
> But God prepared a worm when the morning rose the next day, and it smote the gourd that it withered.' (Jonah IV, 6–7)

Willing read this after he had painted *Place*, with its flourishing, shade-inducing plant. Little wonder he distrusted critical interpretations. 'I hope that if my paintings get to you, they do so before the sensible person has had time to draw any conclusion about them at all. I have found that if you paint an image irrationally, then the people who look at that image will be seized by it on an irrational level. Having painted something irrationally, I, like you, begin to rationalise it. I construct theories and fit titles to those theories. And yet I am convinced that if I painted my pictures as the result of a rational succession of thoughts, they would not work for people the way they seem to – perhaps they would not afford them the chance to rationalise in turn. Certainly the viewer would be denied the chance to respond intuitively at the outset.'

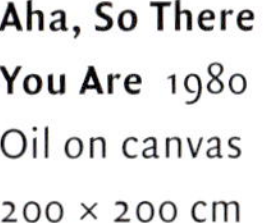

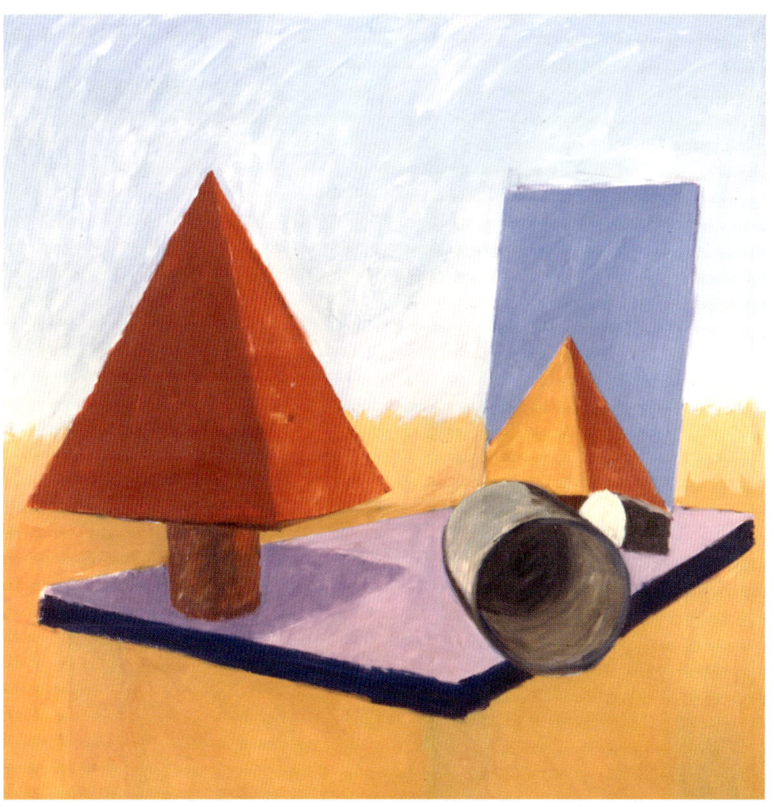

Aha, So There You Are 1980
Oil on canvas
200 × 200 cm

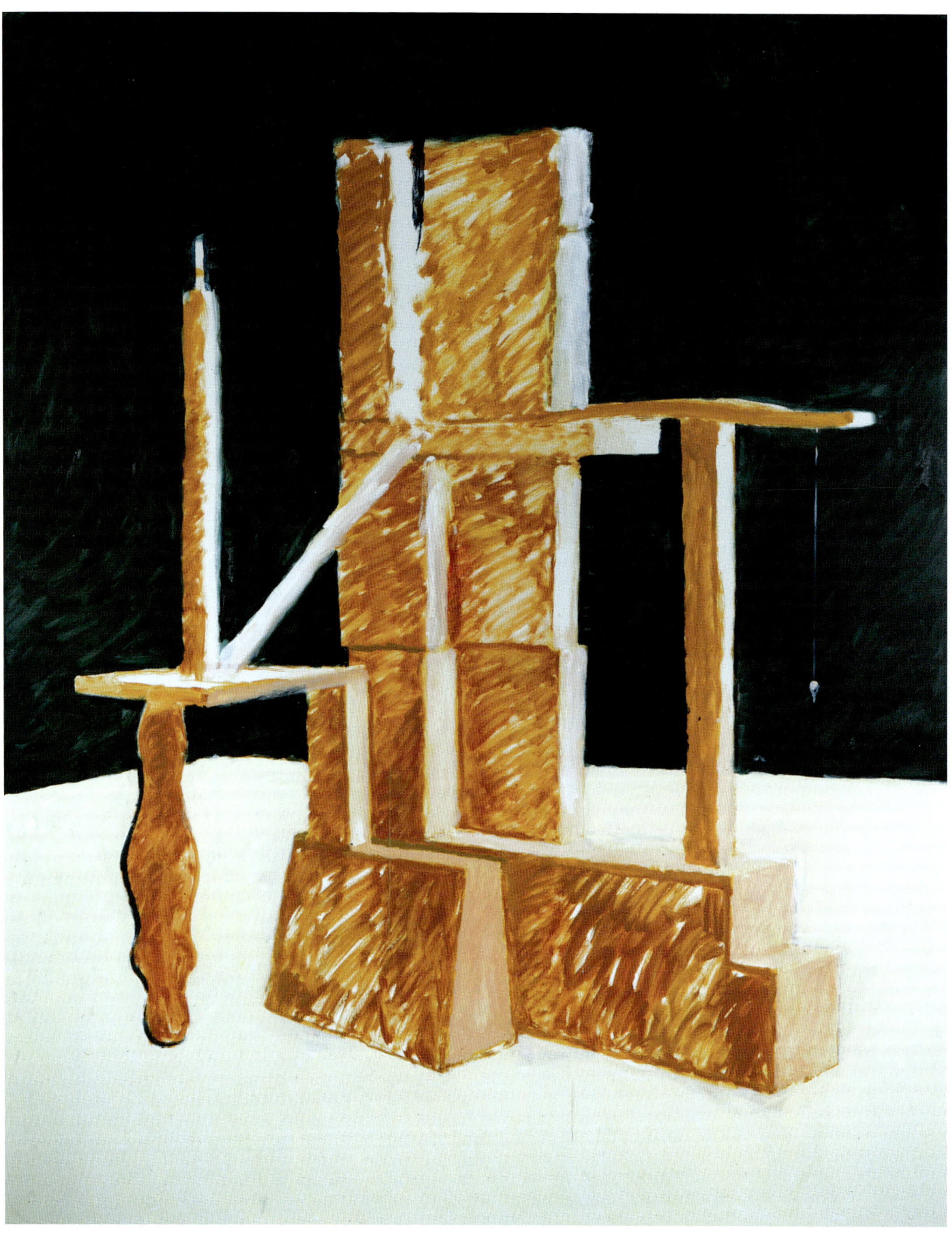

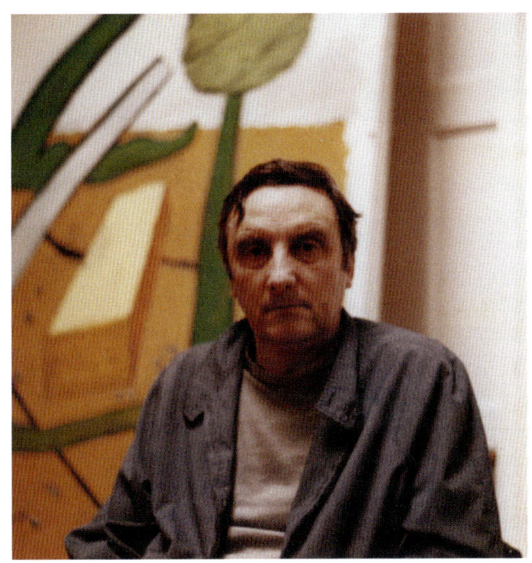

ABOVE
Victor Willing in his London studio, 1981

RIGHT
Paula Rego
Vic (Study for the family) 1987
Pencil on paper
23 × 23 cm

OPPOSITE
Judge 1982
Oil on canvas
250 × 200 cm
Pallant House Gallery, Wilson Gift through The Art Fund (2006)

Willing owed his general rationalization to the art historian Erwin Panofsky. 'Panofsky pointed out that in the Renaissance, artists introduced perspective, a measurable space, into pictures because time had become measurable. This meant that the notion of future and past time was made believable and practical, which in turn had all sorts of socioeconomic results.... What we've had in the twentieth century is an abrupt reminder of our own imminent disaster.... To reverse Panofsky's principle, it might be said that the lack of a credible future explains the flatness of modern painting, because we've been forced into thinking principally of the present. I believe in the continuity of life, enough at least to allow myself a shallow space – but there's an emphatic back wall in my paintings – no distant horizons.'

It was this hold on optimism that not only released these haunting and utterly exclusive drawings and paintings from Willing's imagination, but also rescued him from the darkness of extreme disability and curtailed life, which he confronted with valiant tranquillity to the end.

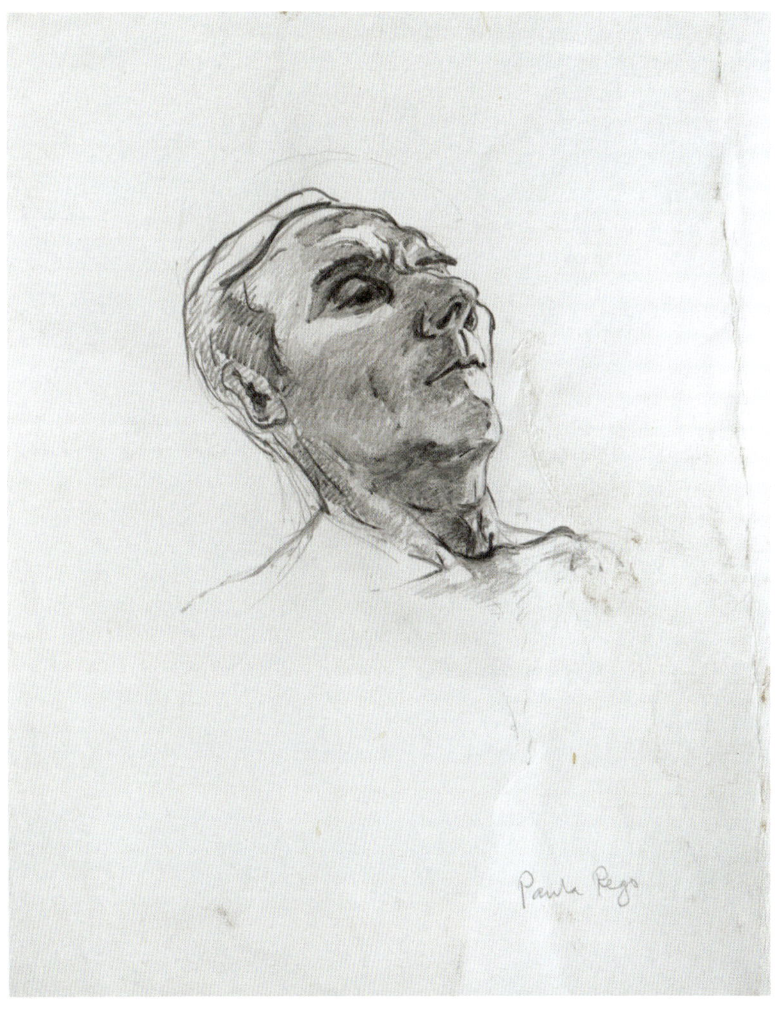

RIGHT
Une Autre Femme (Another Woman) 1987
Oil on canvas
50 × 50 cm

BELOW
The Don's Daughter 1986
Oil on canvas
50 × 50 cm

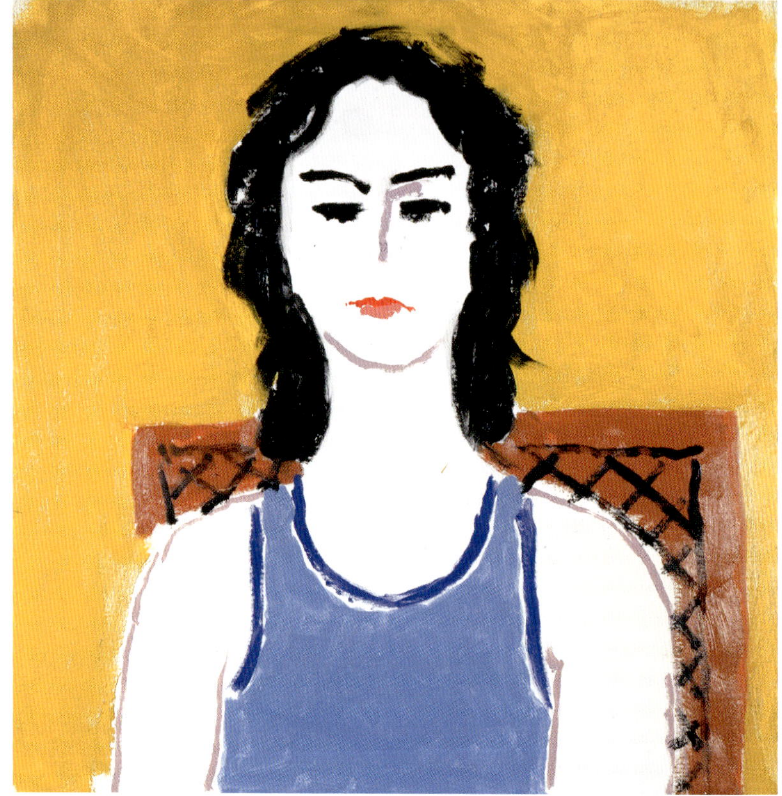

The last of his *Heads* was his final painting. He called it *Une Autre Femme* after Matisse's *Une Femme à la Chaise.* 'Since I knew it would be my last painting, I didn't want it to be gloomy', he said. 'I wanted to paint something nice. And a pretty girl, I thought, would be a nice thing to paint. I think Matisse's painting is absolutely delicious.'

In 1949, when at the Slade, Willing made a stone sculpture. And in his last years he had an unfulfilled wish to make what he called *aediculae. Aedicula* is the diminutive of *aedes*, a temple building. They were temples within temples, in Roman times containing protective shrines with statues of household gods. The most famous is inside Jerusalem's Church of the Holy Sepulchre, where Jesus's body is legendarily said to have lain before his Resurrection. Willing wanted an *aedicula* – he always referred to it in Latin – to be made under his instruction and placed at the centre of his 1986 Whitechapel exhibition. It was to be the climax of that climactic show, his own abode at the heart of his art. It did not happen, but when he could no longer make pictures he had five sculptures made to his specification. Not abodes or shelters, like the one in *Place*, but perhaps shrines of protective consolation. It surely has some bearing on his answer to the last subject we discussed in our Whitechapel catalogue interview:

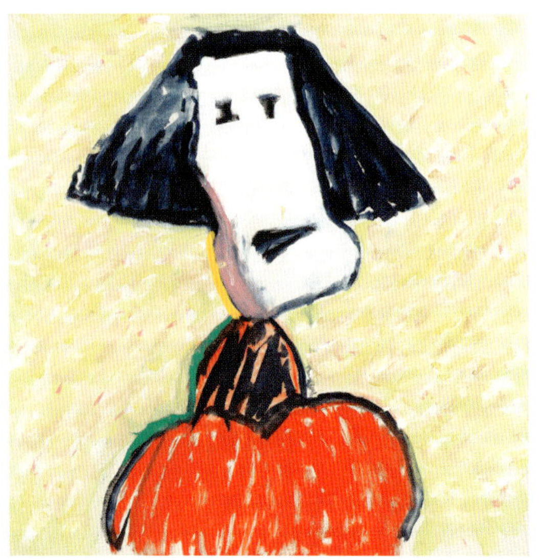

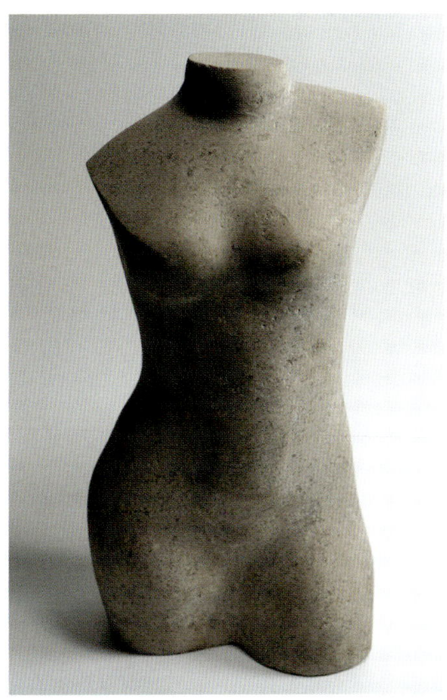

that Panofsky's interpretation of the flatness of modern paintings suggested a rejection of religion.

'You have to accept the lot to be religious. I don't. But as well as that inner reality, I have found myself aware also of those images that have been insistent, that others recognise and which we might call archetypal because they are more than coincidental. A sense of the numinous takes us further than humanist ethics. When we enter caverns measureless to man, we are already treading a path also to religious experience. I have been too timid, in the event, to do more than peep at what might be there.'

ABOVE
Torso *c.* 1949
Stone
30 × 15 cm approx.

BELOW, LEFT TO RIGHT
Magister; Widow; Judge *c.* 1982
Mixed media
each 30 × 15 cm approx.

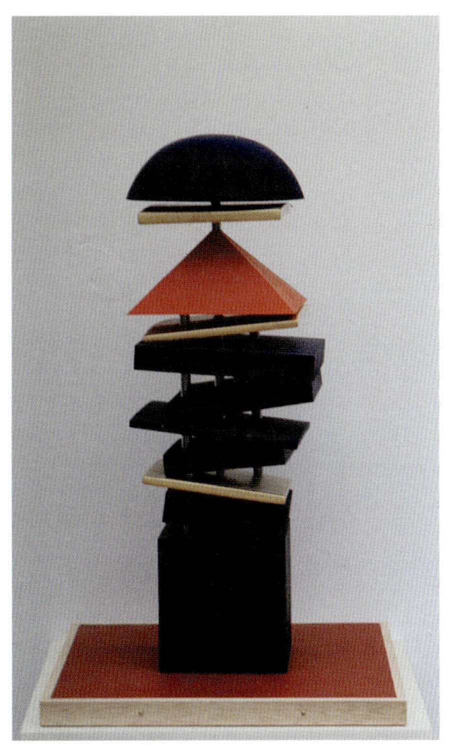

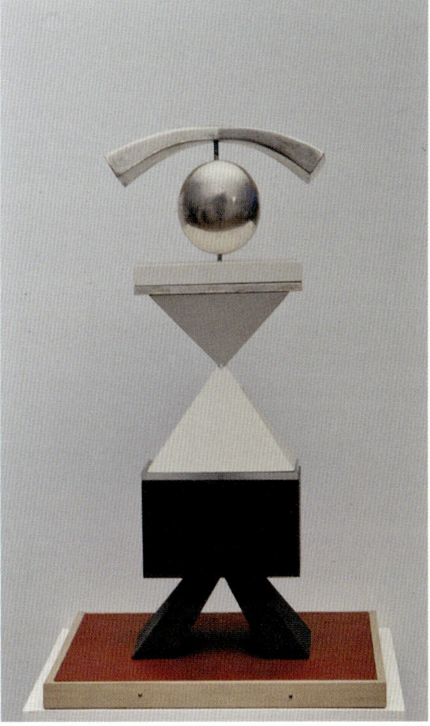

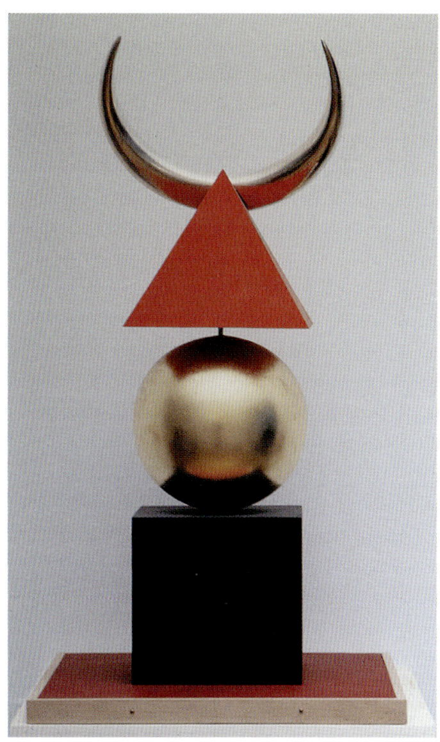

‘I WAS A BIT OF A REBEL AT THE SLADE BUT AS SOON AS I LEFT, I BECAME A SLAVE TO ITS PRESCRIPTIVE WAYS. IT TOOK ME TWENTY YEARS TO RECOVER, THAT’S HOW I LOOK AT IT. IN THE INTERIM, I PAINTED STODGY PICTURES OF NUDES AND FIGURES.’

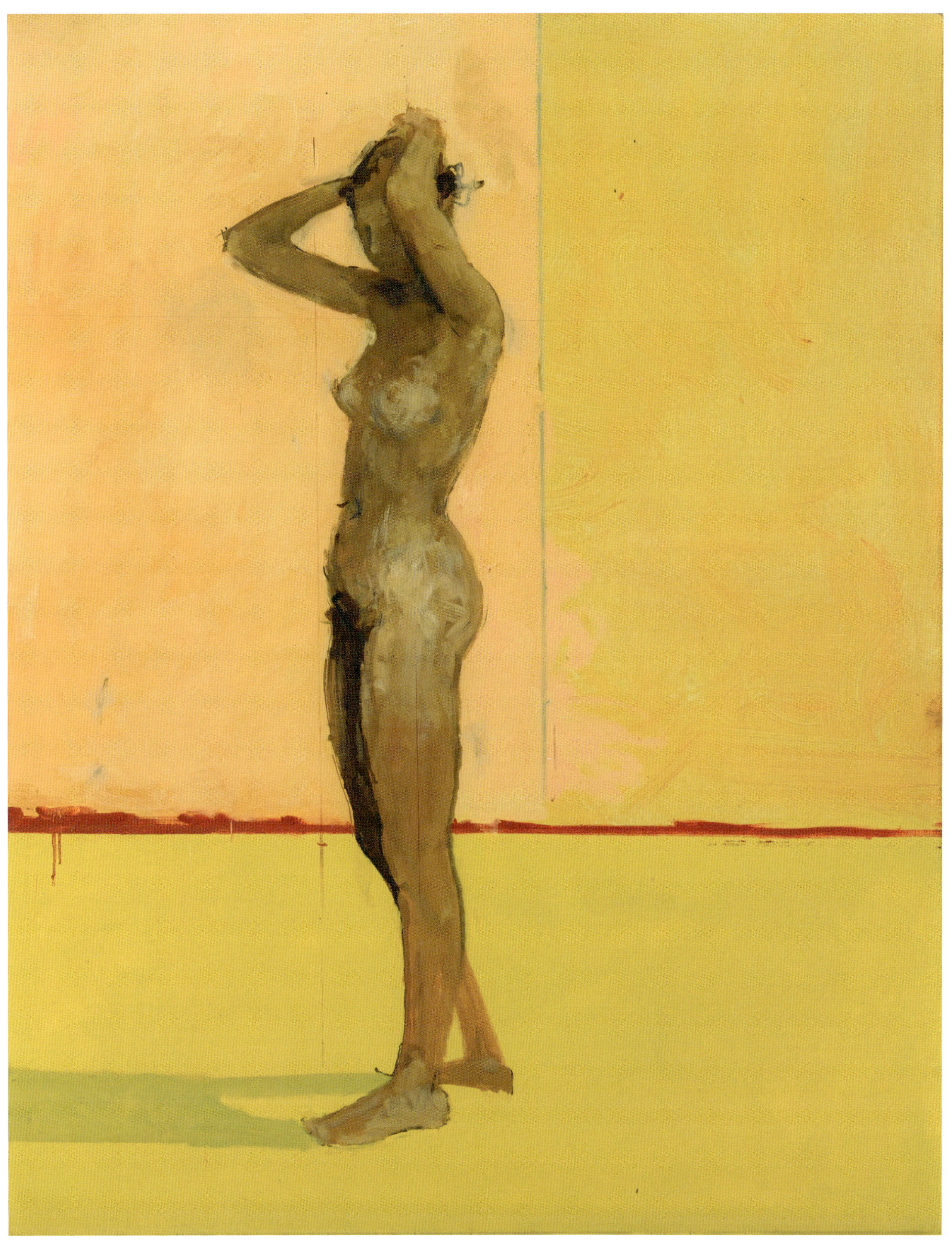

Standing Nude 1955
Oil on canvas
127 × 101.6 cm
Arts Council Collection,
Southbank Centre, London

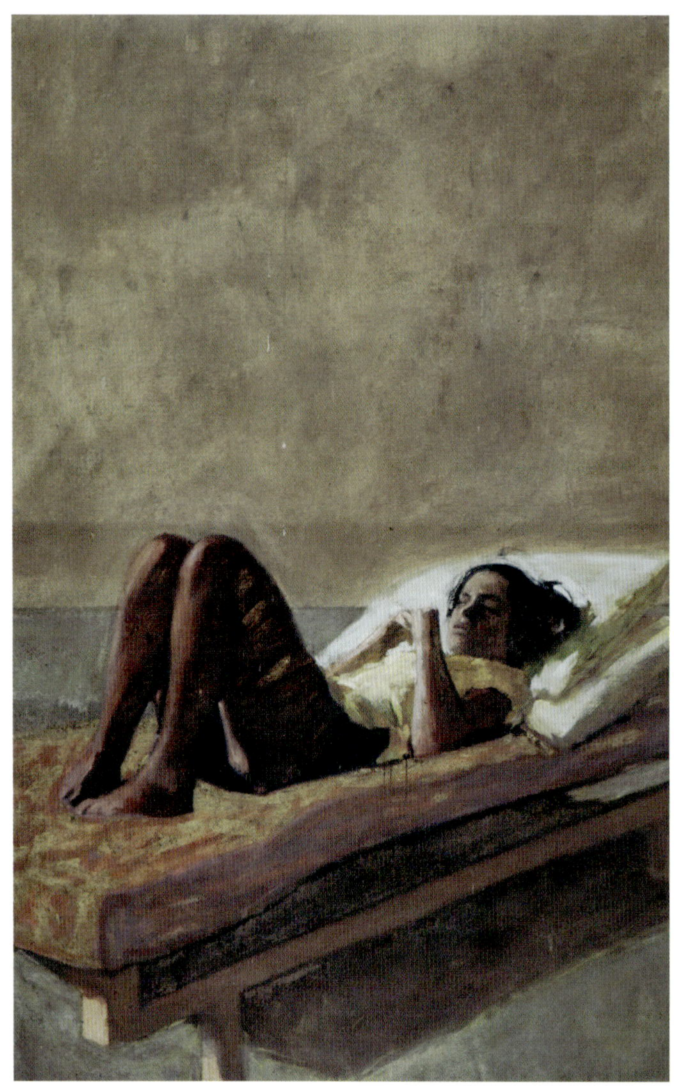

Maneula 1958
Oil on canvas
136.2 × 87.5 cm

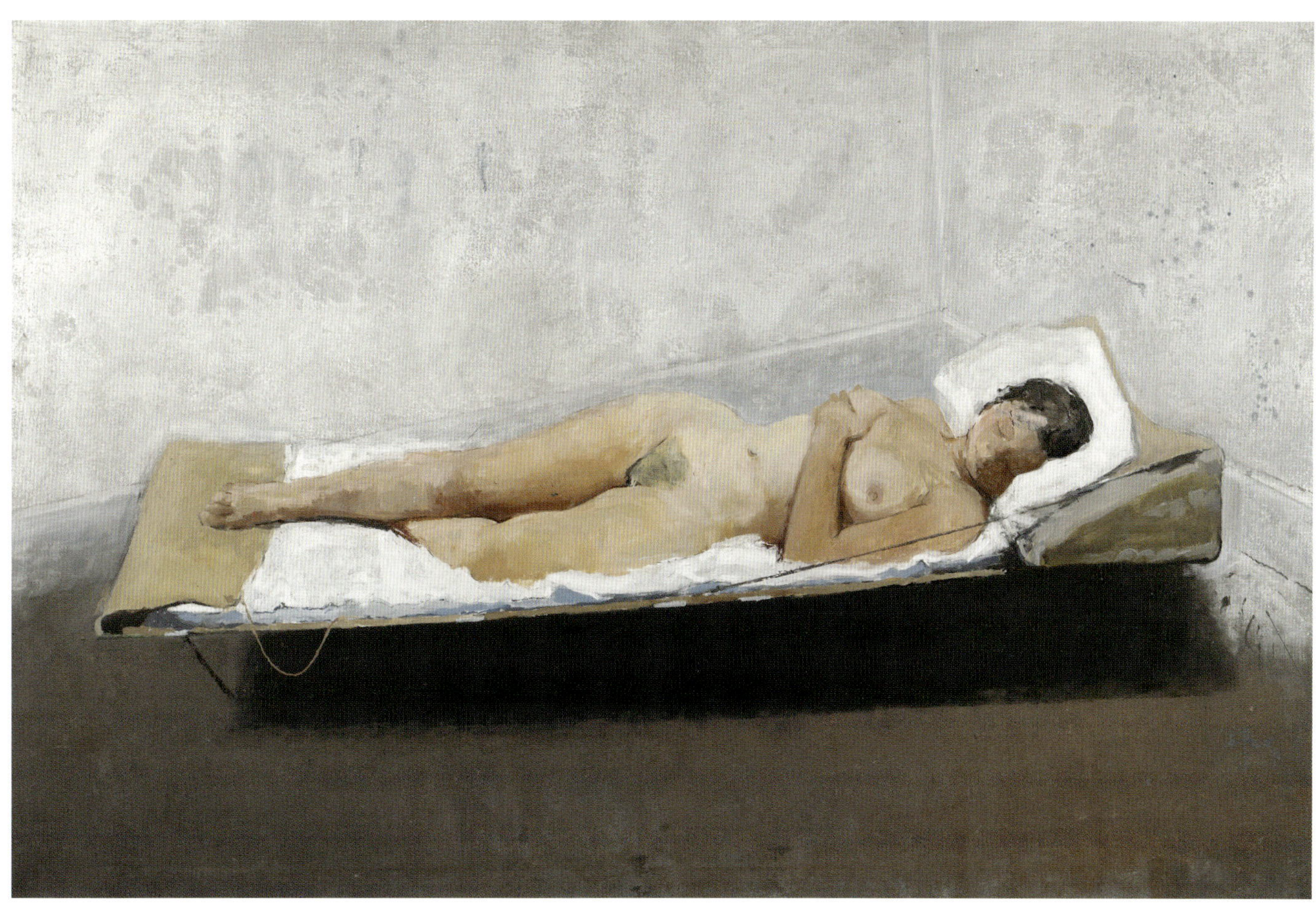

Reclining Nude 1950s
Oil on canvas
121 × 188 cm

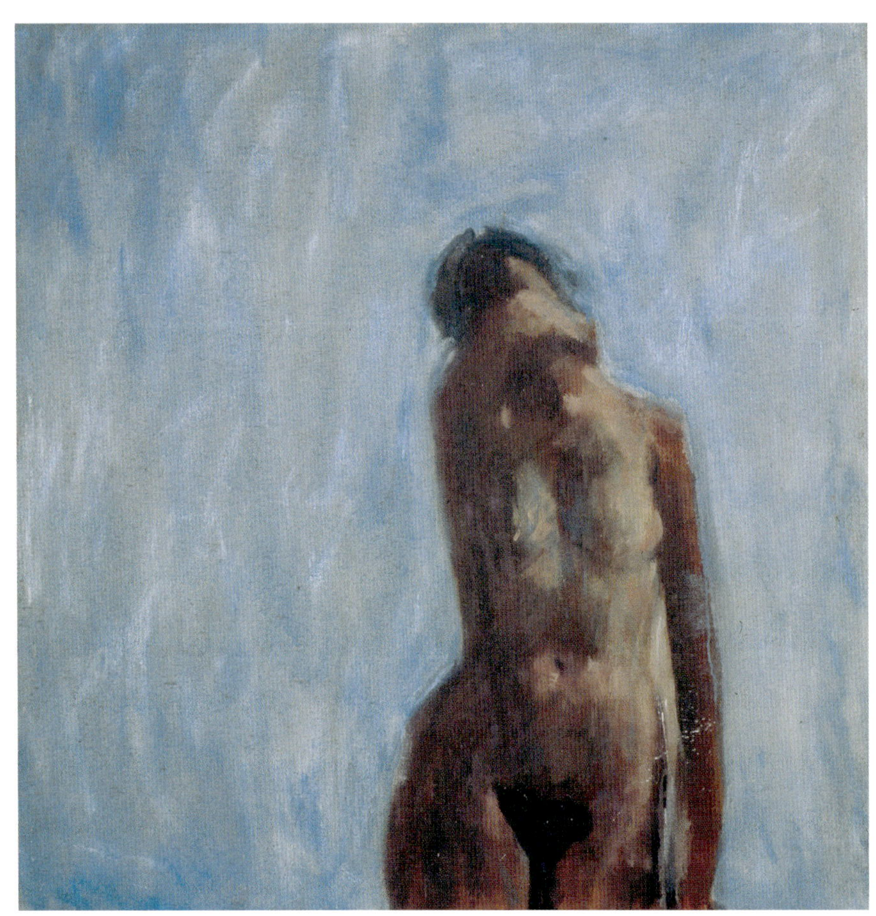

Blue Nude (I)
(Paula Rego) 1958
Oil on canvas
85 × 85 cm

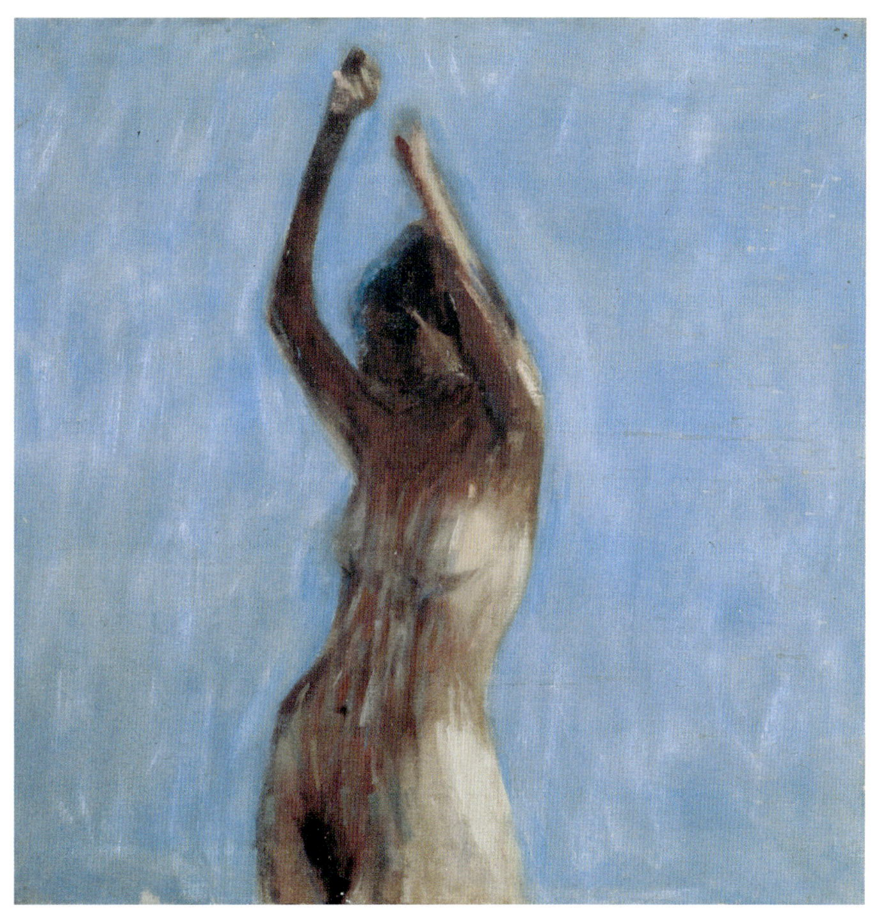

Blue Nude (II)
(Paula Rego) 1958
Oil on canvas
85 × 85 cm

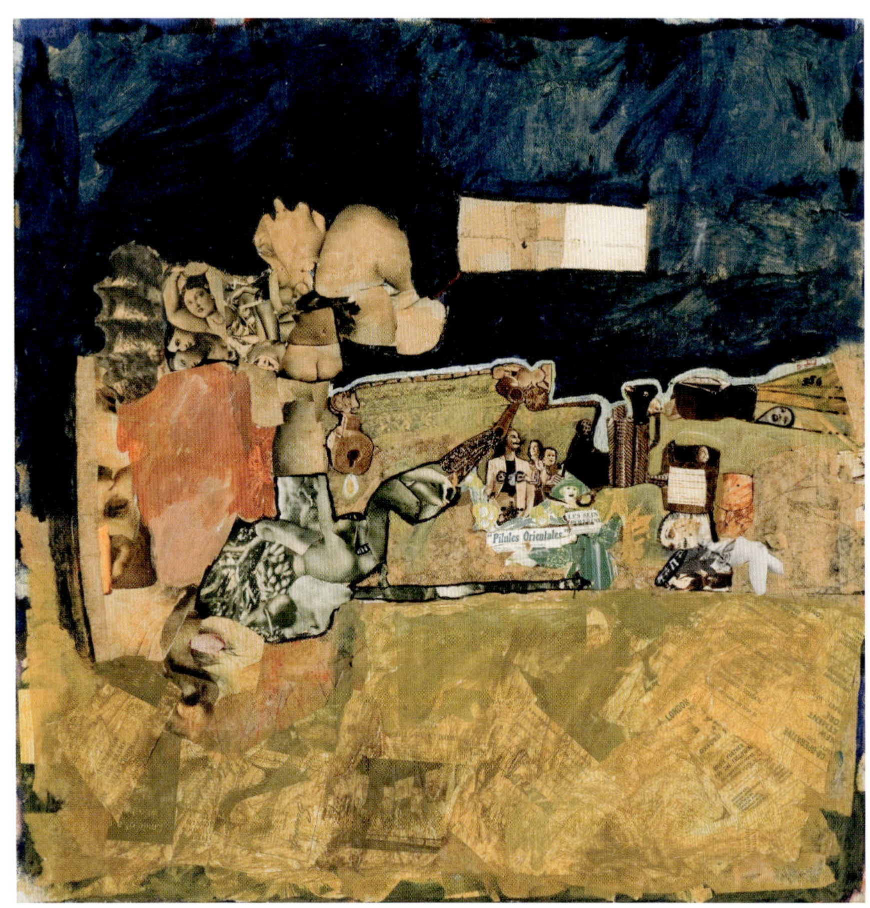

Paula Rego
Turkish Bath 1960
Acrylic, graphite, paper
glued on canvas
84 × 84 cm
(painted on the reverse
of *Nude* [*Paula Rego*])

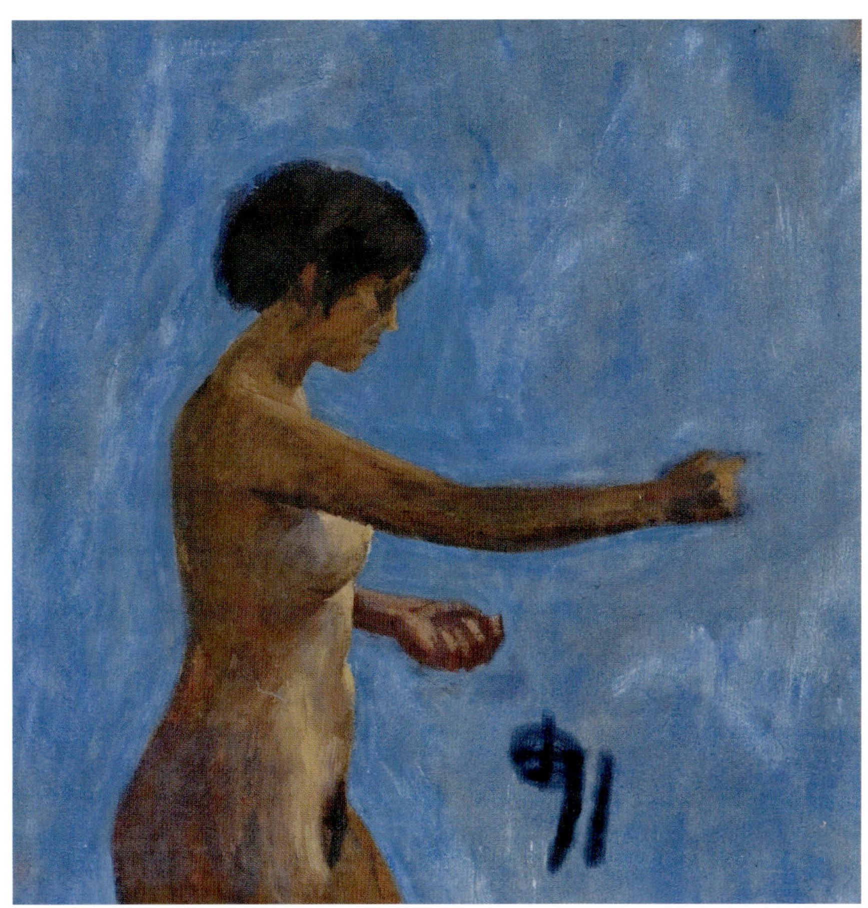

Nude (Paula Rego) 1958
Oil on canvas
84 × 84 cm

Nude (Triptych) 1959–60
Oil on canvas
three parts,
each 138 × 99 cm

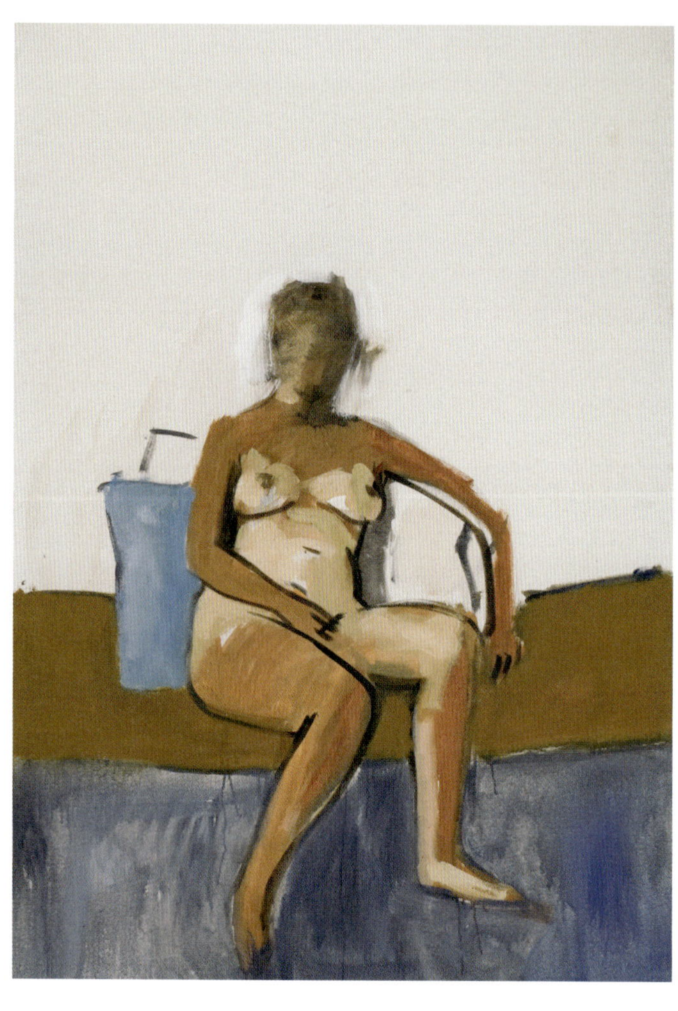

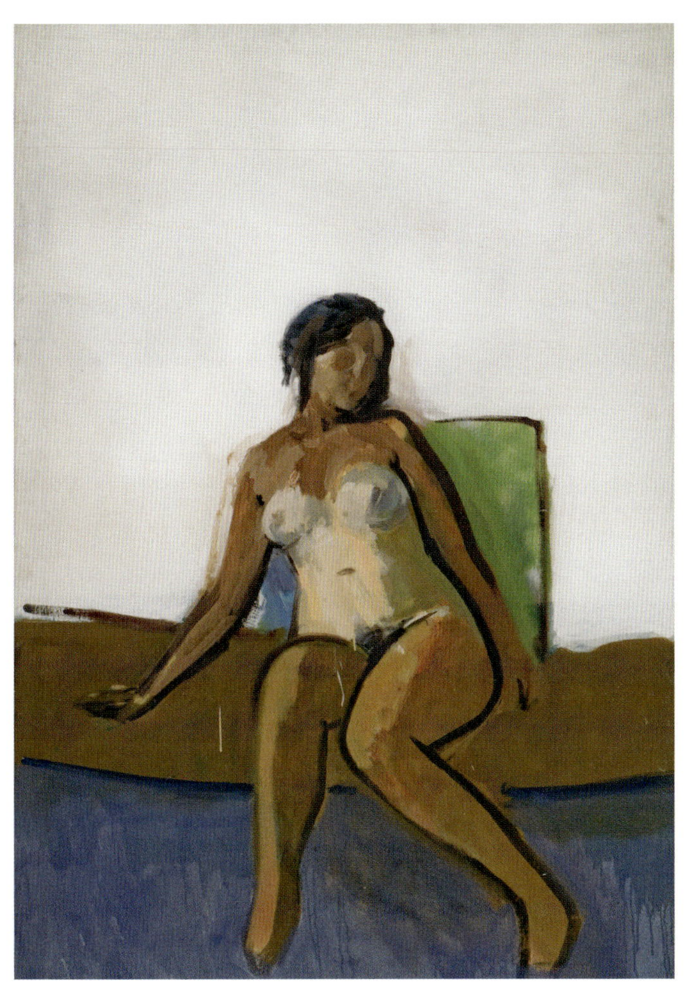
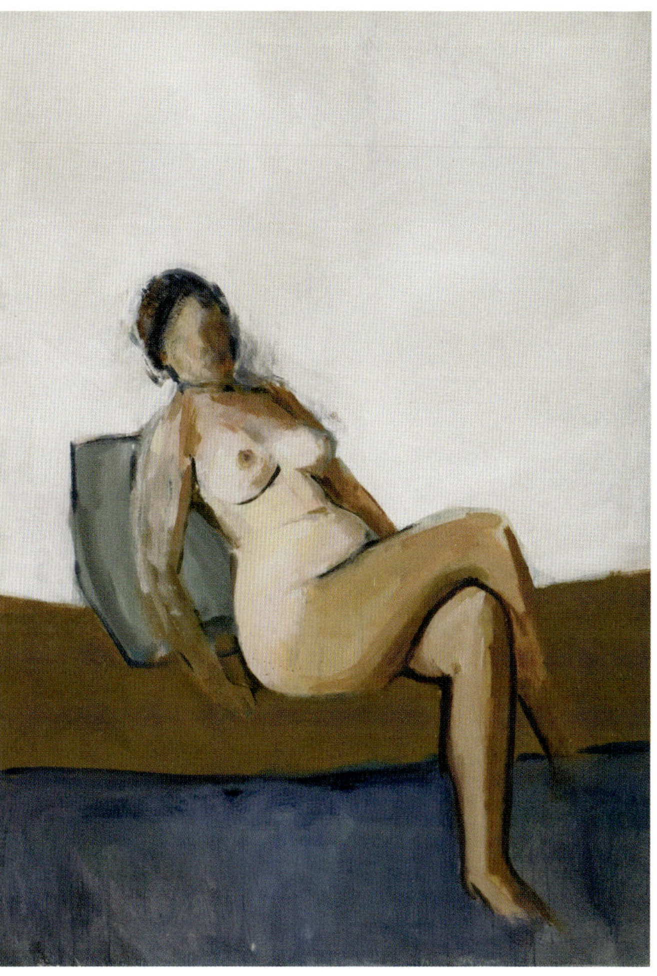

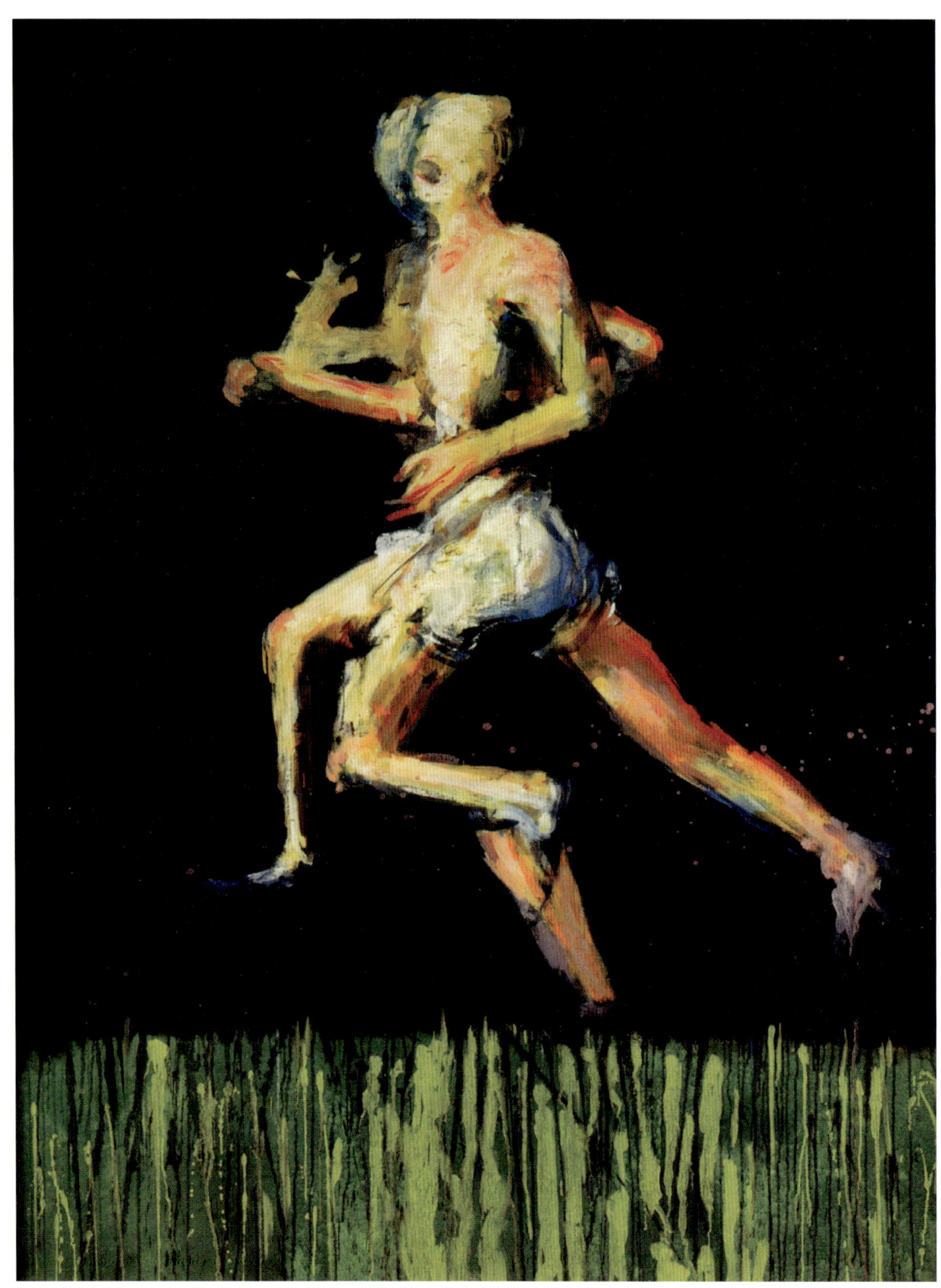

Runners 1955
Oil on canvas
150 × 116 cm

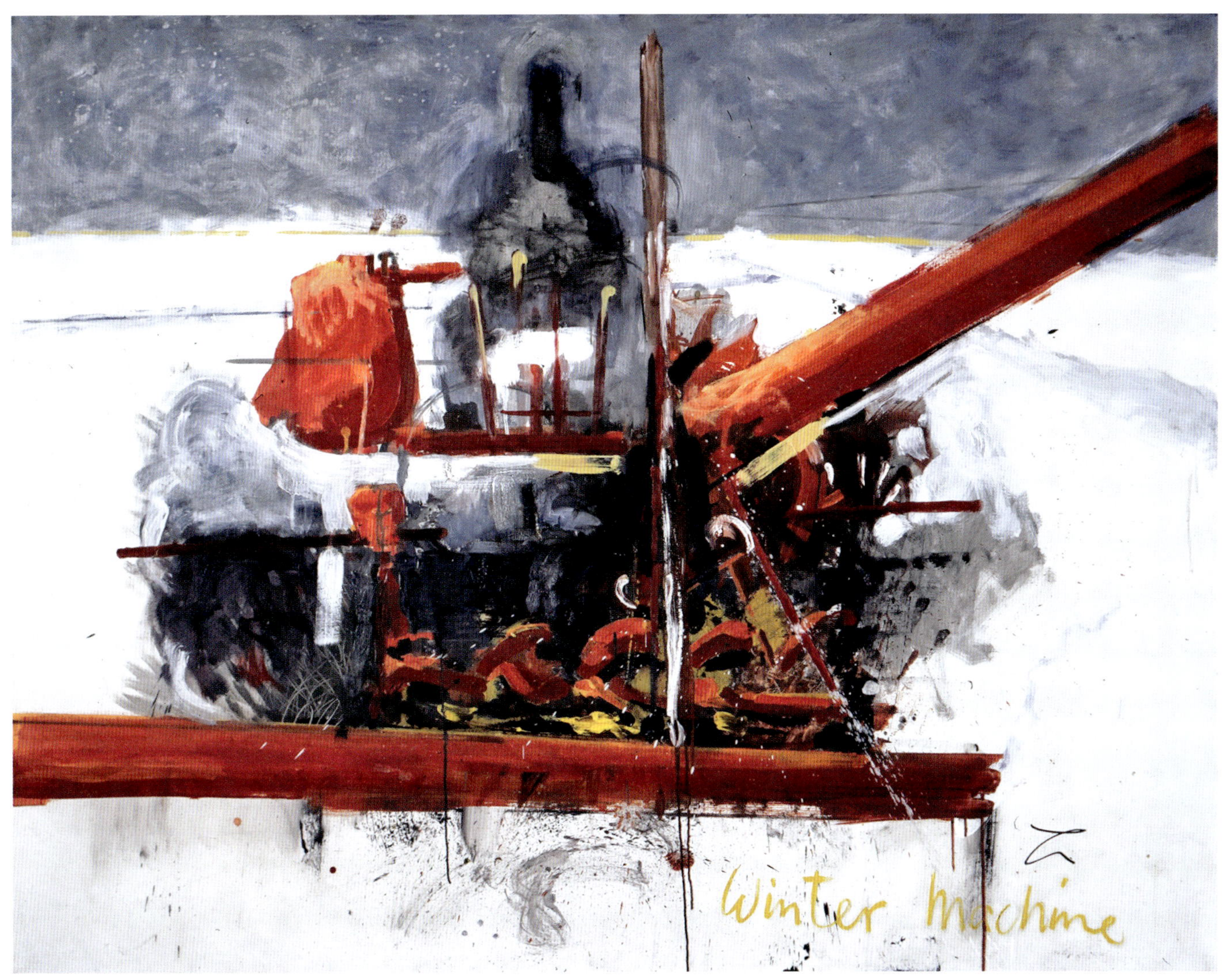

Winter Machine 1954
Oil on canvas
117 × 152 cm
Arts Council Collection,
Southbank Centre, London

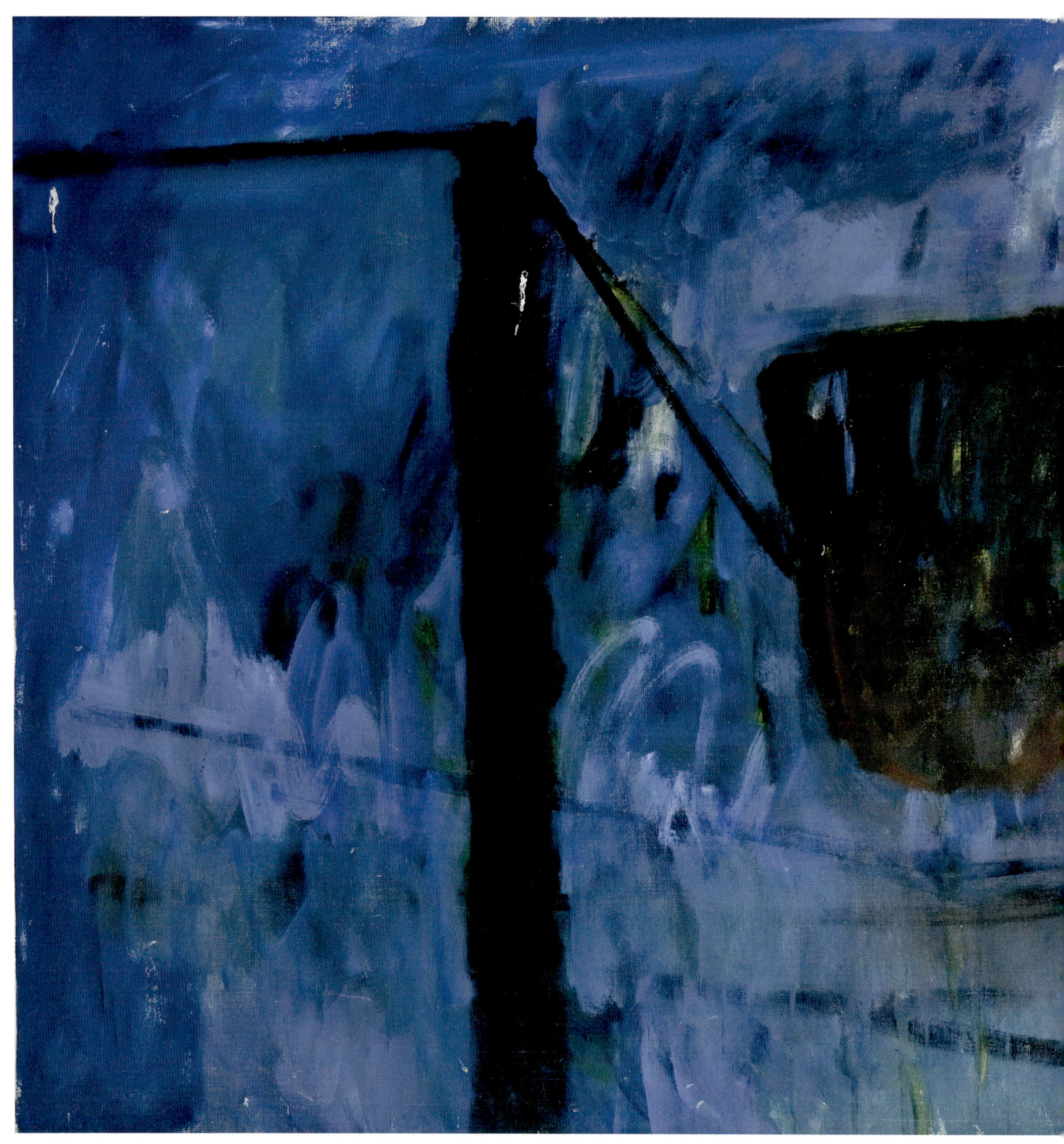

Precarious Drag 1956
Oil on canvas
100 × 200 cm

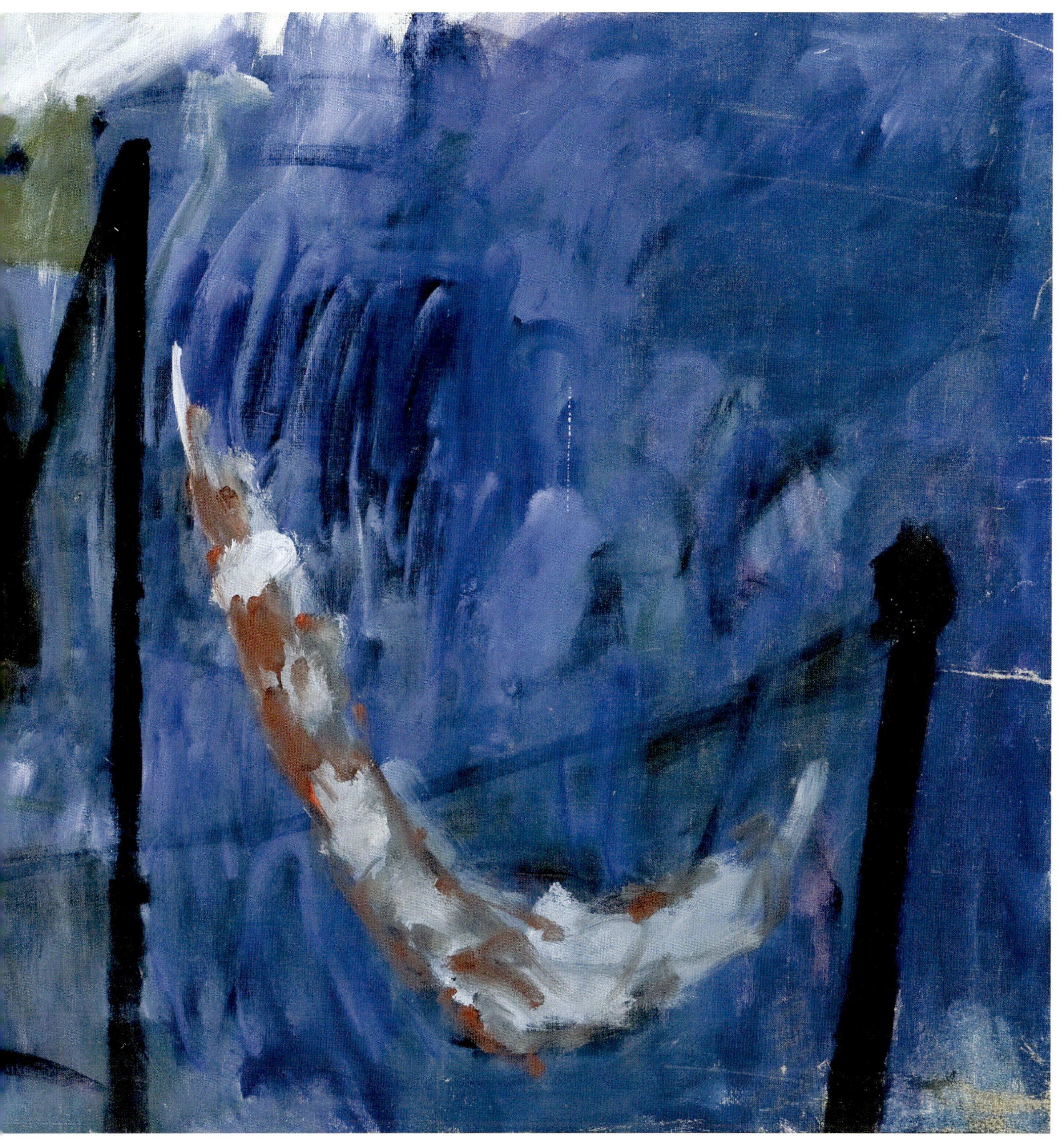

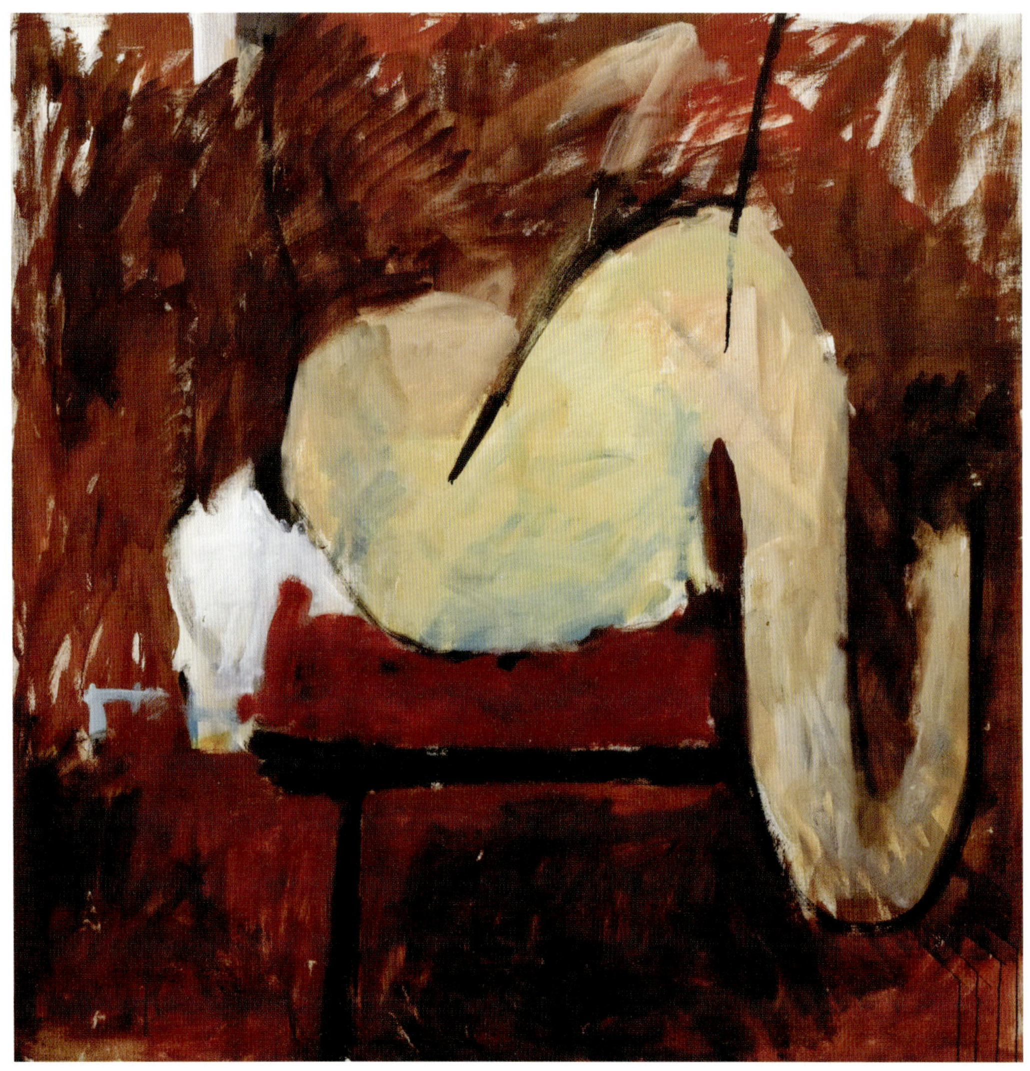

Lech 1957
Oil on canvas
140 × 140 cm

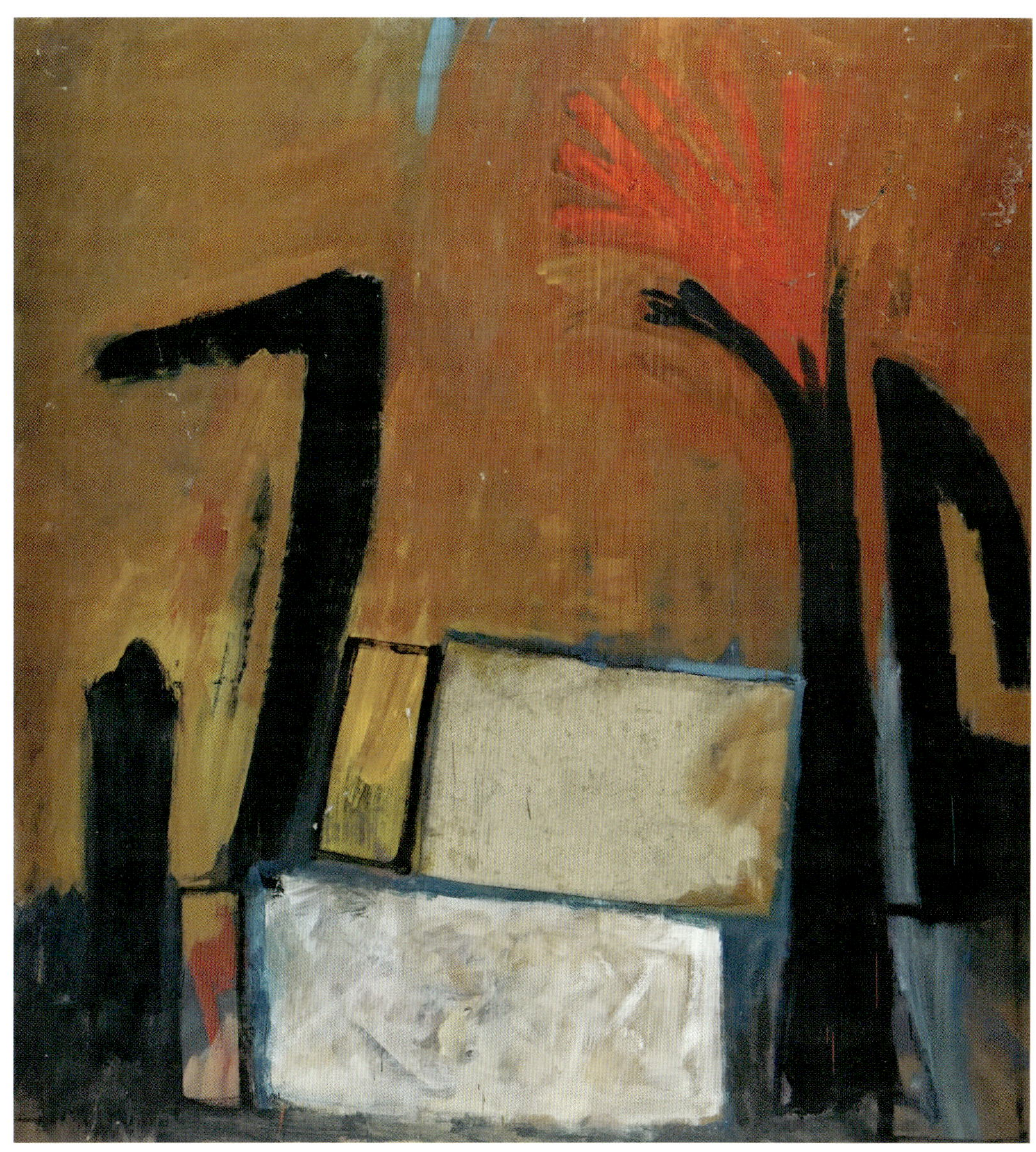

No. 13 1959
Oil on canvas
150 × 143 cm

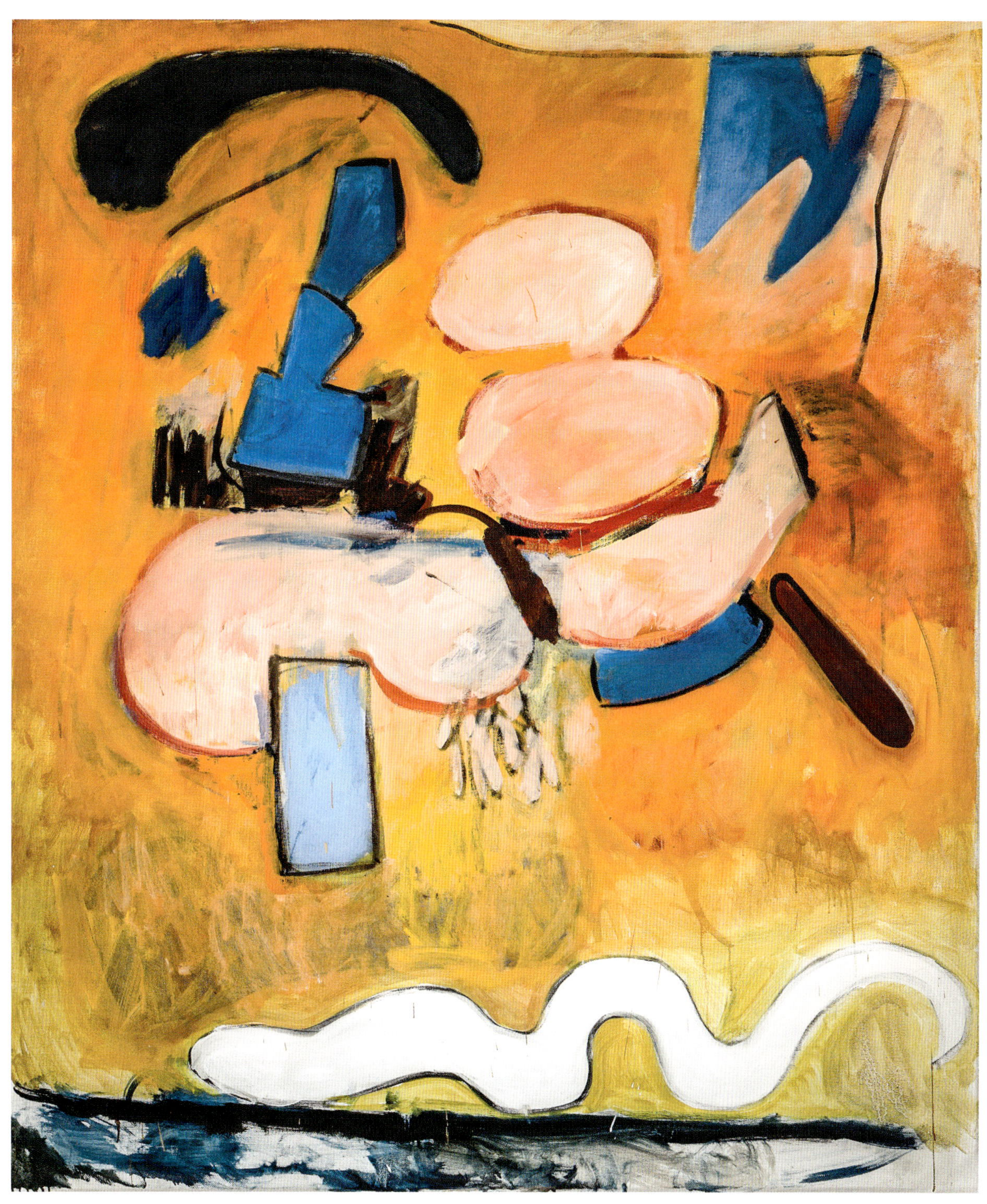

Untitled 1961
Oil on canvas
160 × 150 cm

‘I WAS FORTUNATE IN THAT I HAD THESE HALLUCINATIONS.... THEY HAD THE BENEFICIAL EFFECT OF MAKING ME MUCH MORE RECEPTIVE TO MY IMAGINATION. I NO LONGER PUZZLED ABOUT QUESTIONS OF SIGNIFICANCE OR ORIGINALITY, THE SORT OF QUESTIONS THAT HAD ENCOURAGED MY PERSONAL UNEASE AND NEGATIVITY IN THE PAST.’

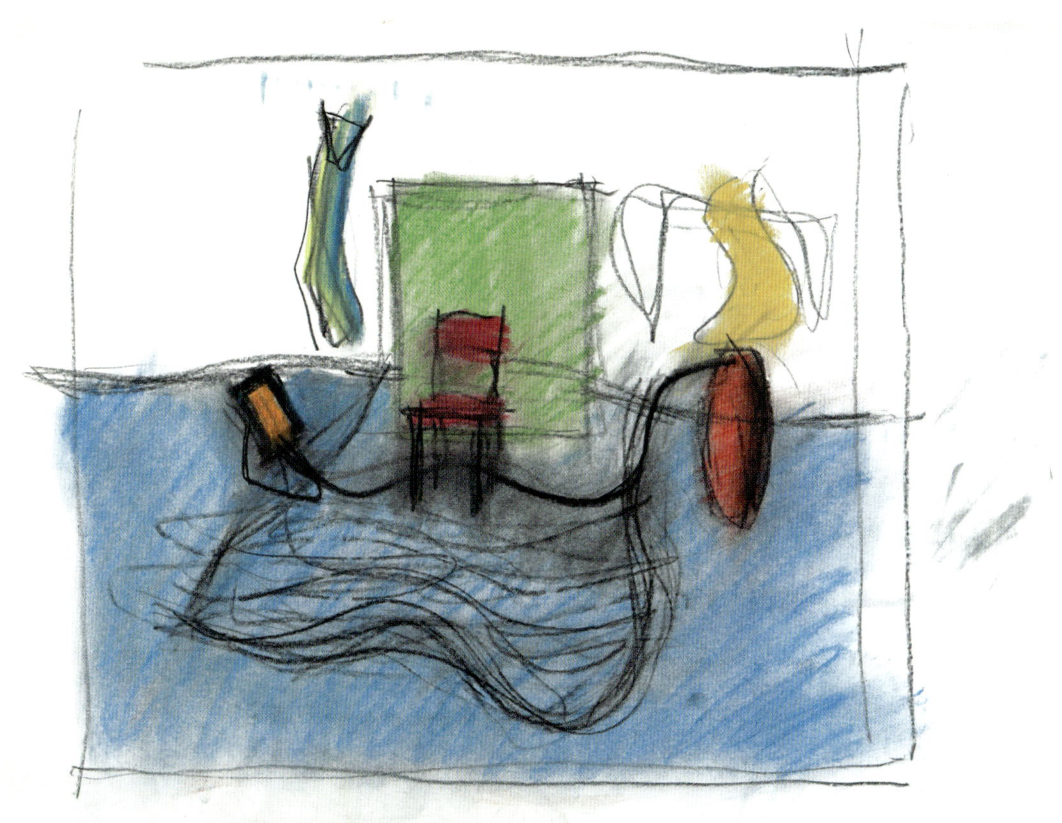

Study for Errant 1978
Charcoal and
pastel on paper
32 × 45 cm

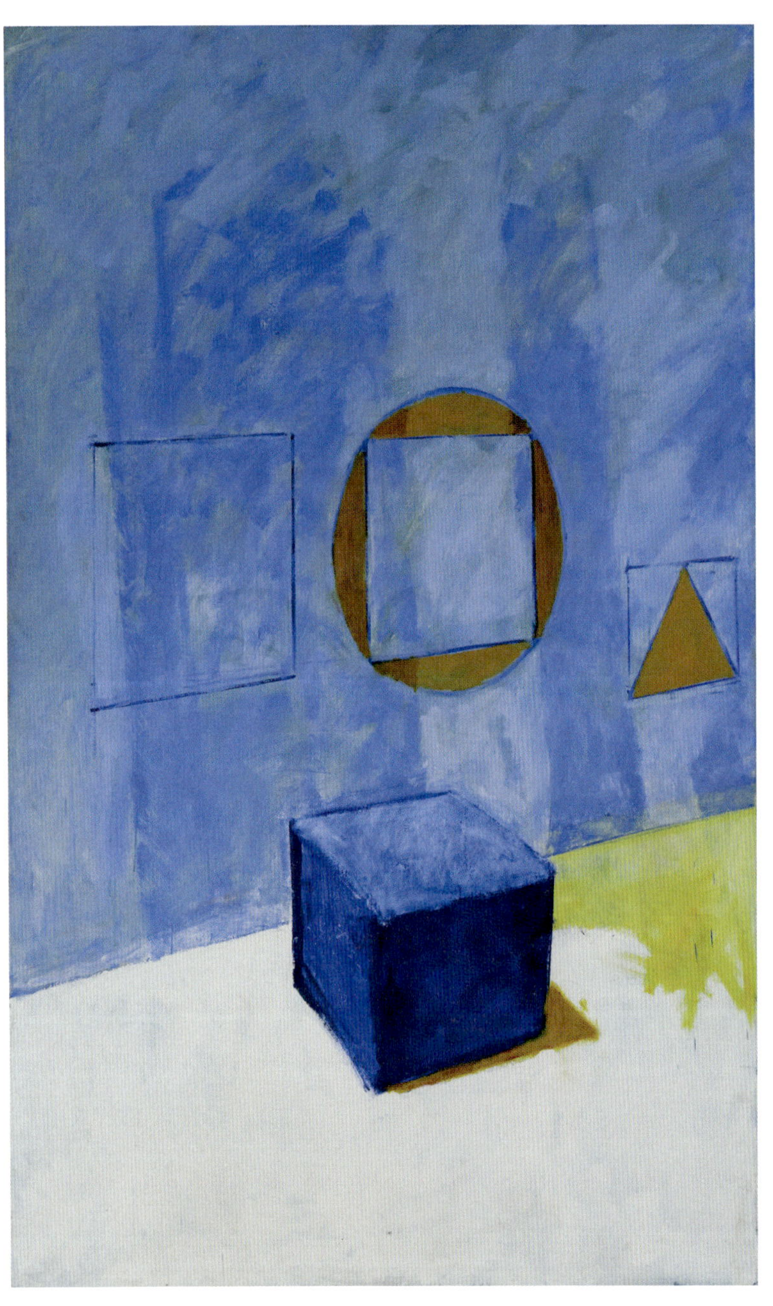

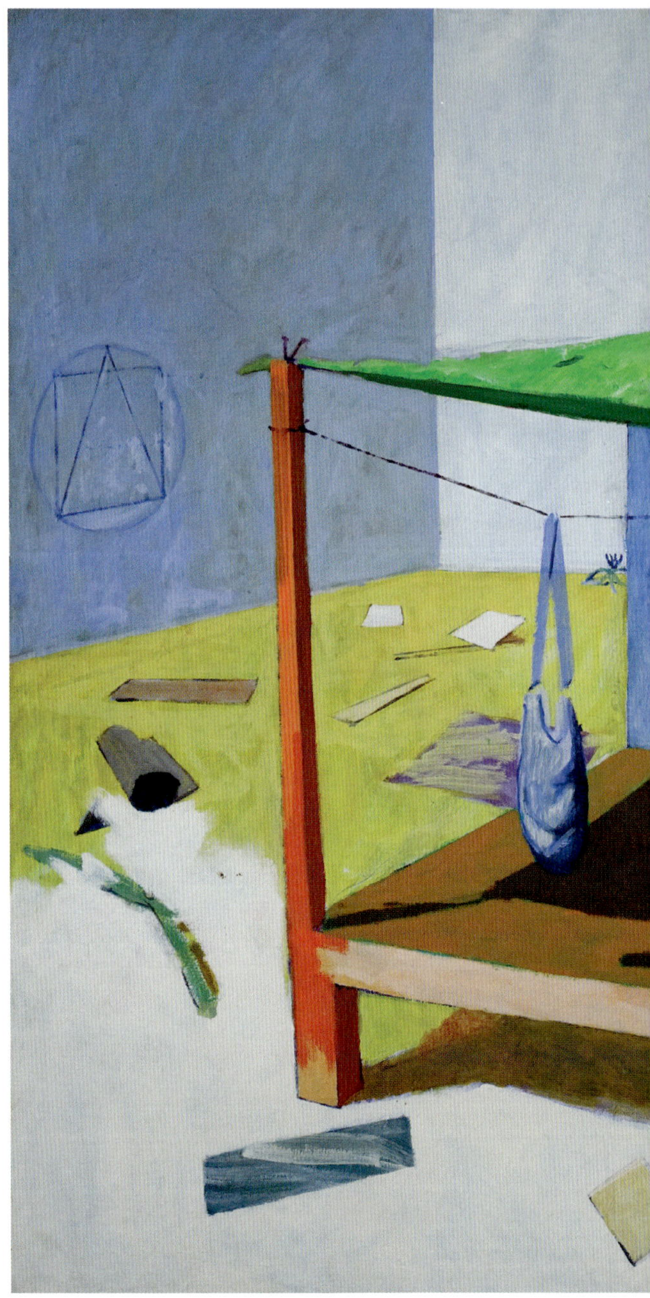

Place 1976–8
Oil on canvas
191 × 426 cm

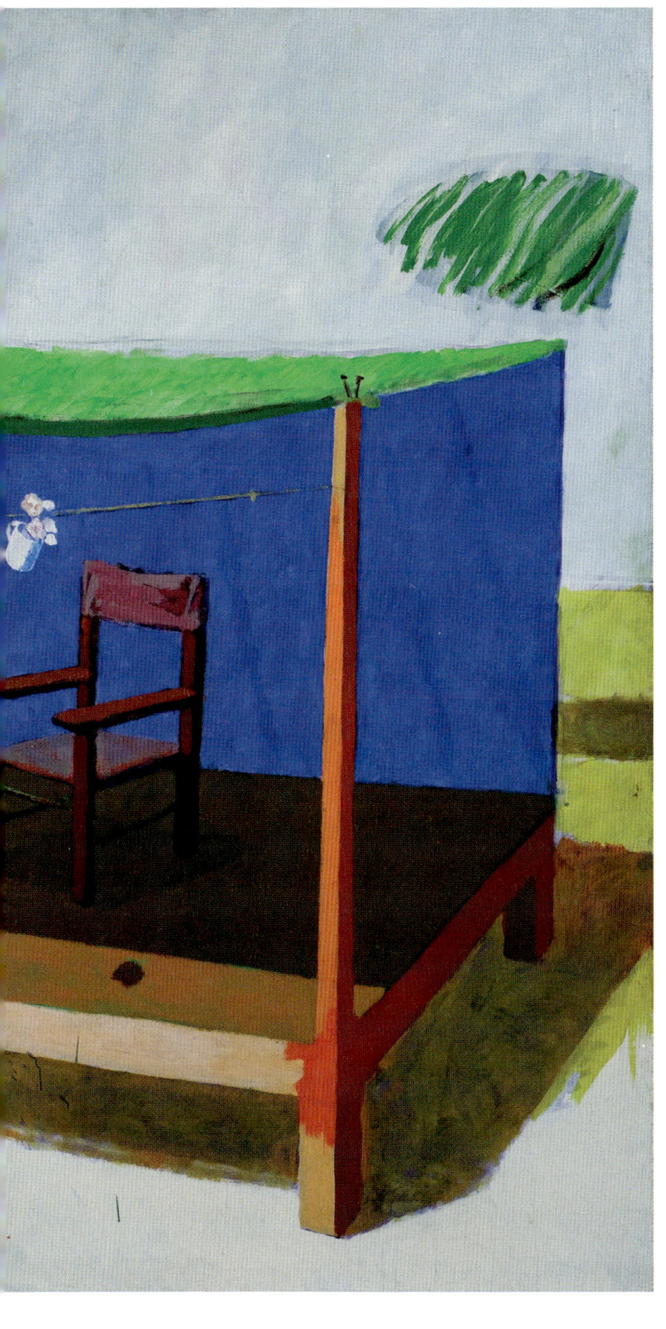

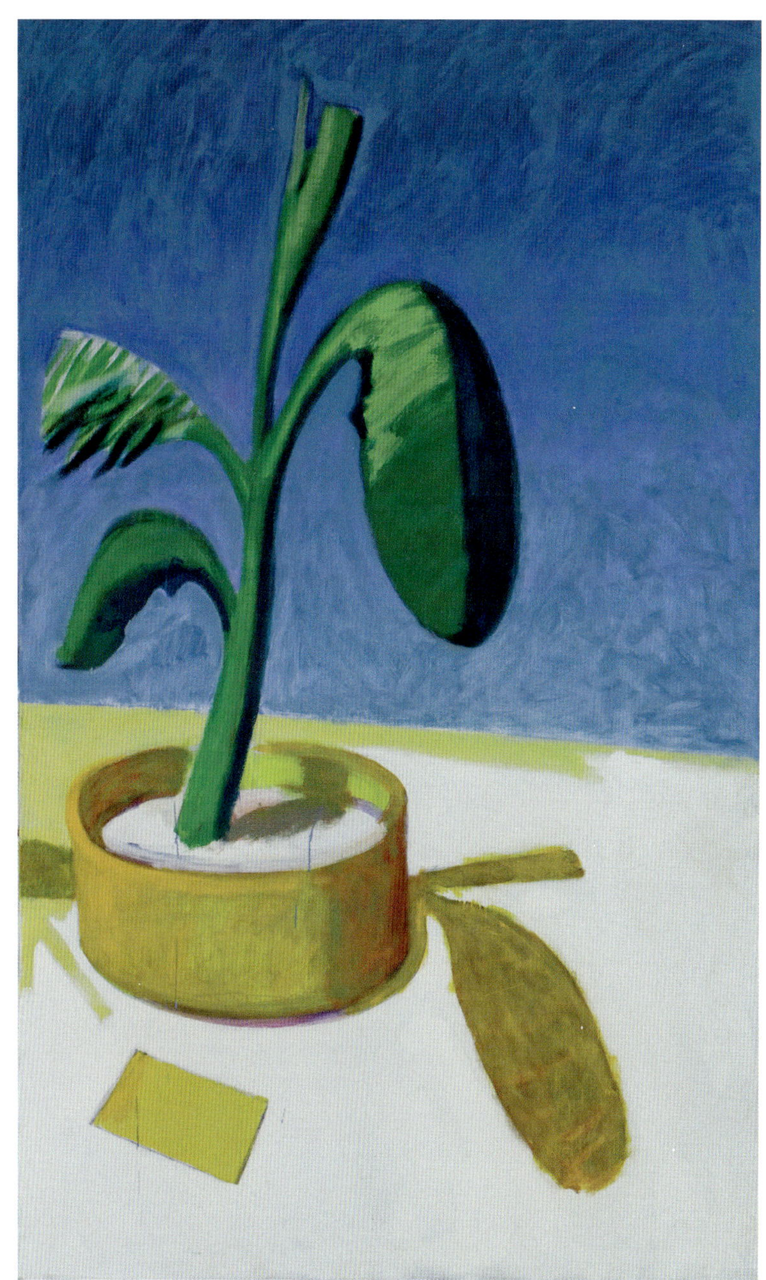

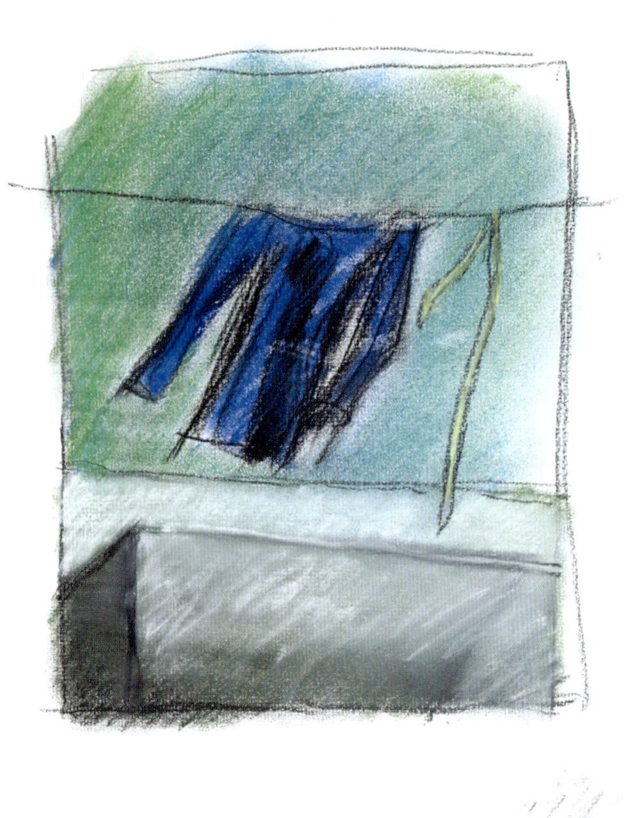

Untitled *c.* 1980
Charcoal and
pastel on paper
30 × 22.5 cm

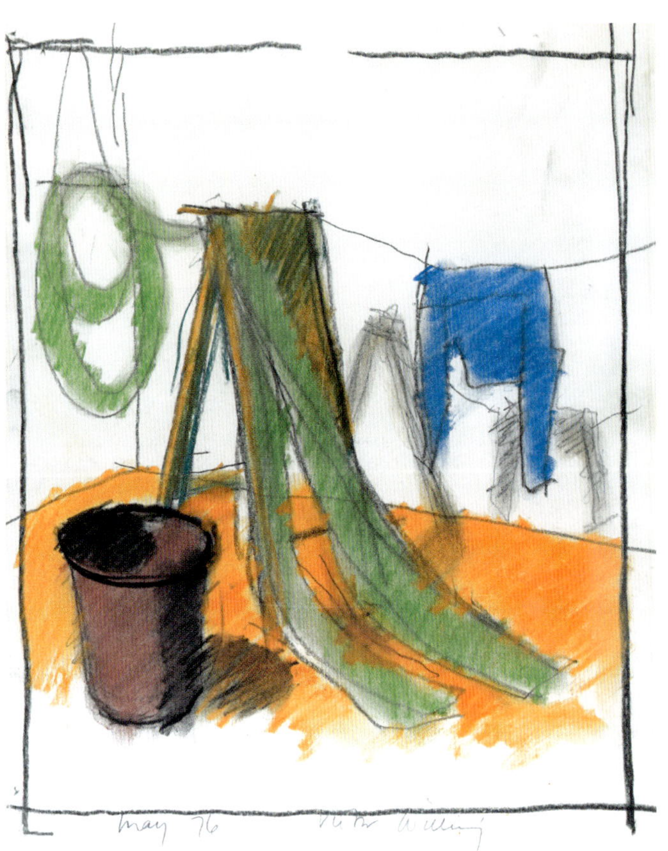

Green Drape 1976
Charcoal and
pastel on paper
45 × 35 cm

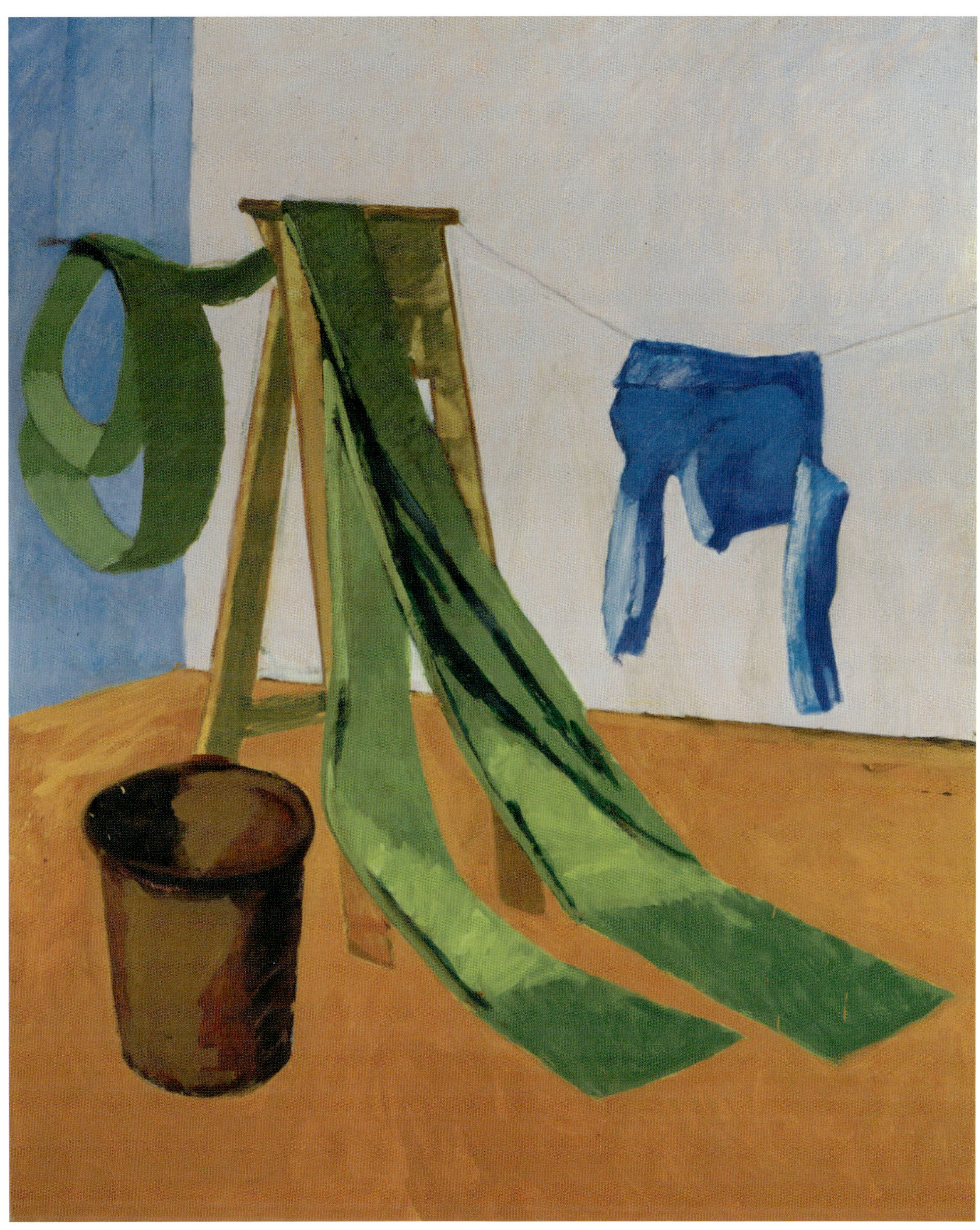

Stepladder 1976
Oil on canvas
183 × 152 cm
Pallant House Gallery,
Chichester, Wilson Loan (2006)

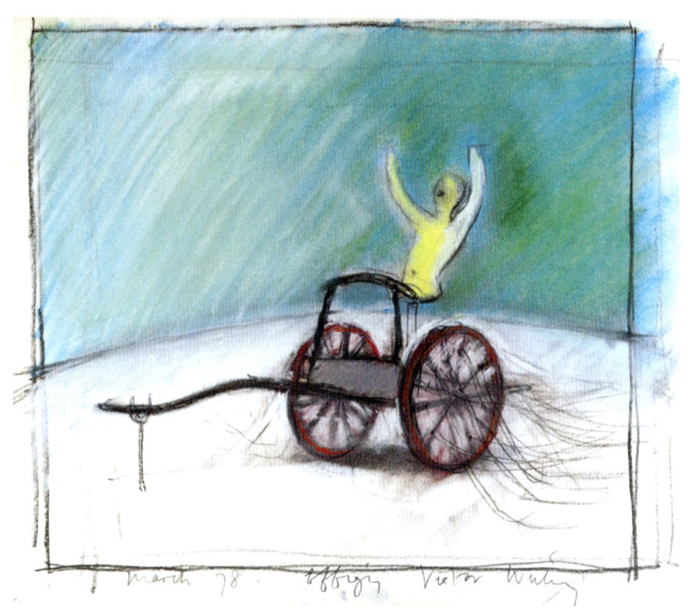

Effigy 1978
Crayon and
pastel on paper
24.5 × 32.5 cm

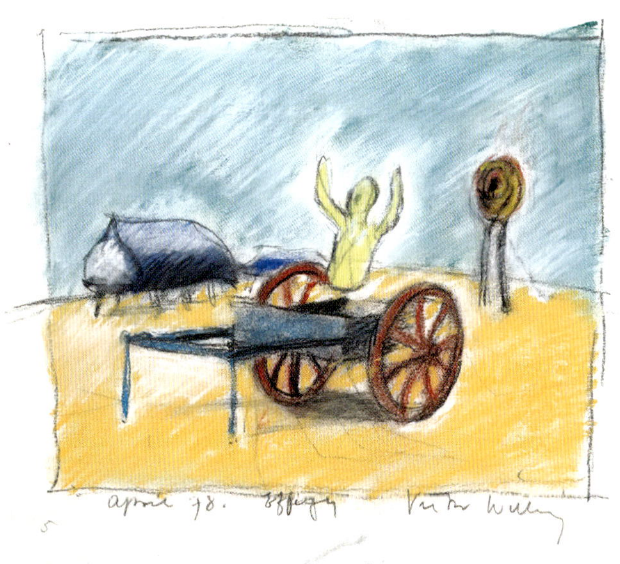

Effigy 1978
Crayon and
pastel on paper
32 × 39.5 cm

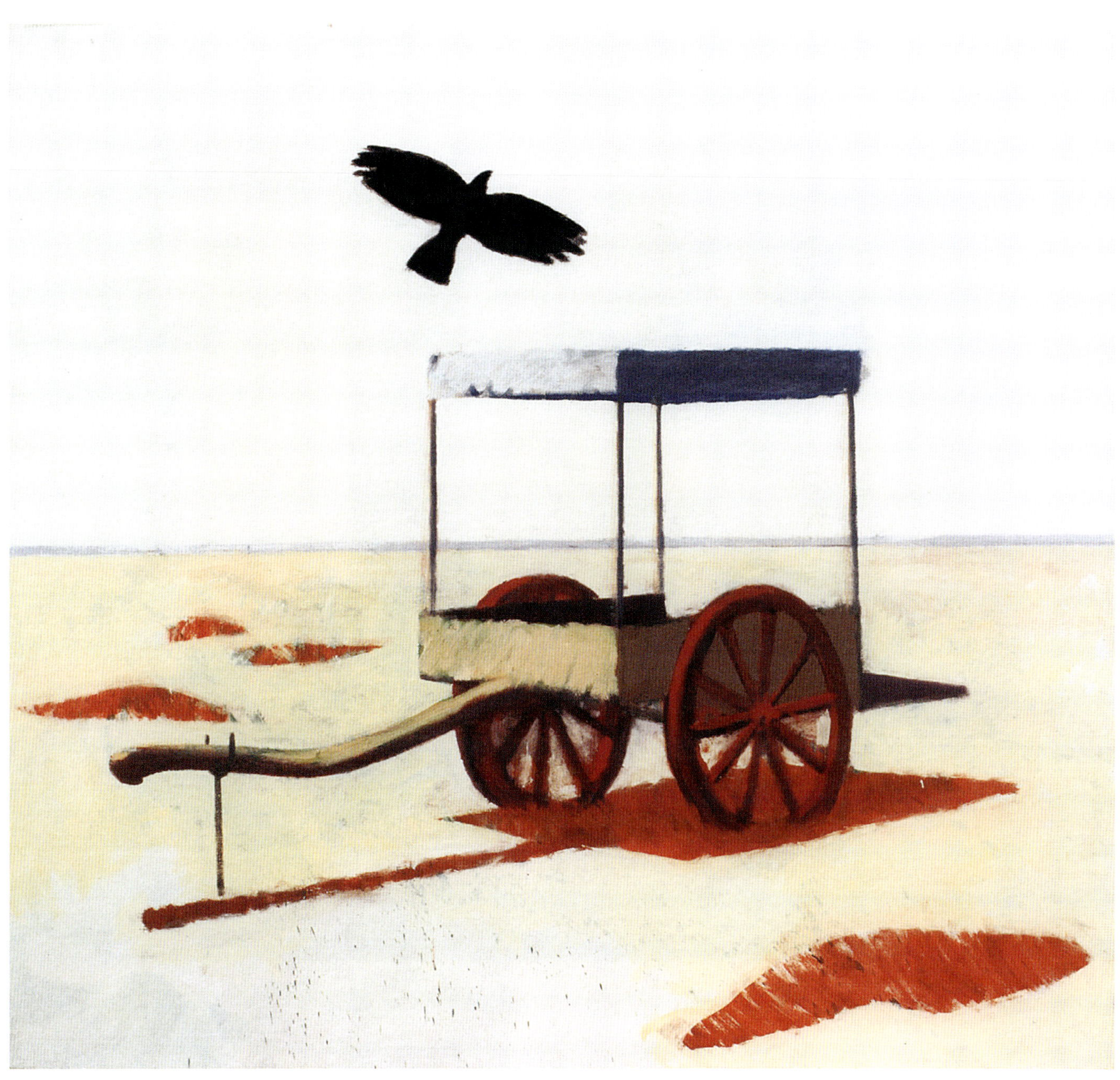

Cart 1978
Oil on canvas
188 × 208 cm

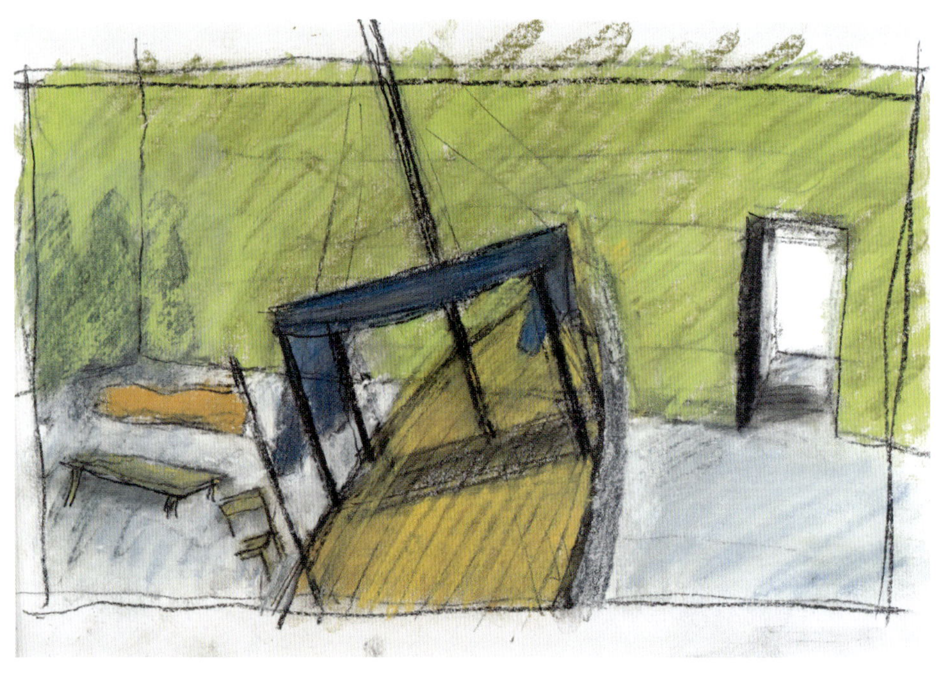

Study for Night 1978
Charcoal and
pastel on paper
41 × 54 cm

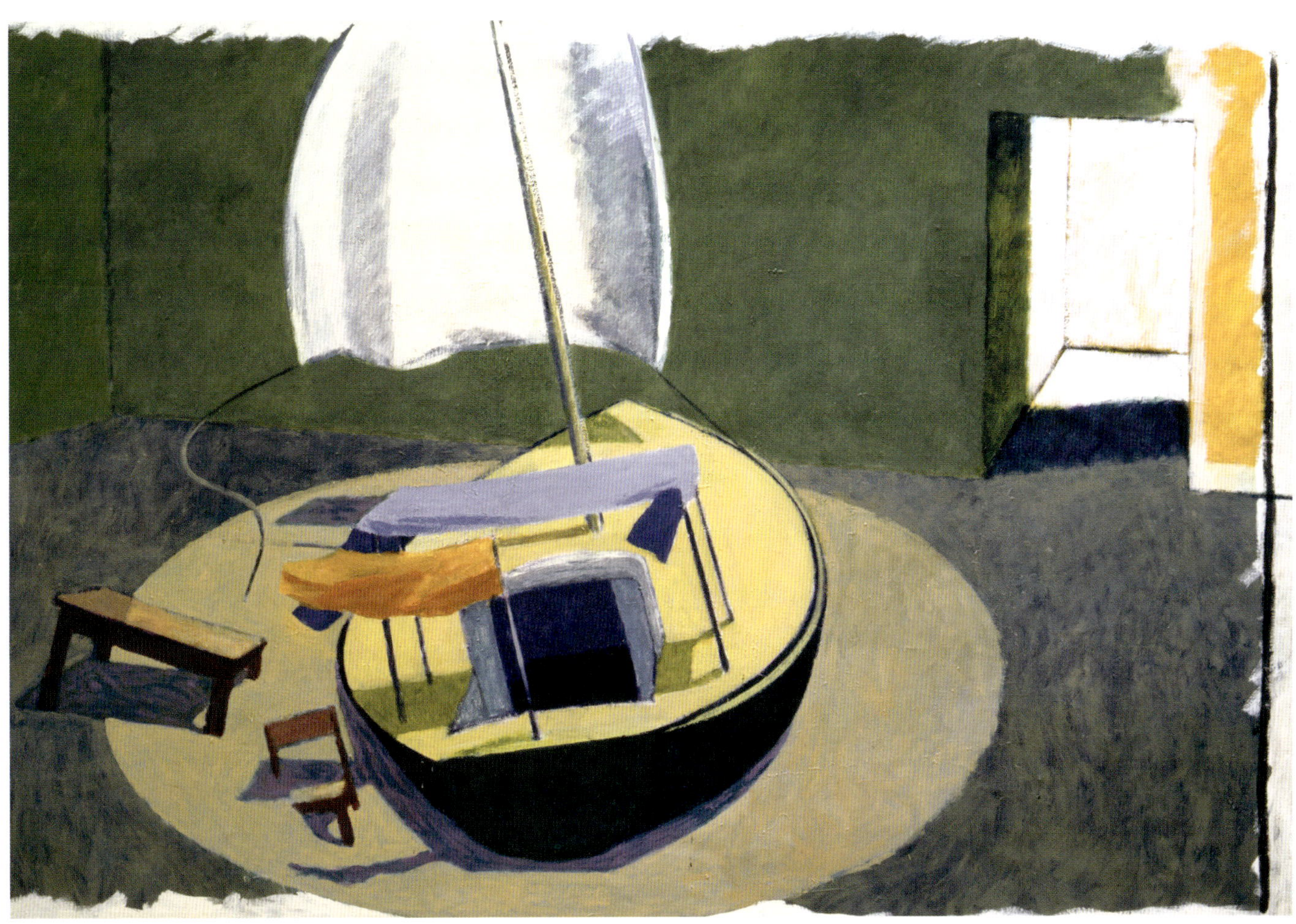

Night 1978
Oil on canvas
228 × 315 cm
Pallant House Gallery,
Chichester, Wilson
Gift through The Art
Fund (2006)

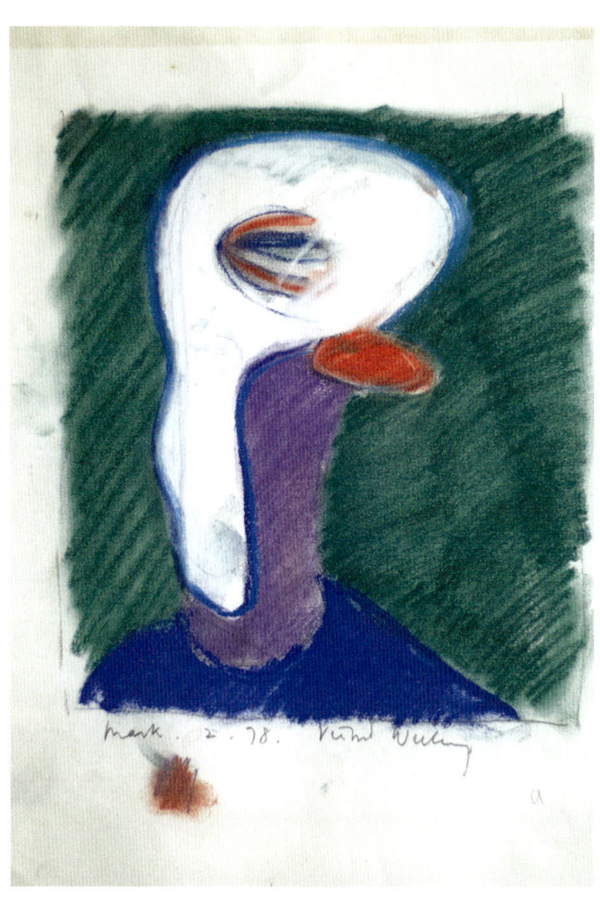

Mask 1978
Crayon and
pastel on paper
38 × 28.5 cm

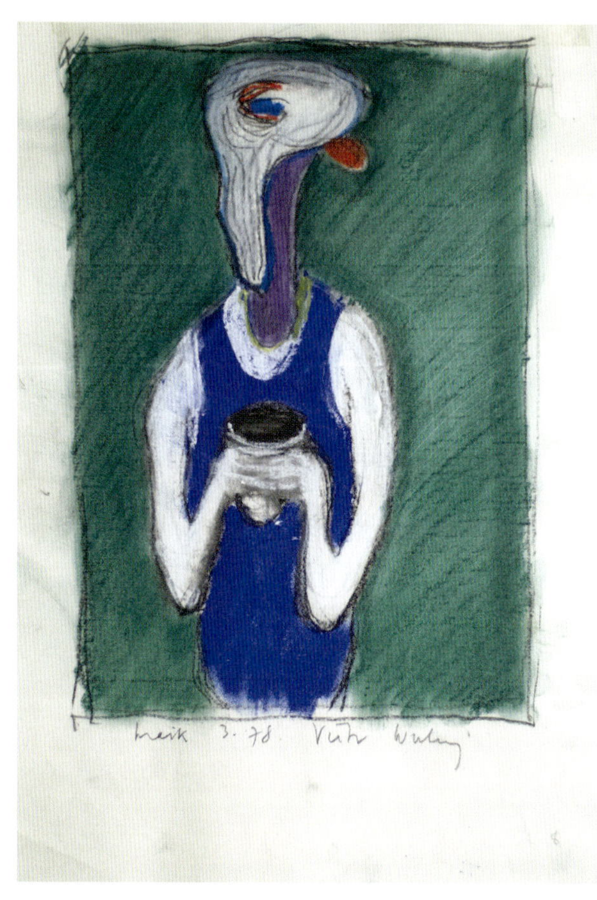

Mask 1978
Crayon and
pastel on paper
38 × 28.5 cm

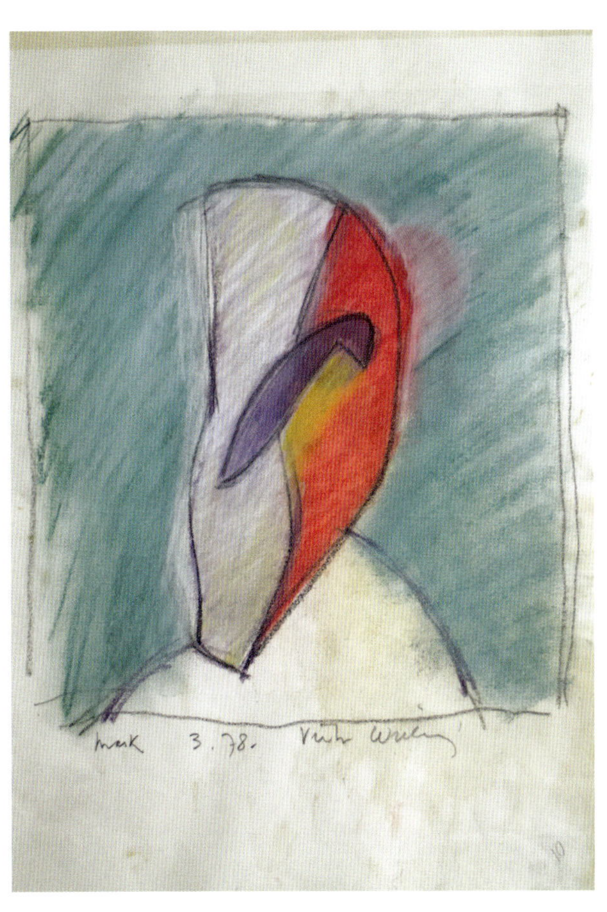

Mask 1978
Crayon and
pastel on paper
38 × 28.5 cm

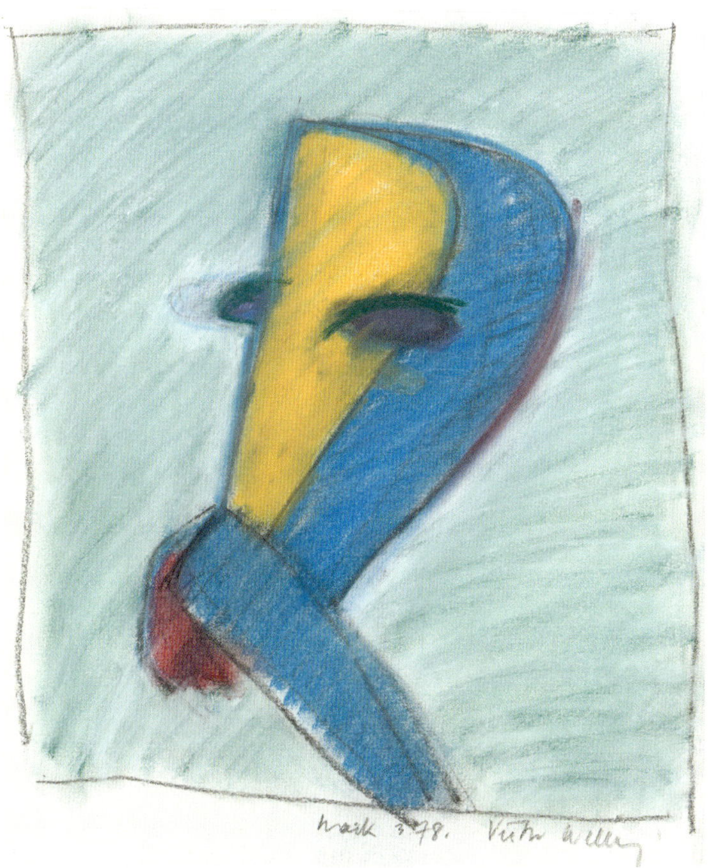

Mask 1978
Crayon and
pastel on paper
38 × 28.5 cm

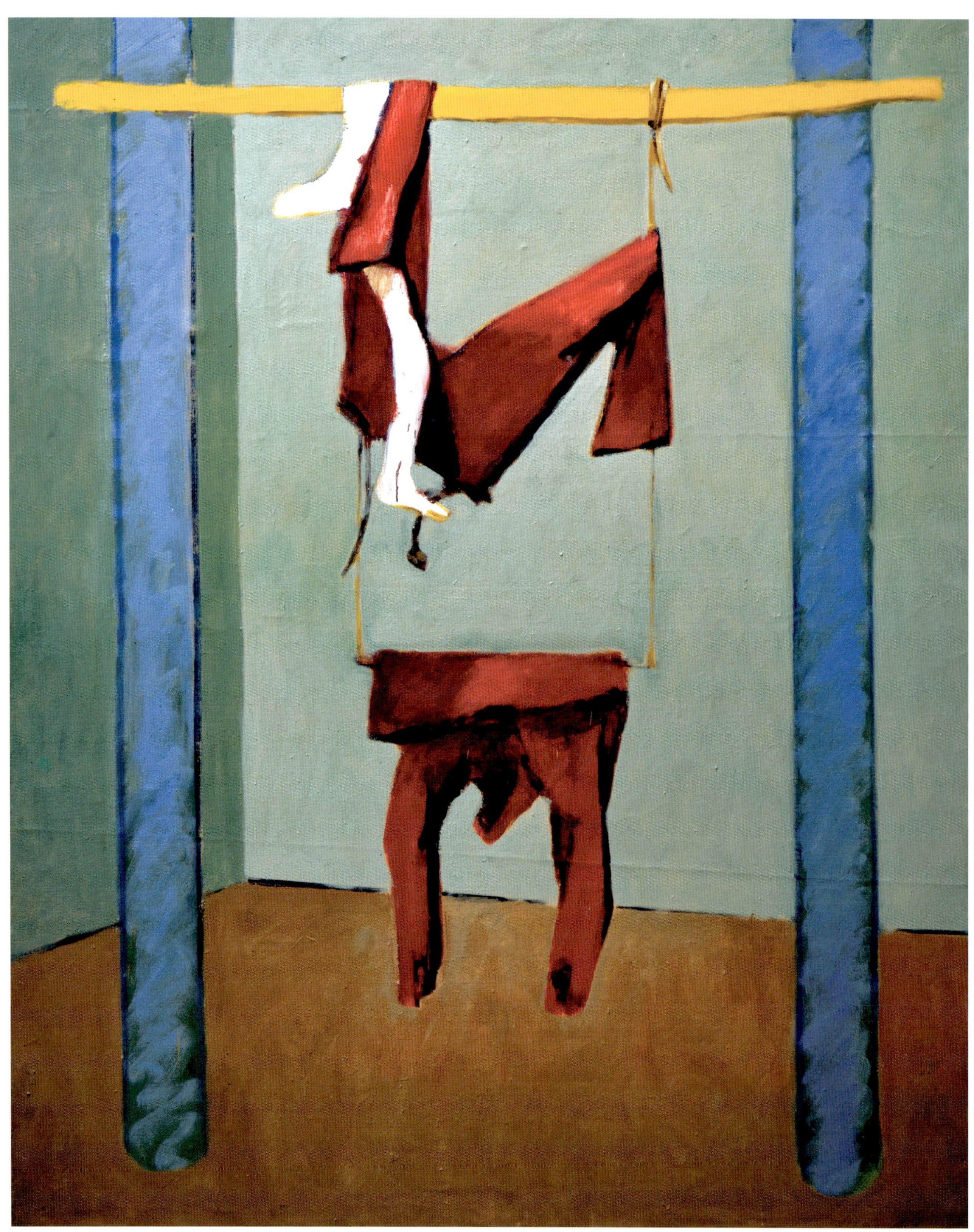

Swing 1978
Oil on canvas
183 × 152 cm
Pallant House Gallery,
Chichester, Wilson Loan
(2006)

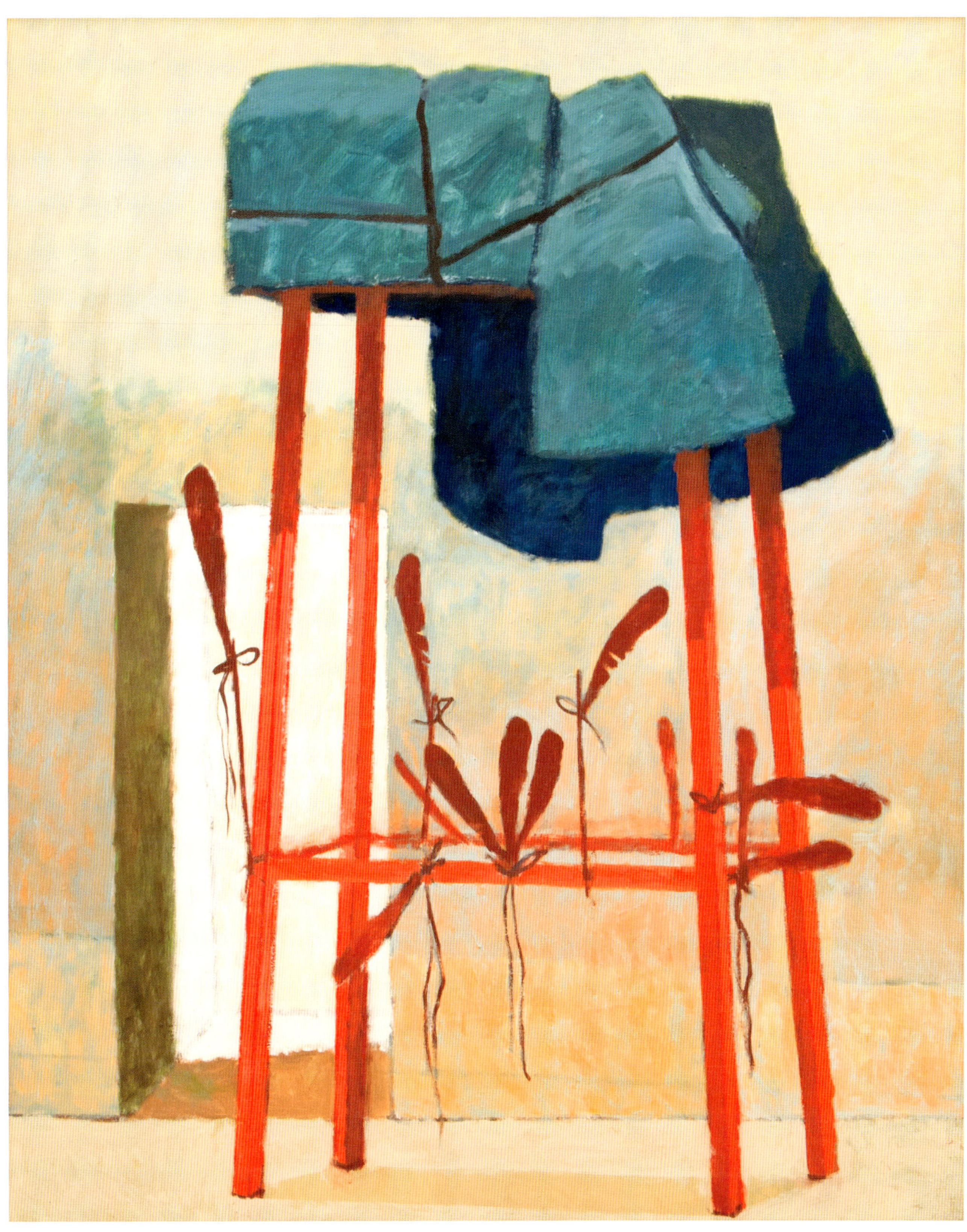

Feathers 1979
Oil on canvas
179 × 153 cm
Rugby Art Gallery and
Museum Art Collections

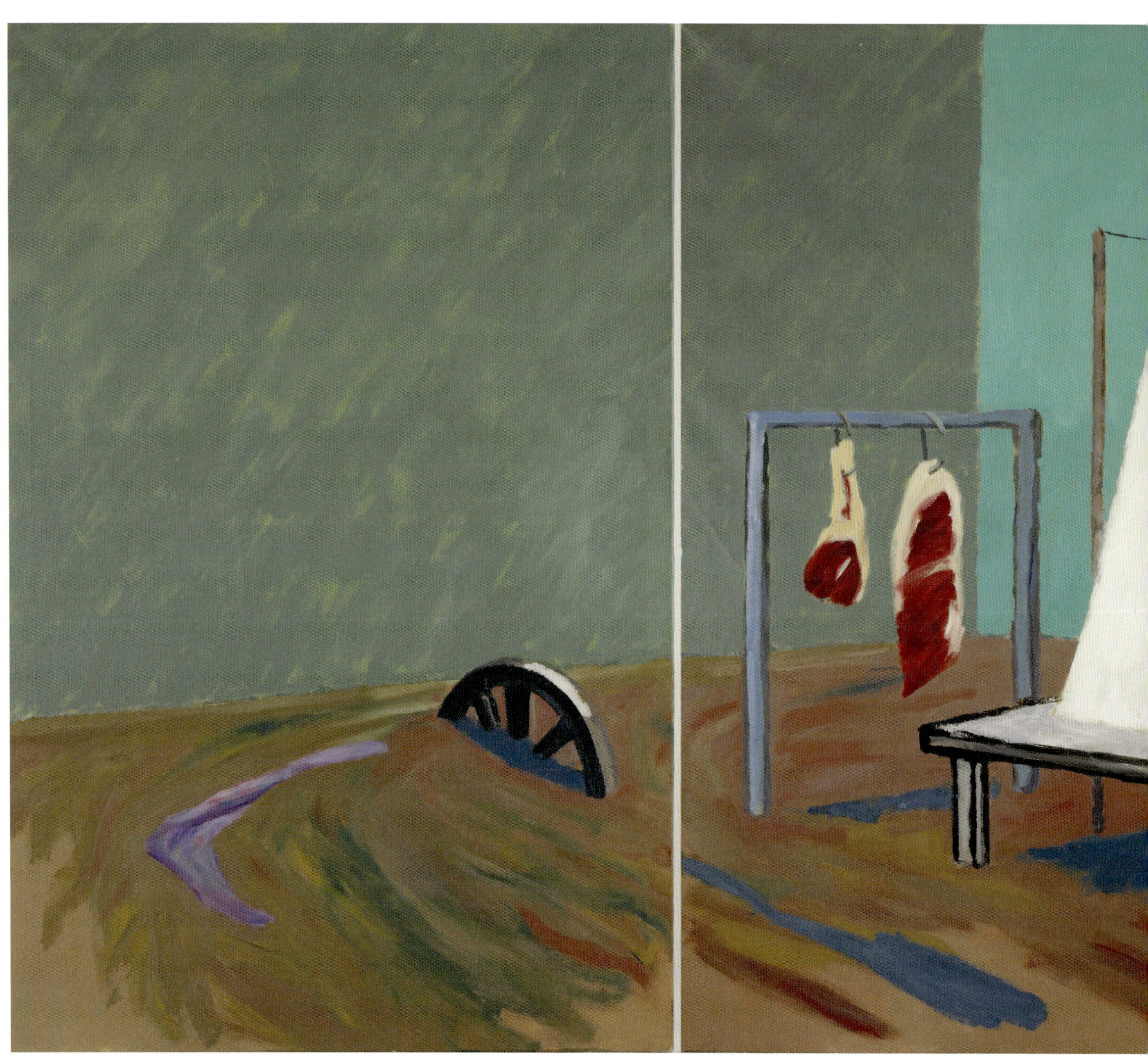

Mud 1979–80
Oil on canvas
183 × 426 cm
Arts Council Collection,
Southbank Centre, London

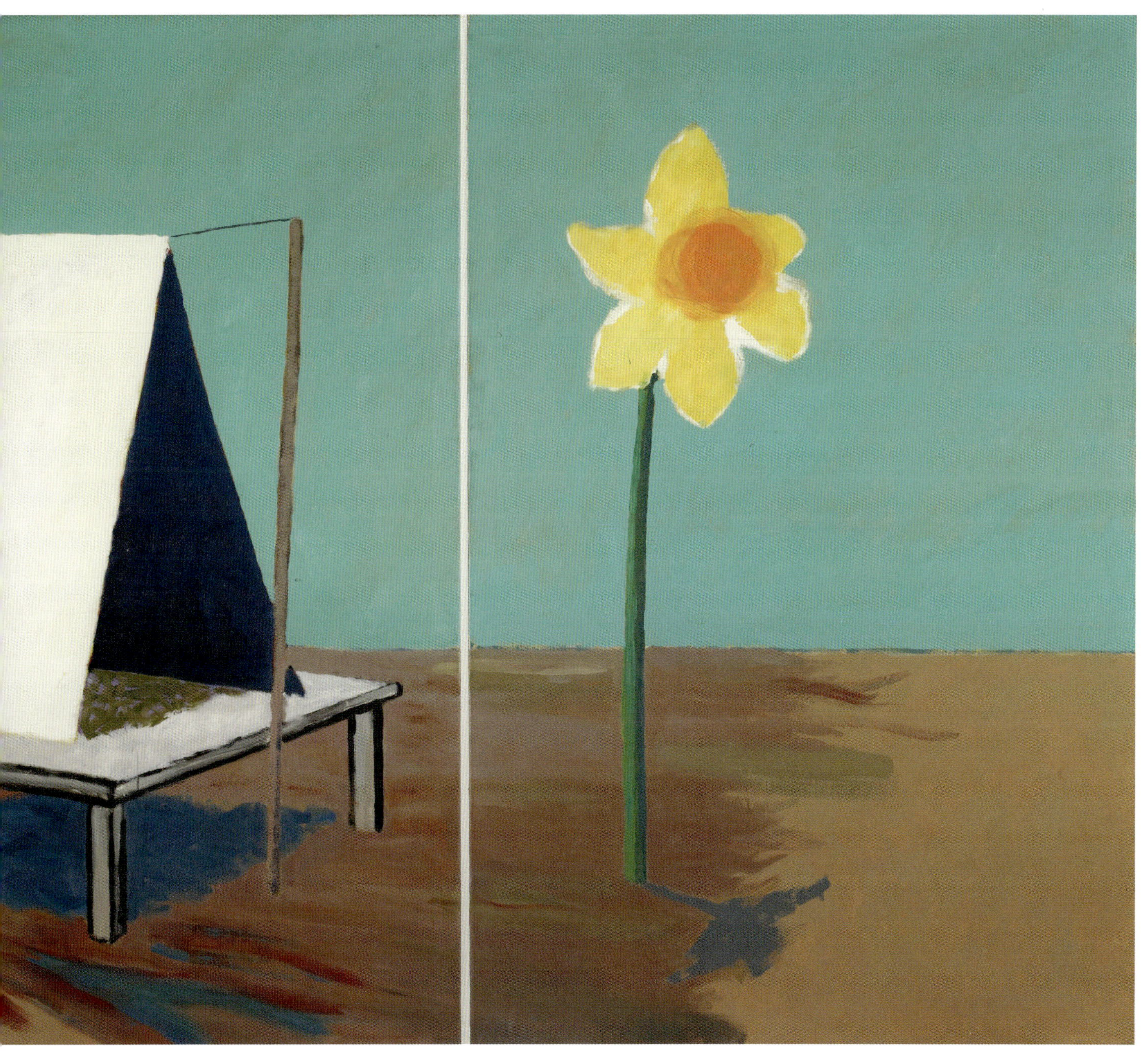

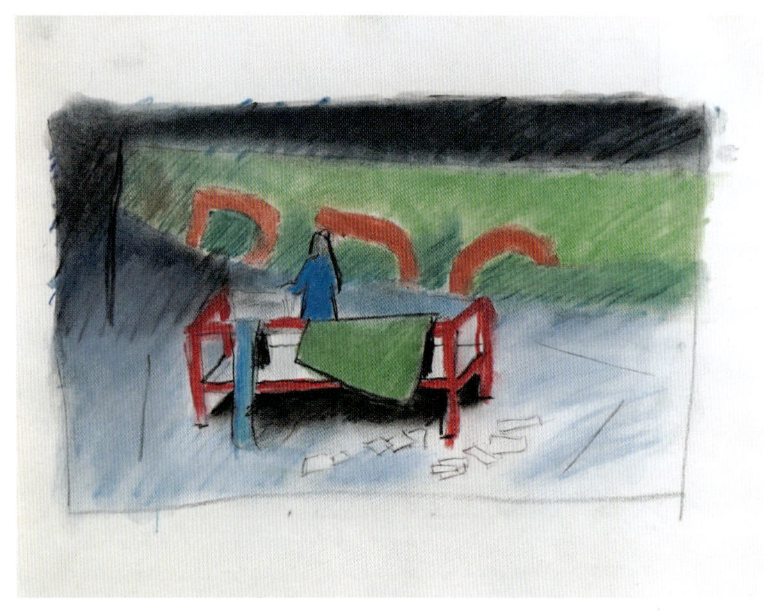

Untitled date unknown
Crayon and
pastel on paper
32 × 42 cm

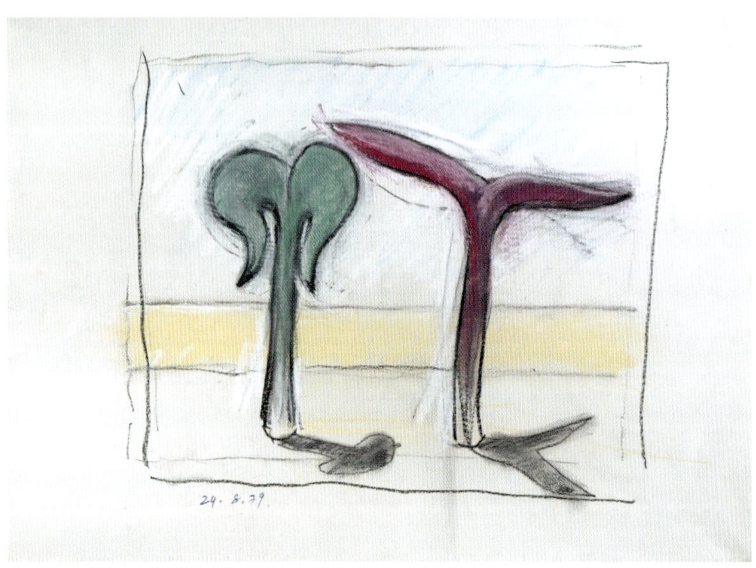

Untitled 1979
Crayon and
pastel on paper
32 × 42 cm

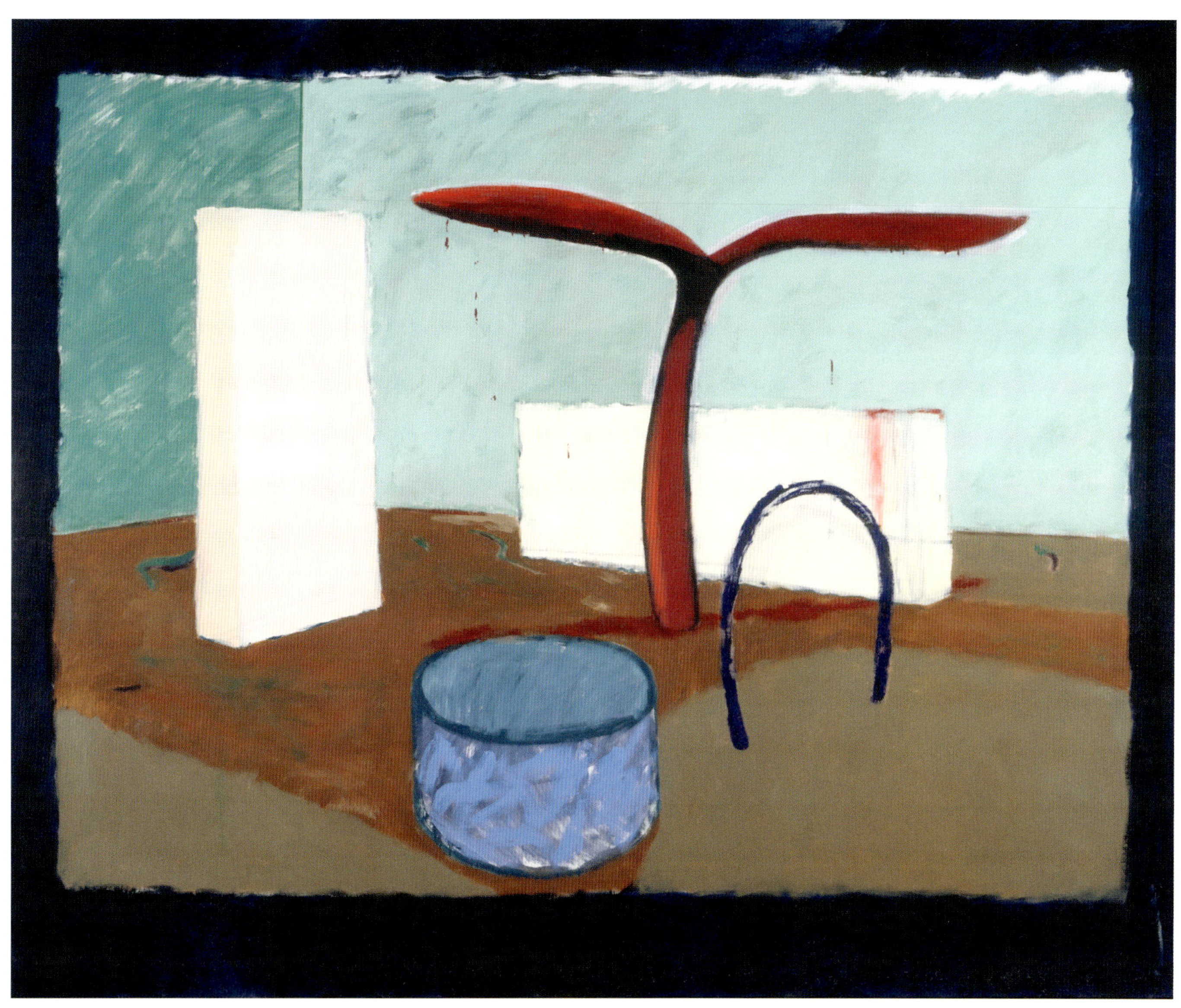

Place with a Red Thing 1980
Oil on canvas
200 × 250 cm
Tate: Purchased 1980

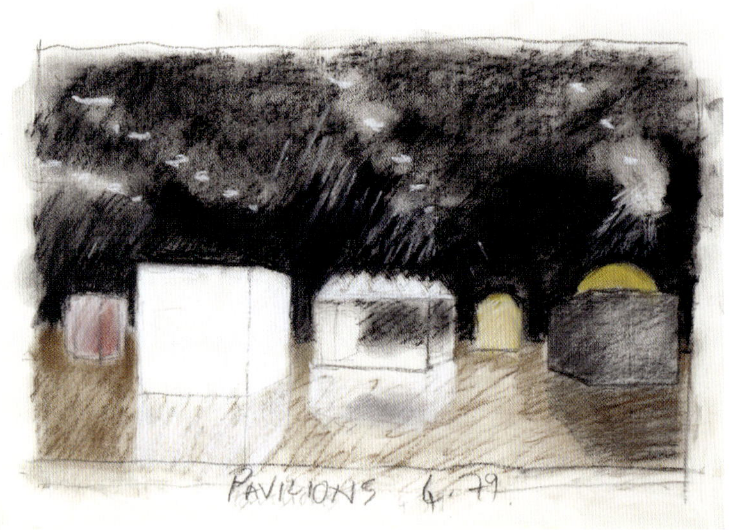

Pavilions 1979
Crayon and
pastel on paper
30 × 42 cm

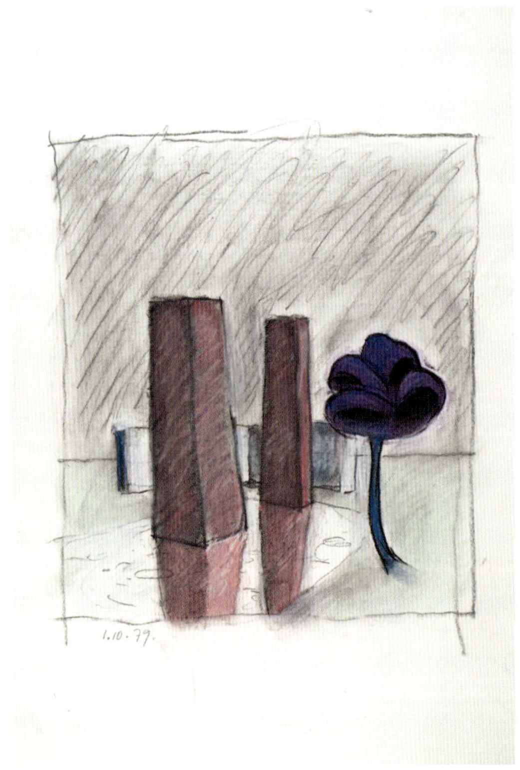

Untitled 1978
Crayon and
pastel on paper
42 × 30 cm

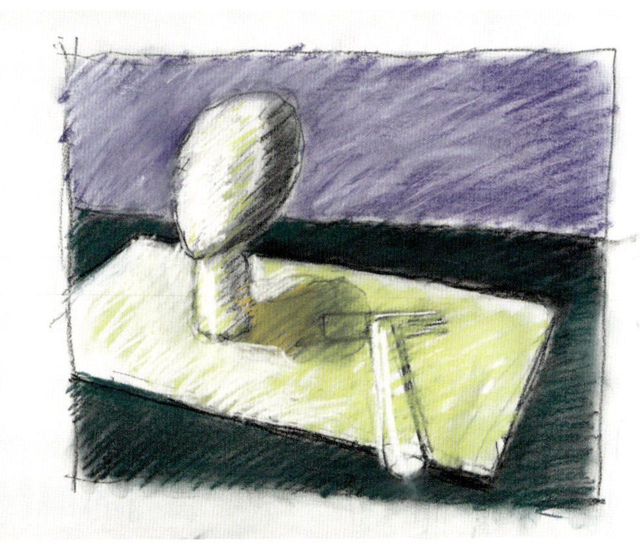

Mask and Hammer *c.* 1980
Crayon and
pastel on paper
30 × 42 cm

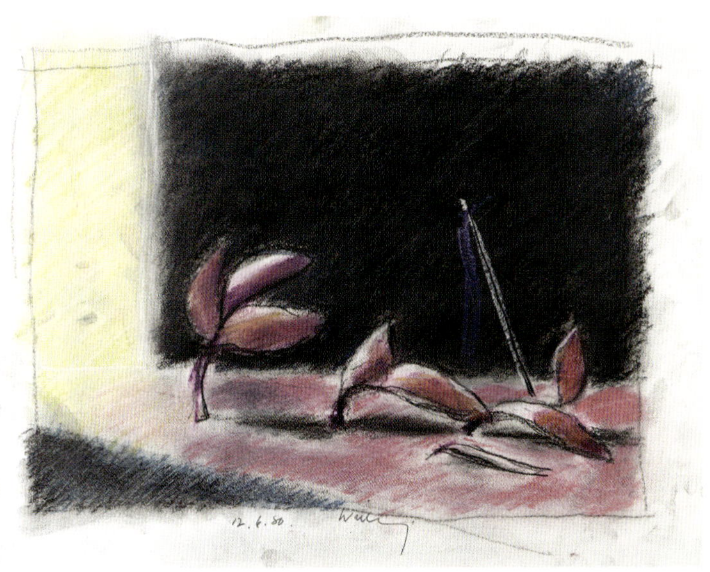

Untitled 1980
Crayon and
pastel on paper
28 × 37.8 cm

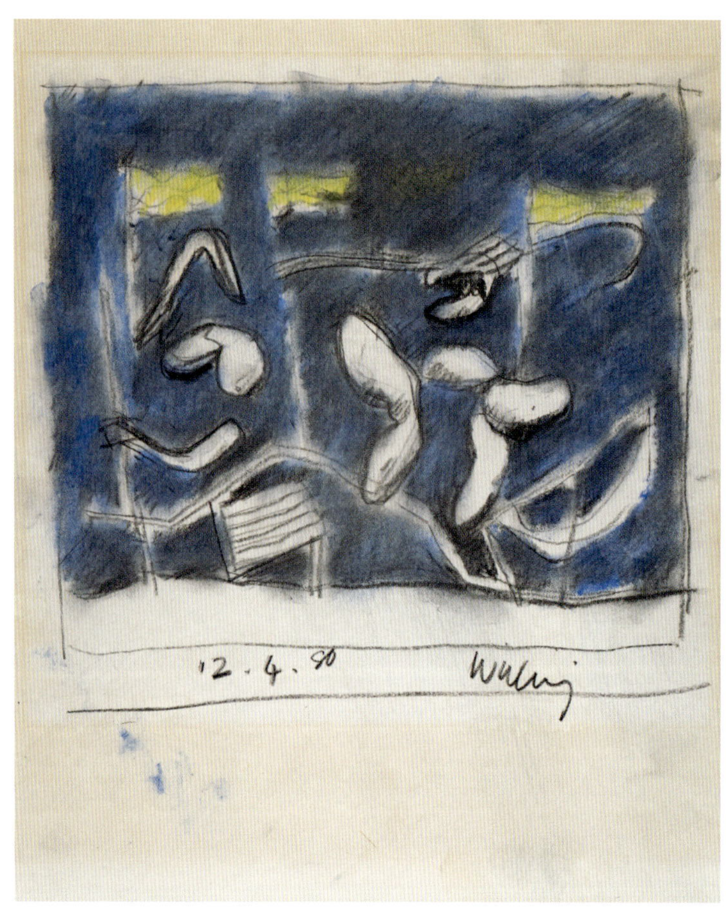

Study for Mother 1980
Crayon and
pastel on paper
38 × 29.5 cm

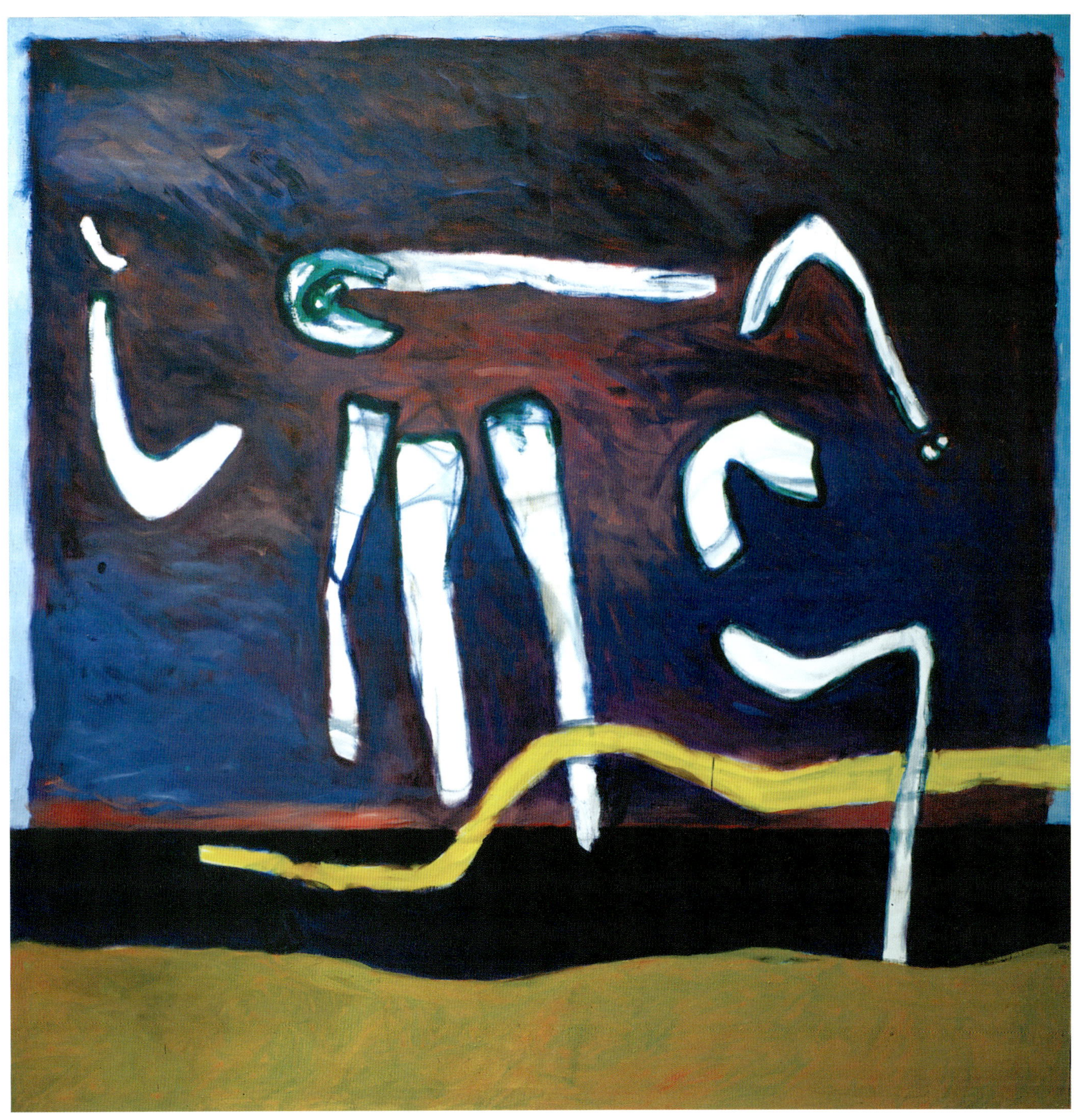

Mother 1980
Oil on canvas
200 × 200 cm

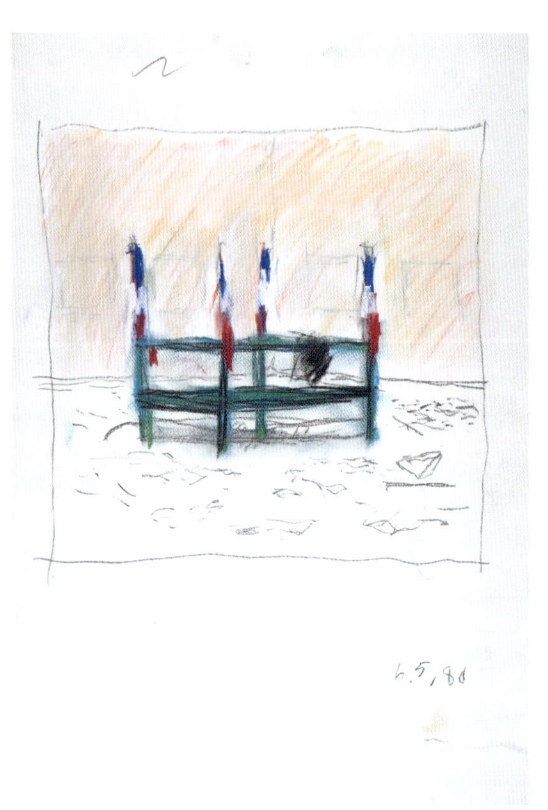

Untitled 1980
Crayon and
pastel on paper
42.5 × 30 cm

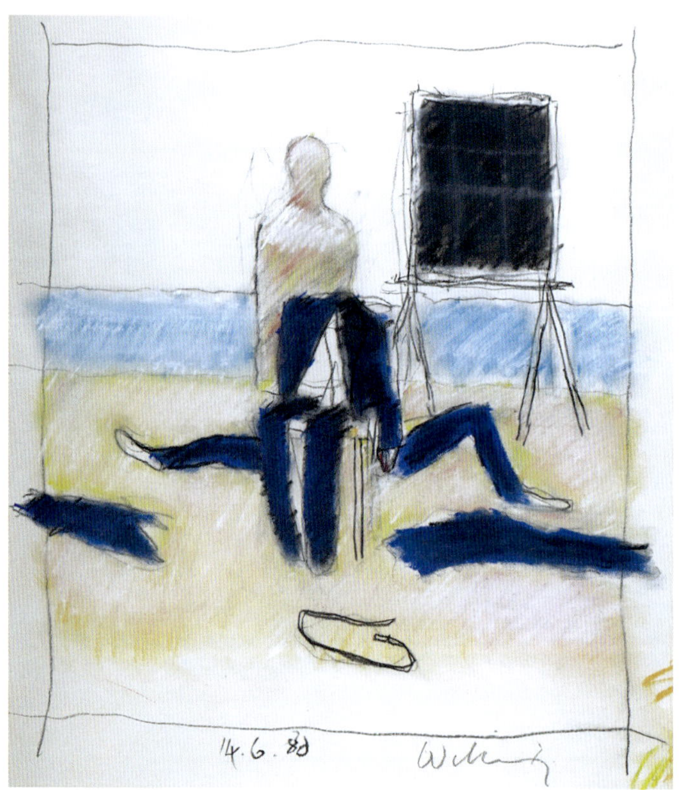

Study for Rien 1980
Crayon and
pastel on paper
82 × 73 cm (framed)

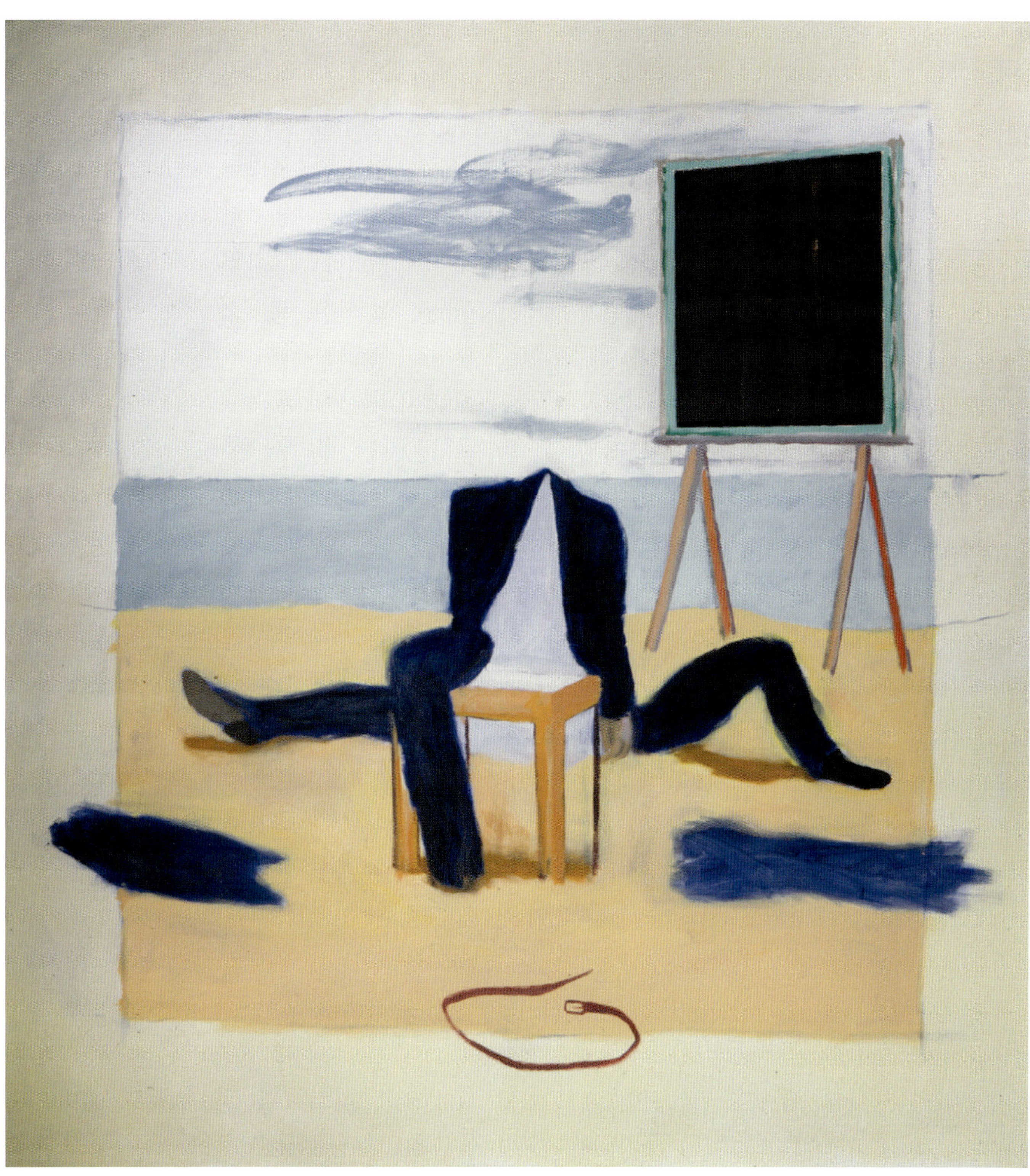

Rien 1980
Oil on canvas
200 × 183 cm
Tate: Purchased 1980

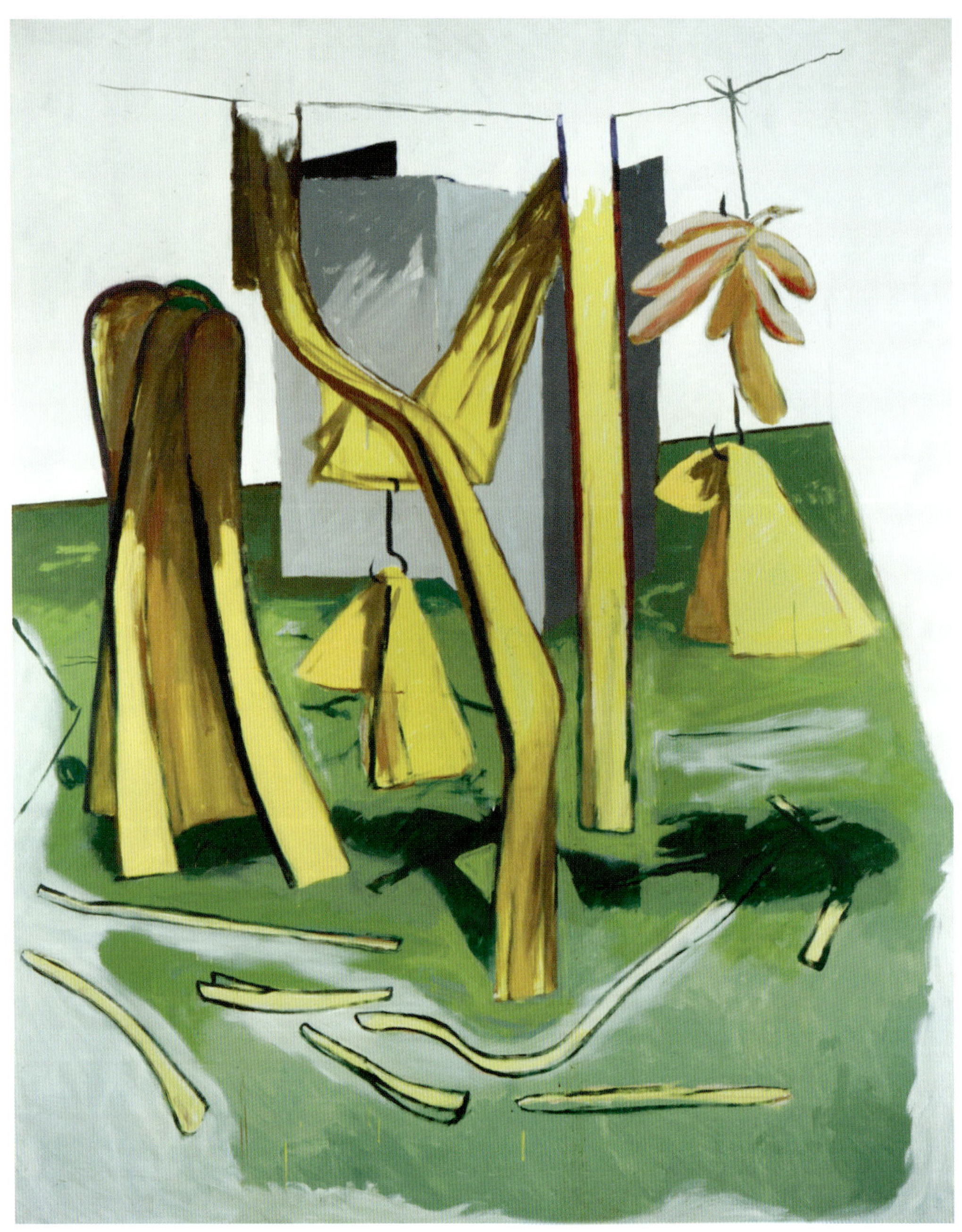

Tatters 1981
Oil on canvas
250 × 200 cm

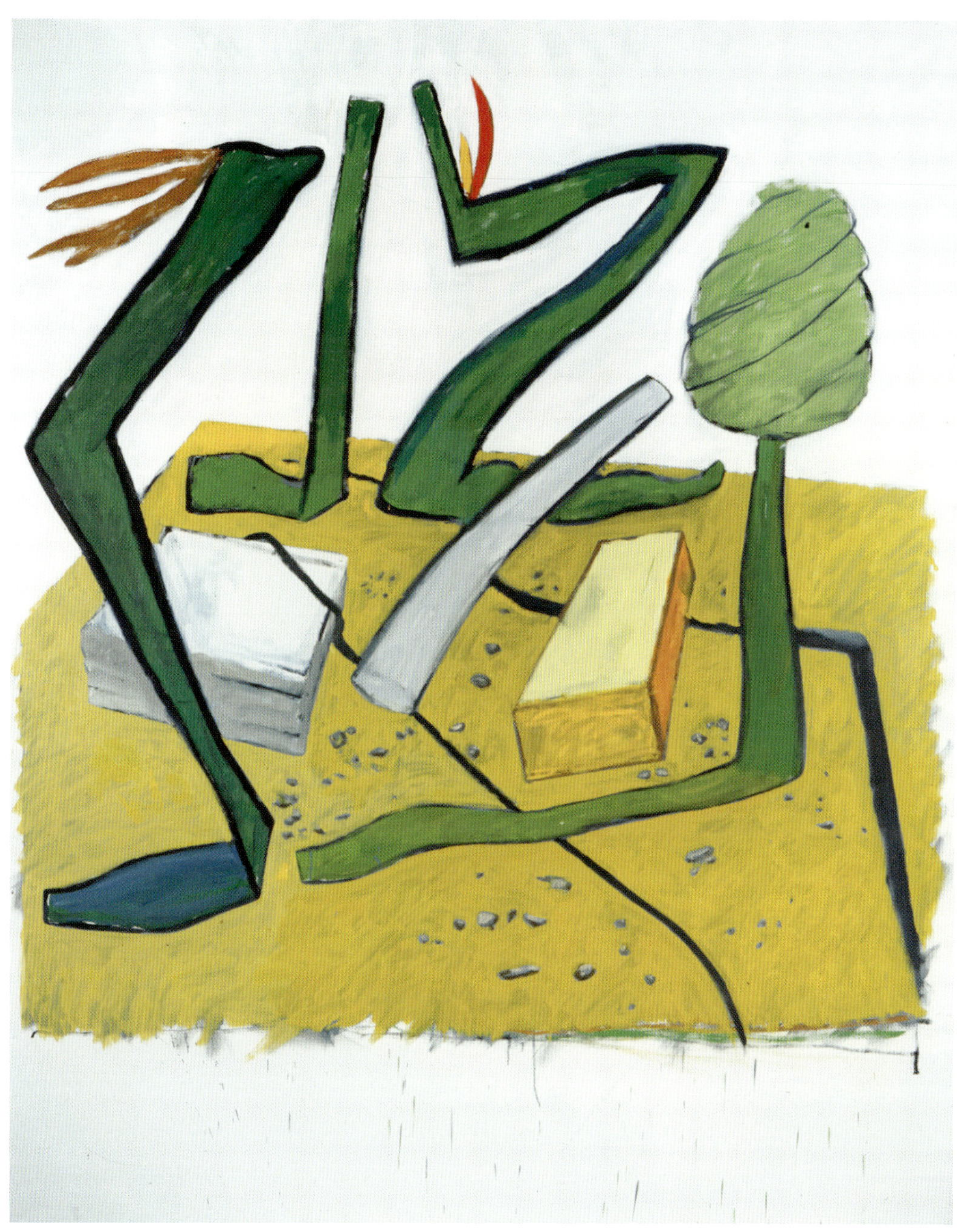

Plants 1981
Oil on canvas
250 × 200 cm

‘THE ADVANTAGE OF HAVING VISIONS WAS THAT I WAS ABLE TO ACCEPT THE IMAGES THAT JUST DROPPED INTO MY IMAGINATION WITHOUT CENSORING THEM, WITHOUT ASKING MYSELF “WHAT DOES IT MEAN?” WHICH IS A DREADFUL QUESTION TO ASK YOURSELF, BECAUSE INEVITABLY YOU DECIDE THAT IT DOESN’T MEAN ANYTHING AND YOU CUT IT OUT.’

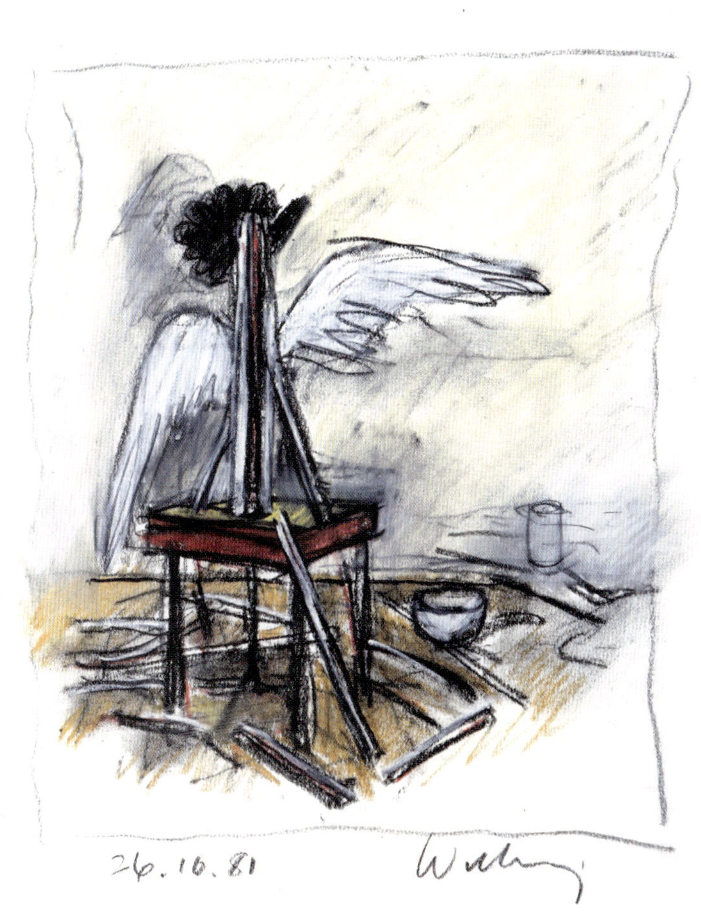

Griffin
(26.10.81) 1981
Charcoal and
pastel on paper
40 × 29 cm

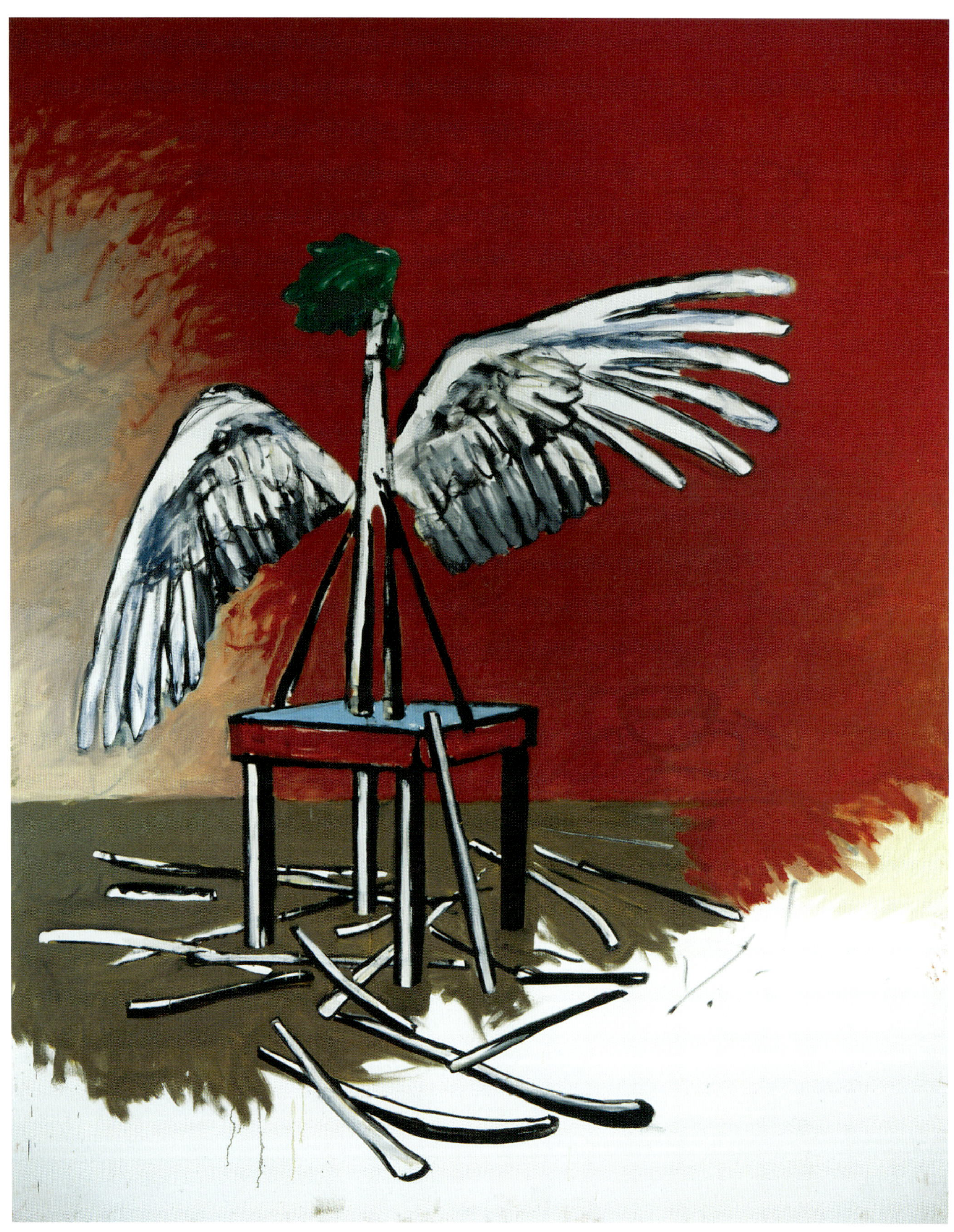

Griffin 1982
Oil on canvas
250 × 200 cm

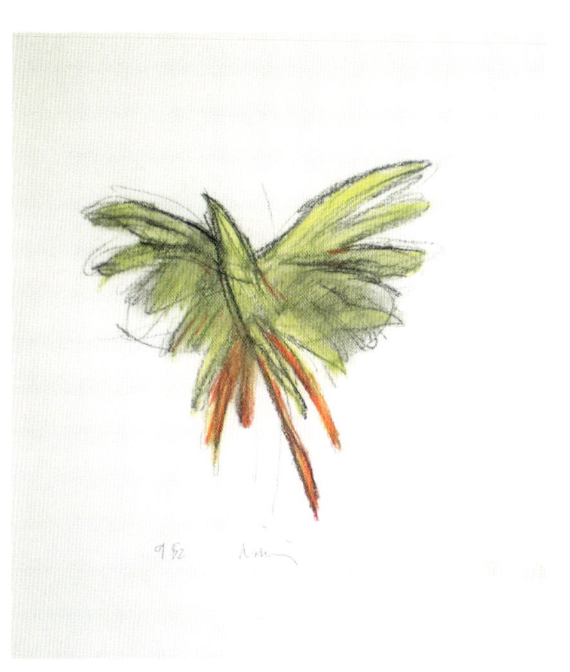

Bird 1982
Pastel on paper
60 × 42.5 cm

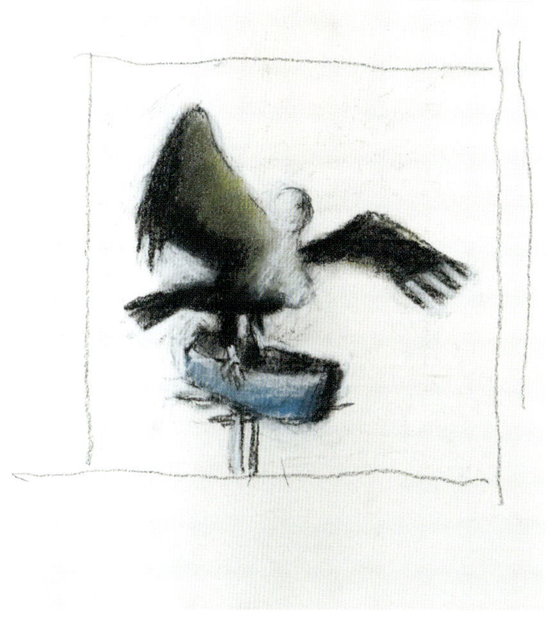

Untitled (Sphinx)
c. 1982 (detail)
Crayon and
pastel on paper
30 × 42 cm

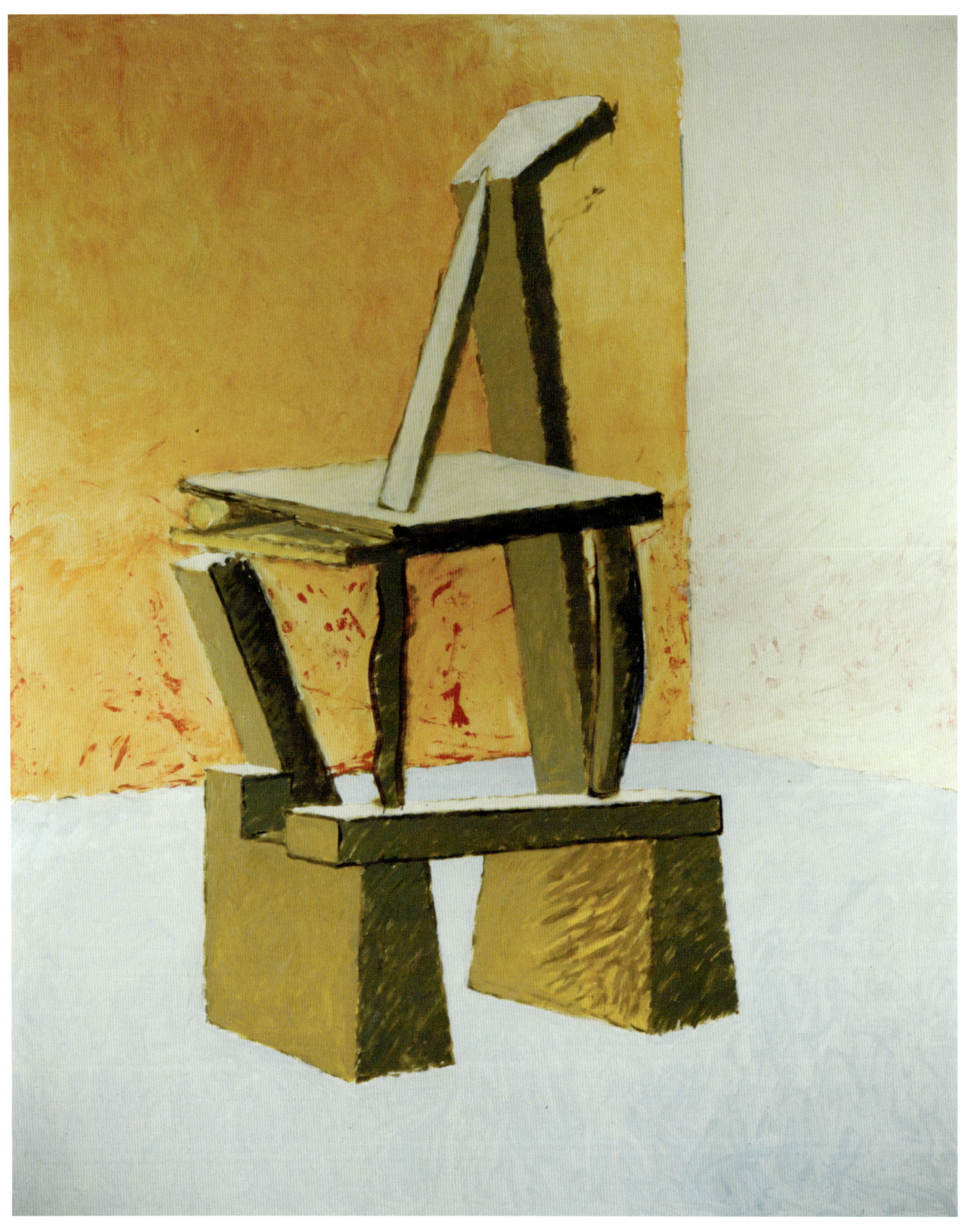

Sphinx 1982
Oil on canvas
250 × 200 cm

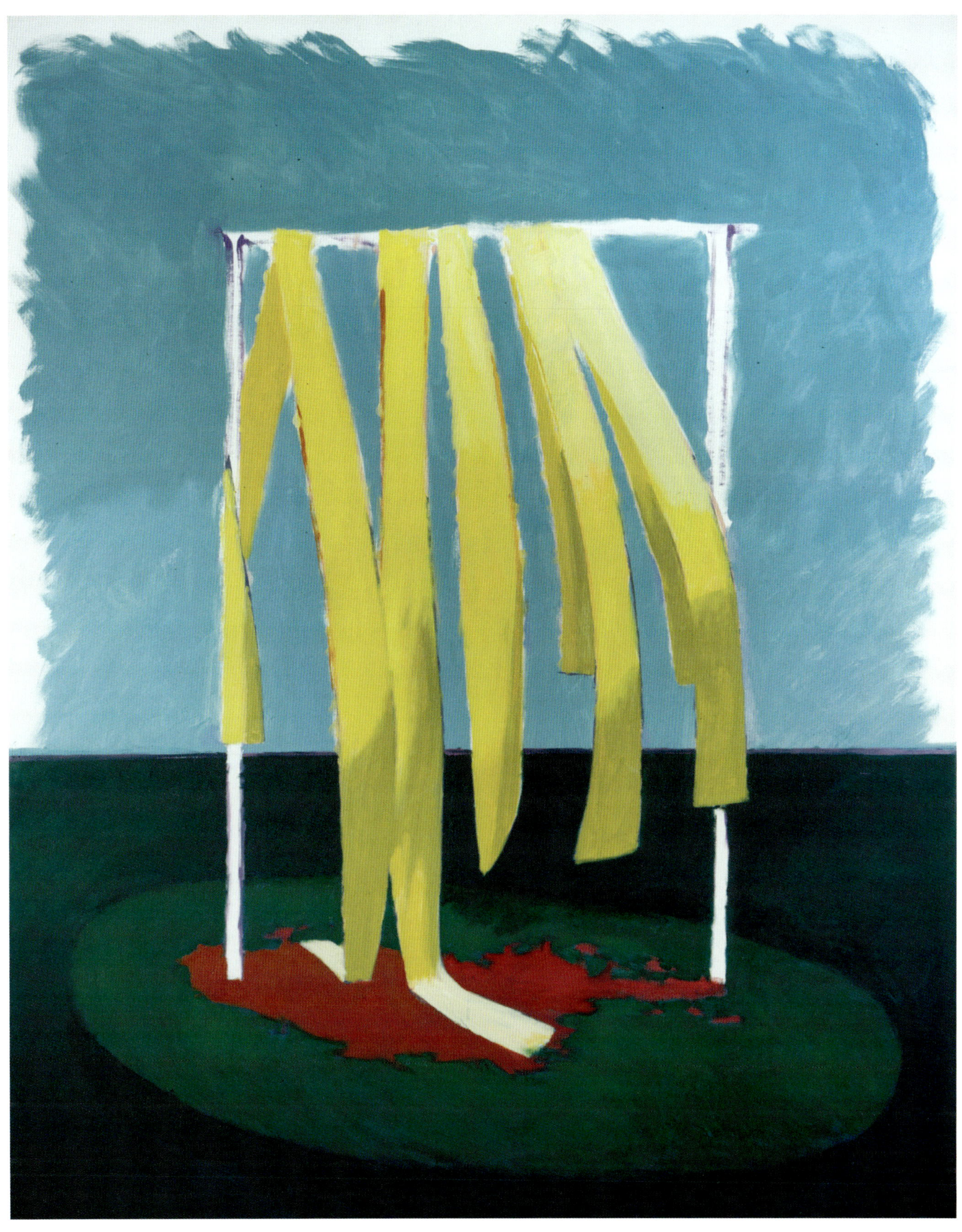

Breathe 1982
Oil on canvas
250 × 200 cm

Cythère 1982
Oil on canvas
240 × 400 cm

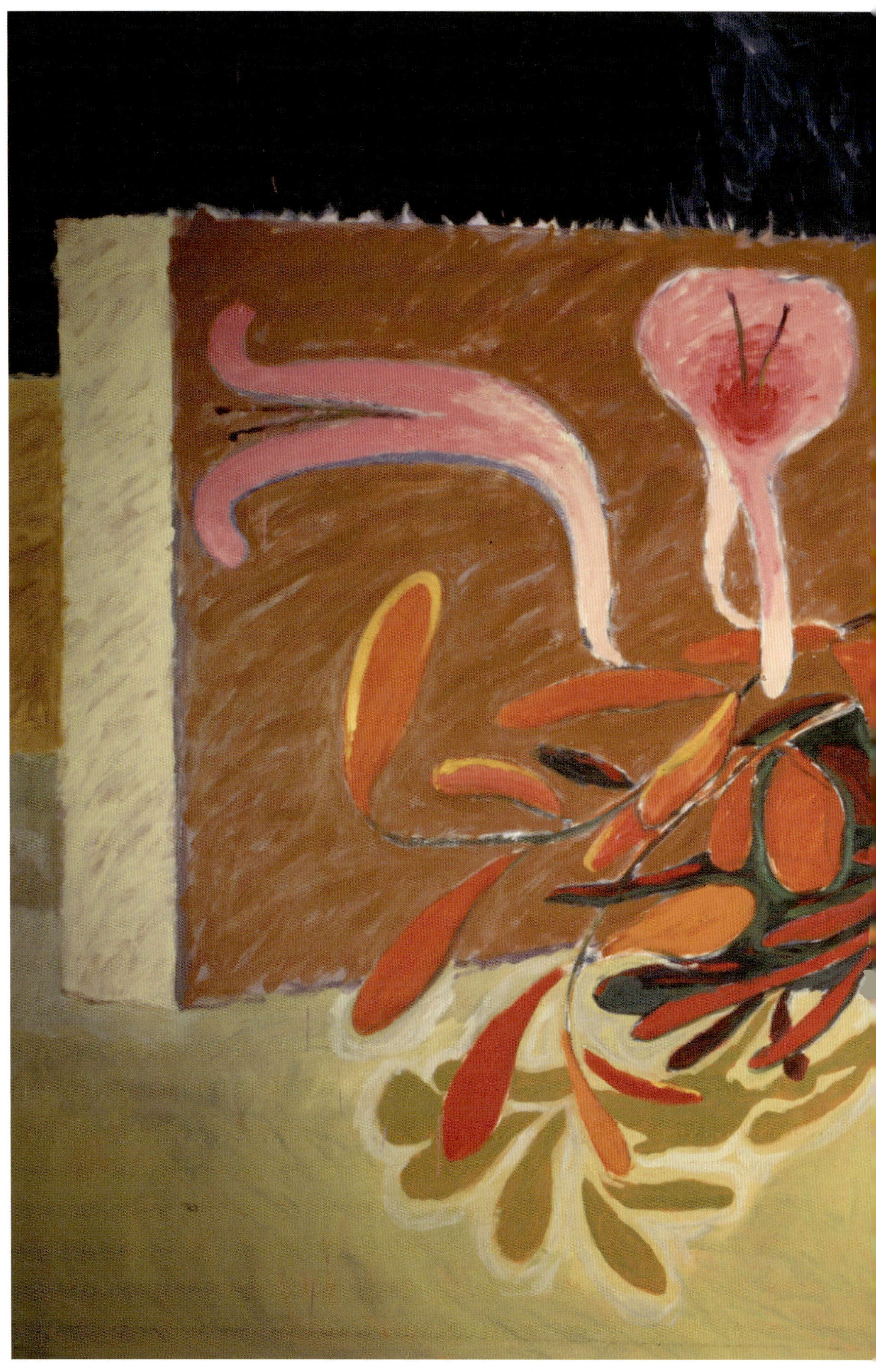

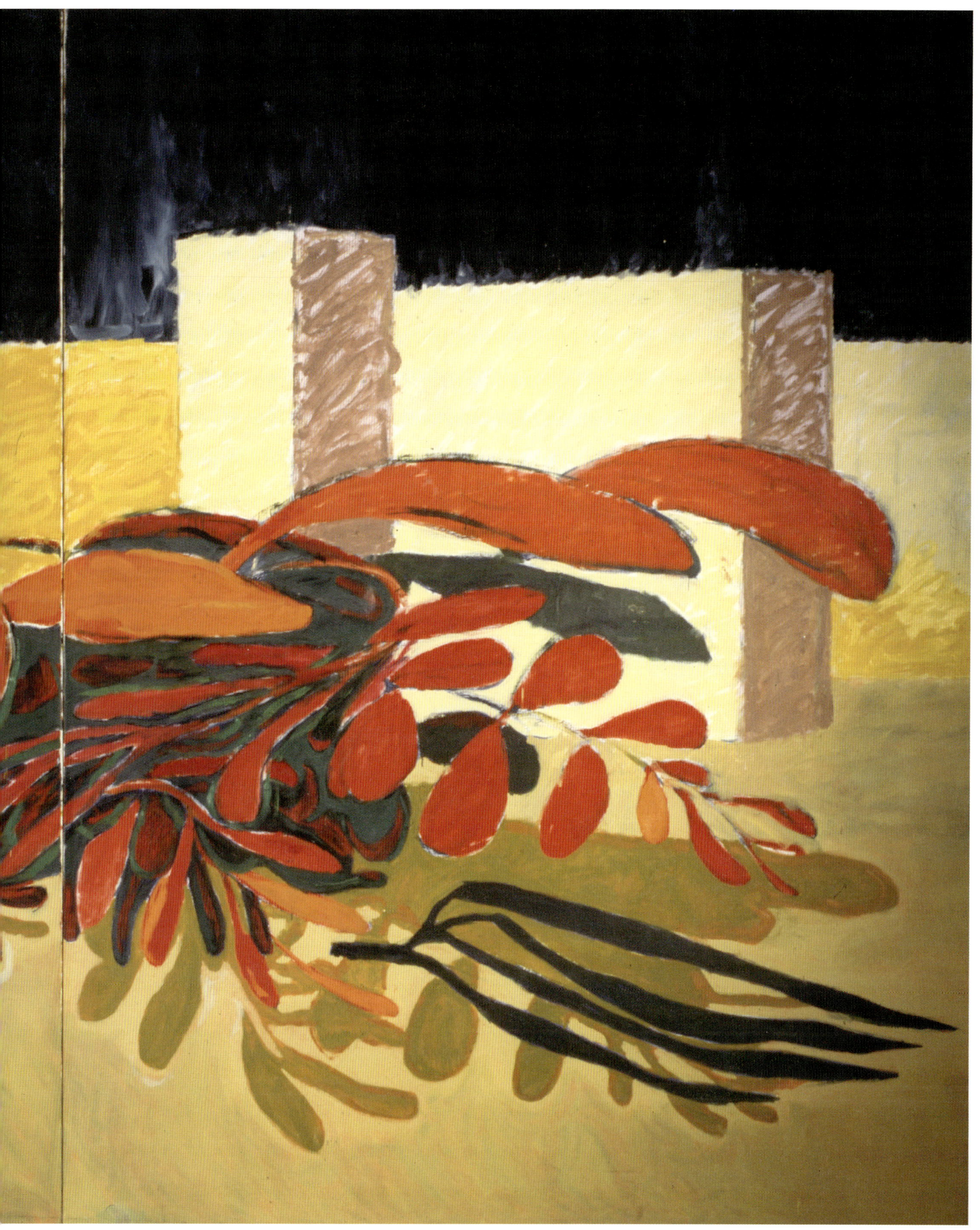

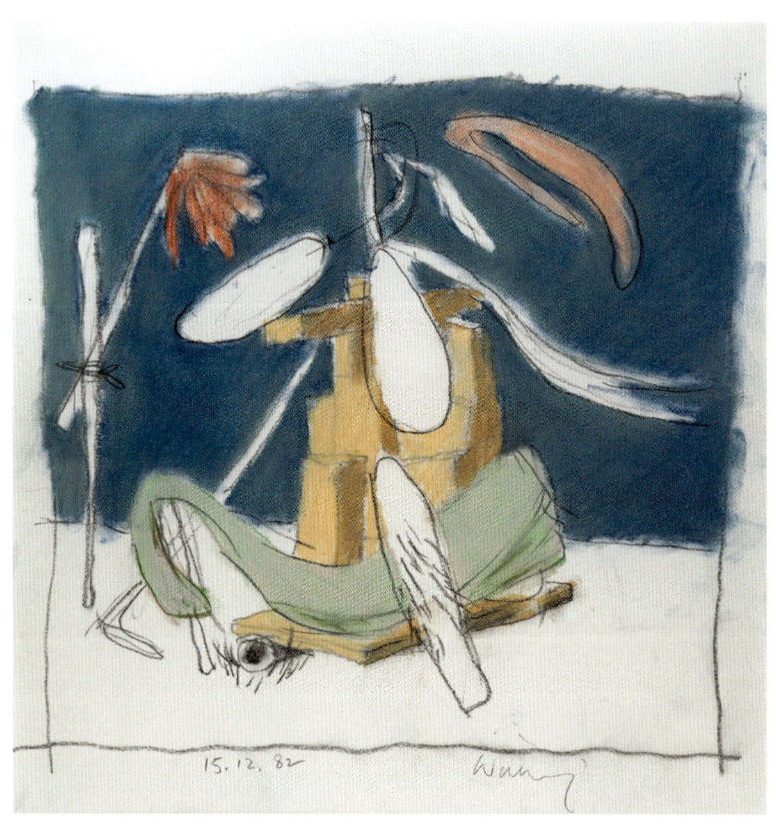

Callot: Harridan
(15.12.82) 1982
Charcoal and pastel
on paper
36 × 28 cm

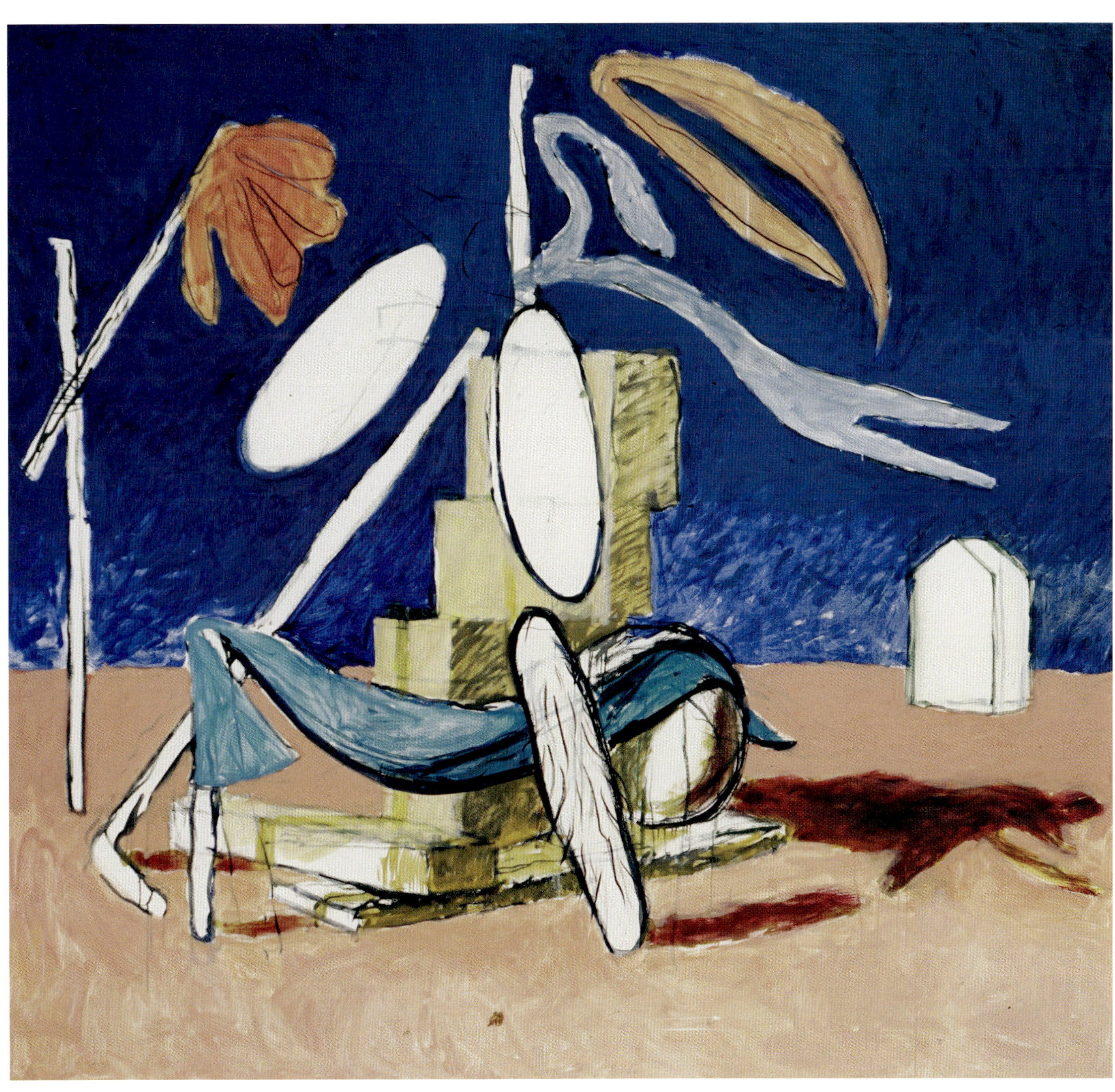

Callot: Harridan 1982
Oil on canvas
200 × 220 cm

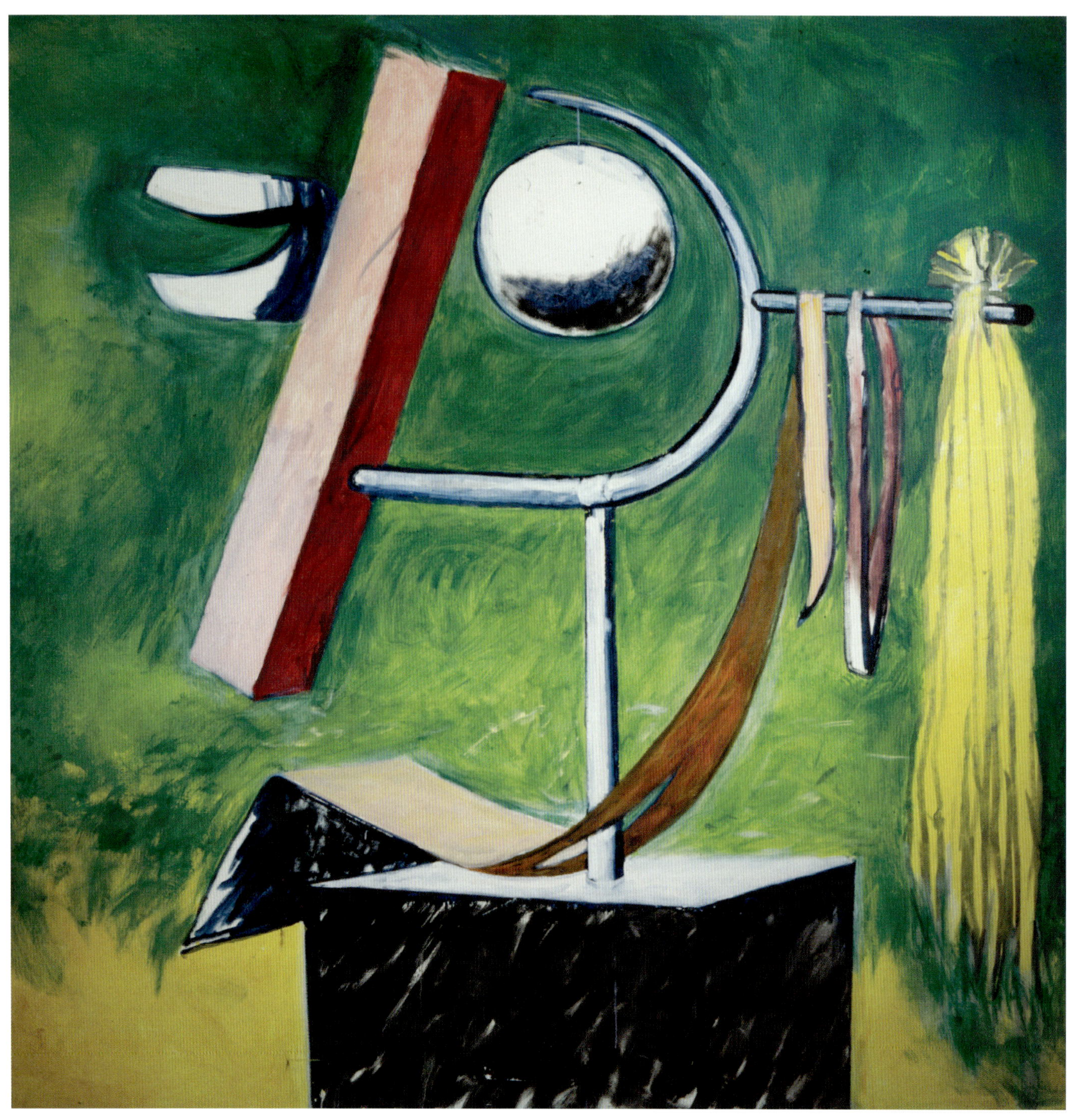

Callot: Fusilier 1983
Oil on canvas
252 × 252.8 cm
Tate: Presented by
Charles Saatchi 1992

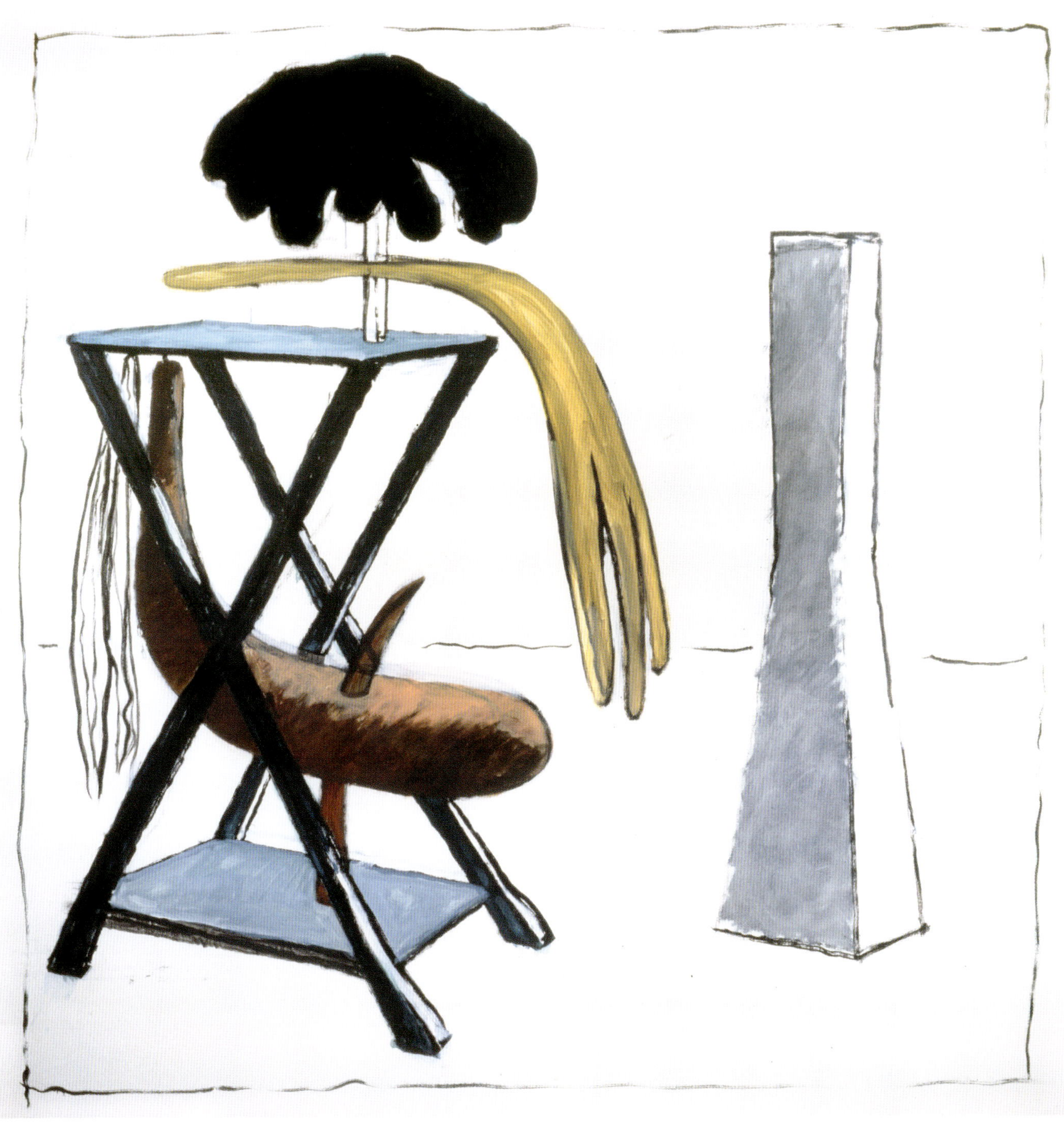

Callot: Cavalier 1983
Oil on canvas
248 × 249 cm

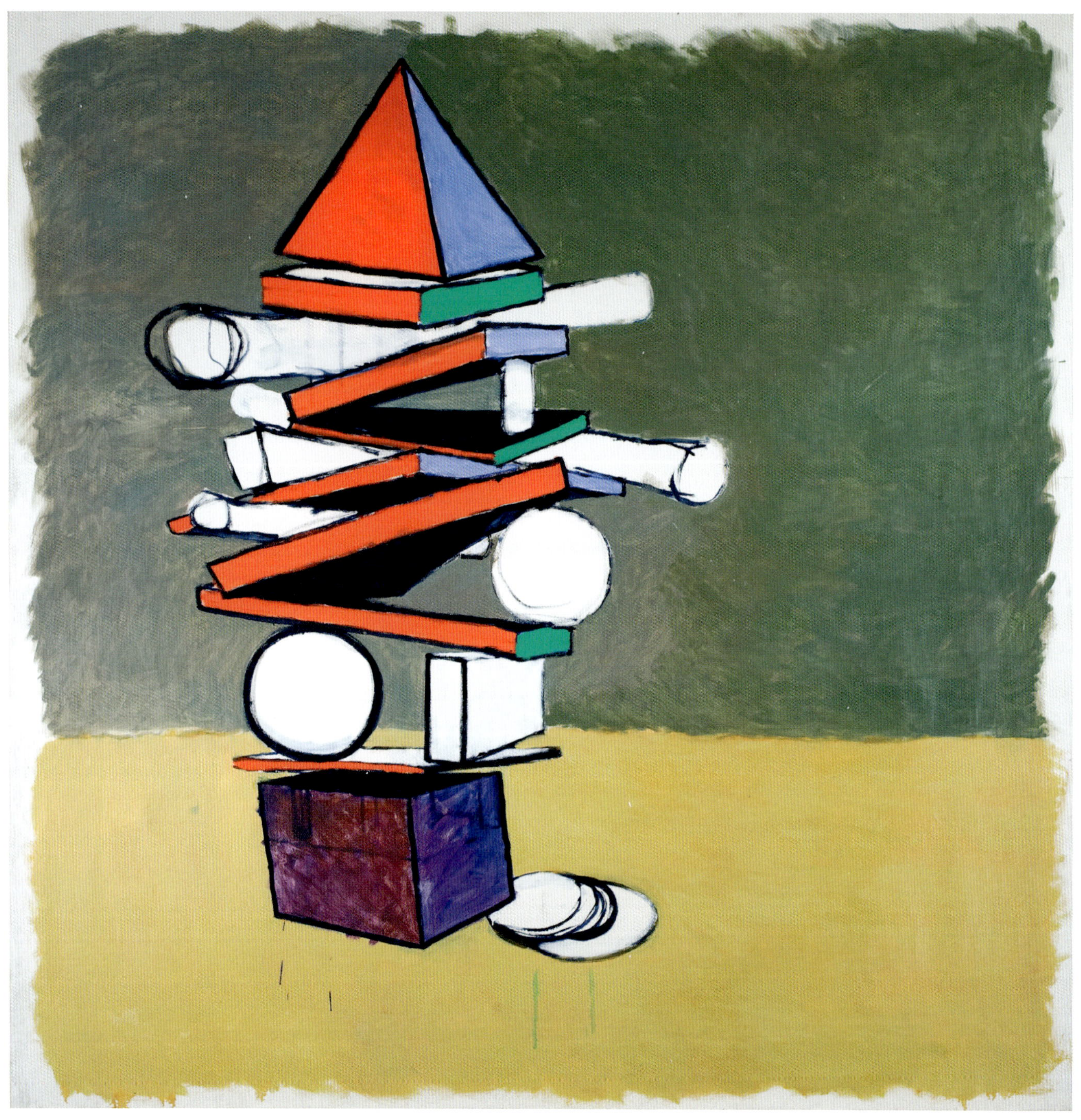

Callot: Judge 1983
Oil on canvas
250 × 250 cm

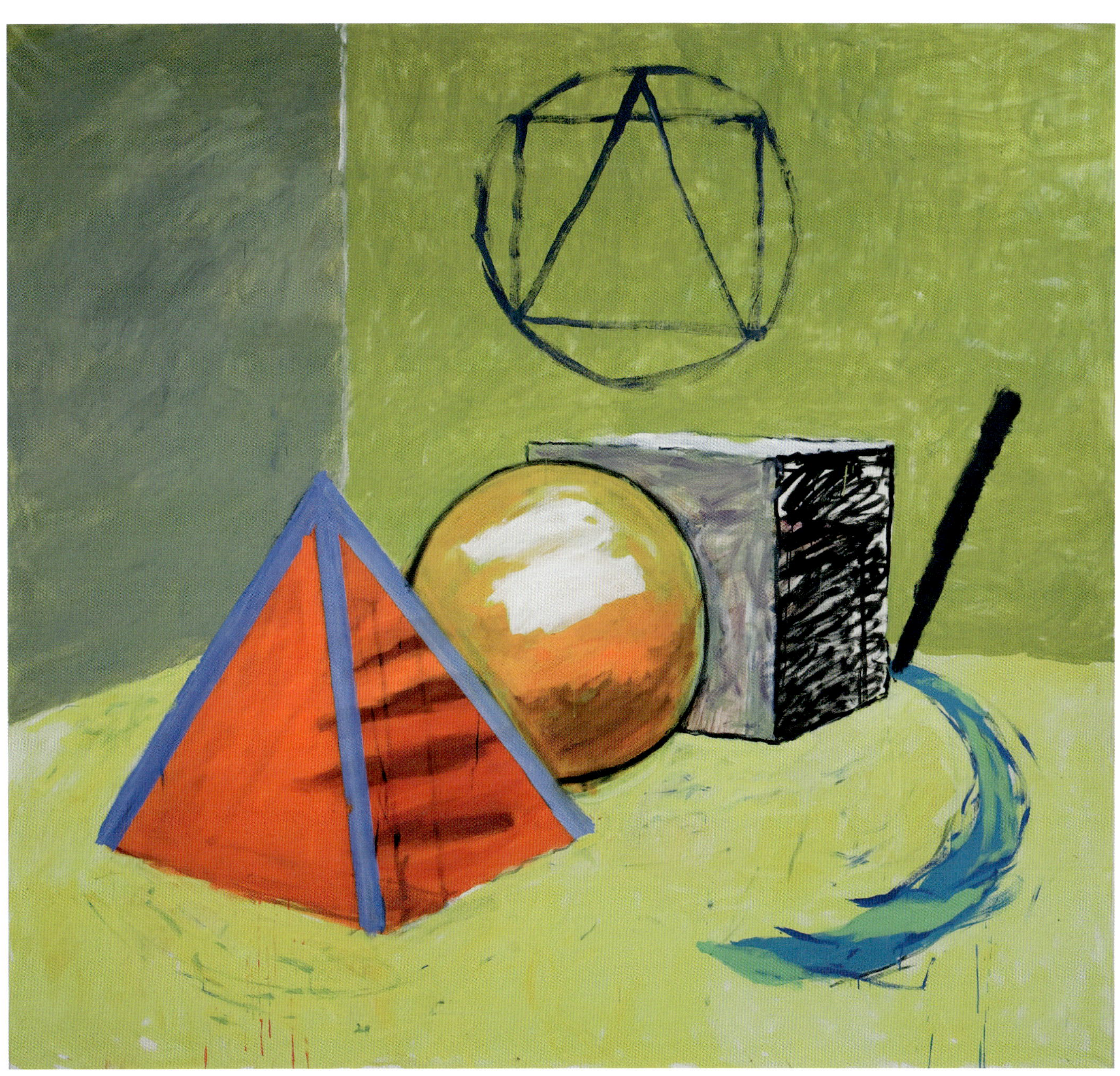

Three Into Two Won't Go 1984
Oil on canvas
220 × 250 cm

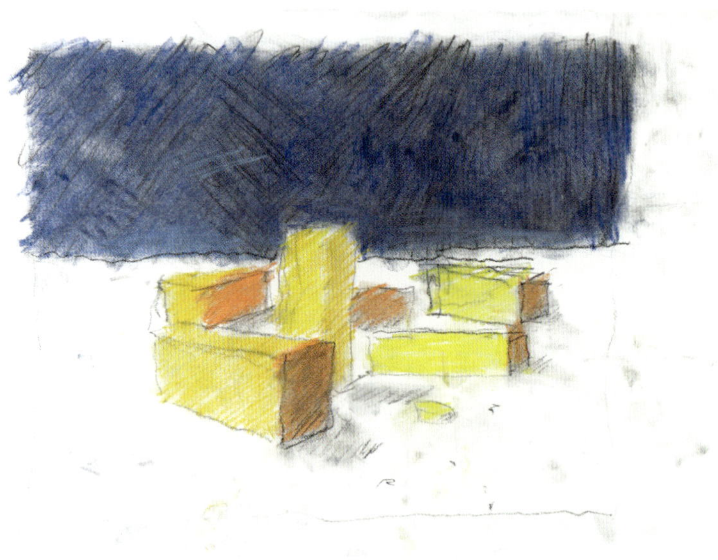

Untitled *c.* 1984
Crayon and
pastel on paper
28 × 37.5 cm

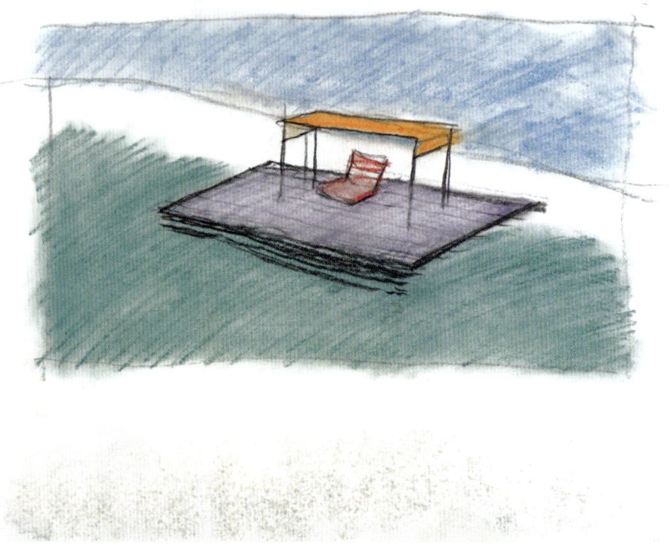

Untitled *c.* 1984
Crayon and
pastel on paper
32 × 45 cm

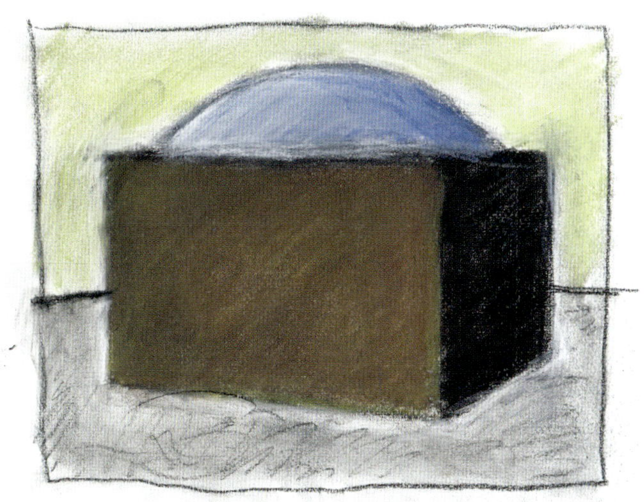

Untitled *c.* 1984
Crayon and
pastel on paper
22.5 × 30 cm

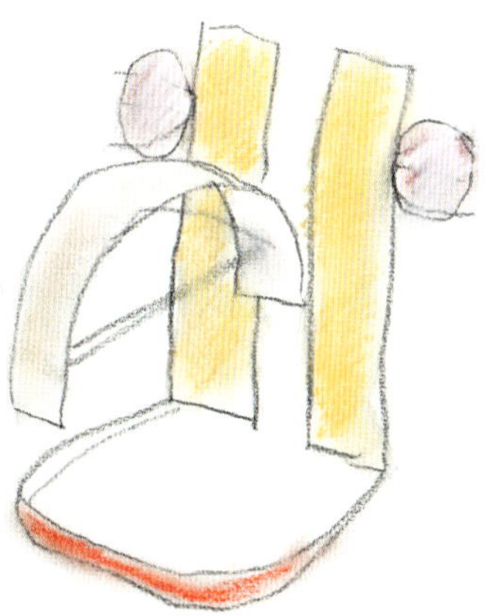

Untitled *c.* 1986
Crayon and
pastel on paper
22.5 × 30.8 cm

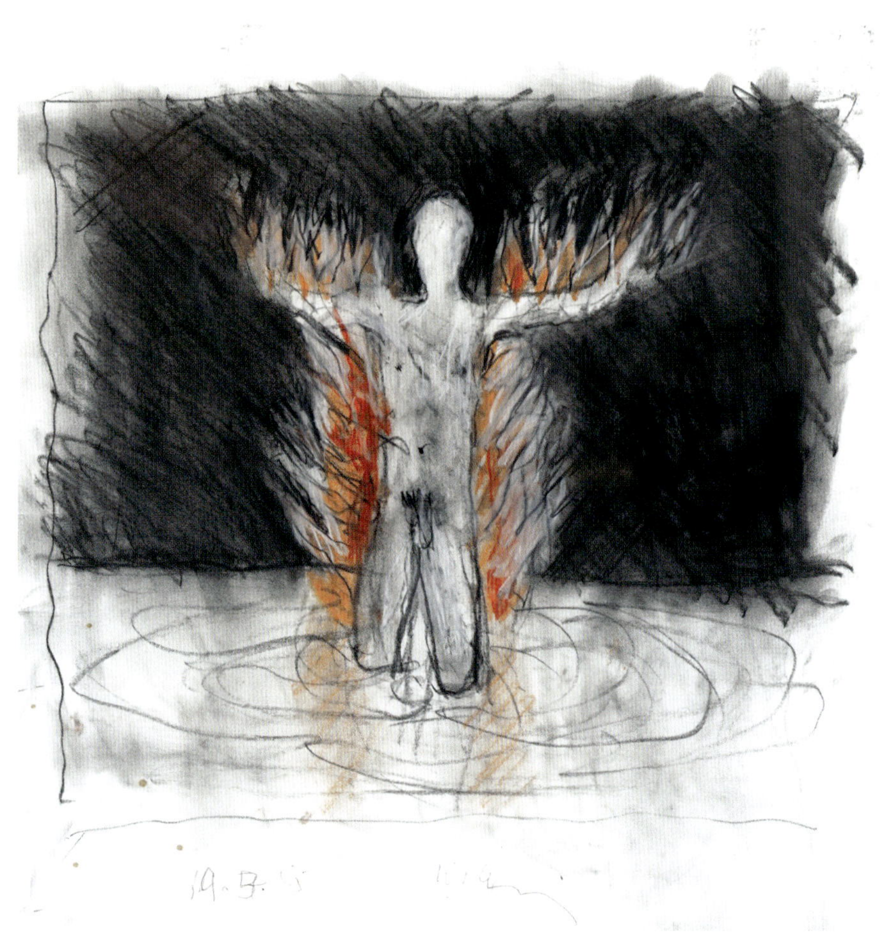

Man in Flames
(19.3.85) 1985 (detail)
Charcoal and pastel
on paper
57 × 38 cm

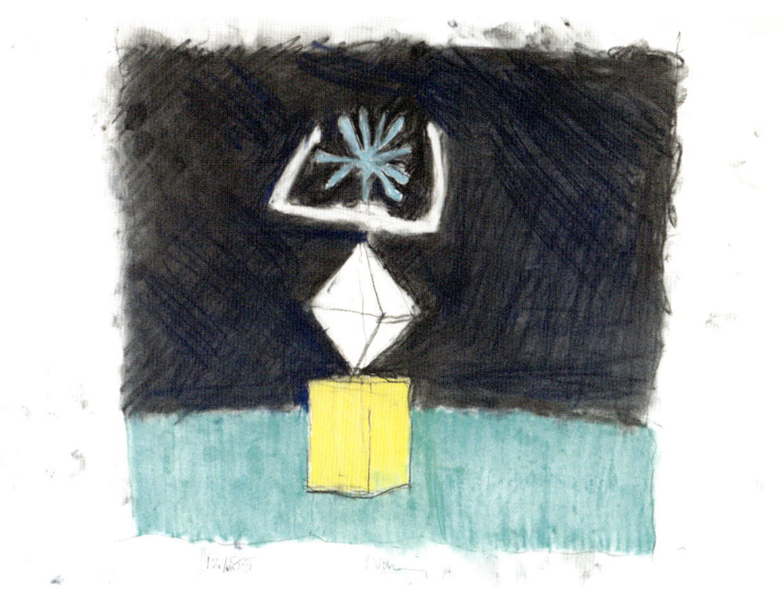

Untitled 1985
Crayon and pastel
on paper
39 × 57 cm

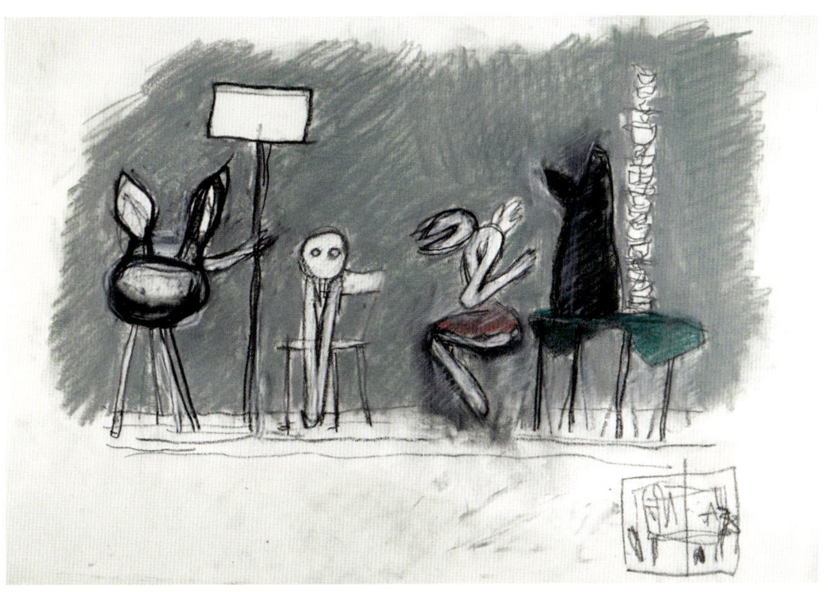

Untitled *c.* 1986
Crayon and pastel
on paper
39 × 57 cm

‘THESE HEADS HOVER UNCERTAINLY BETWEEN TWO DISPARATE, POSSIBLY CONFLICTING, EMOTIONS.... BUT THEY ARE RATHER TWO-DIMENSIONAL AS PERSONALITIES. THE FACT THAT I CAN’T GIVE INDICATIONS OF A LAYERED PERSONALITY, WHICH A MORE SLOWLY PAINTED PORTRAIT MAY CONVEY, IS DUE TO MY PHYSICAL LIMITATIONS. I HAD TO PAINT QUICKLY.’

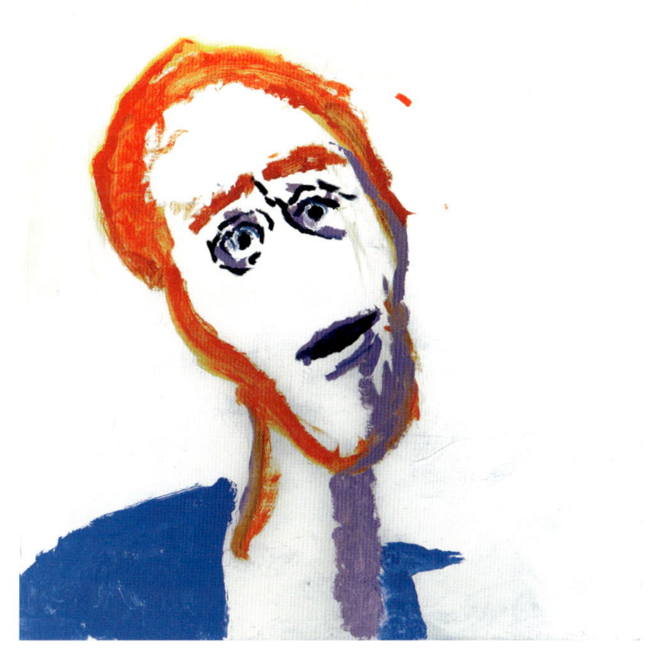

Loser 1986
Oil on canvas
50 × 50 cm

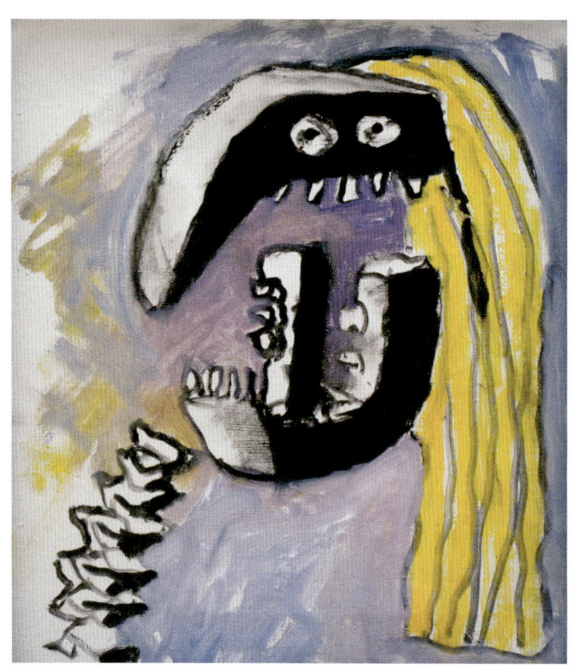

Head VI 1985
Oil on canvas
44 × 39 cm

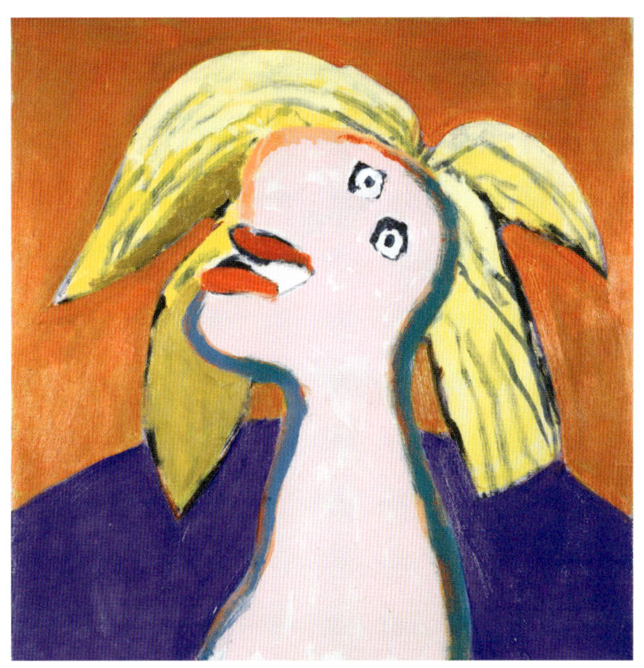

MTW 1987
Oil on canvas
50 × 50 cm

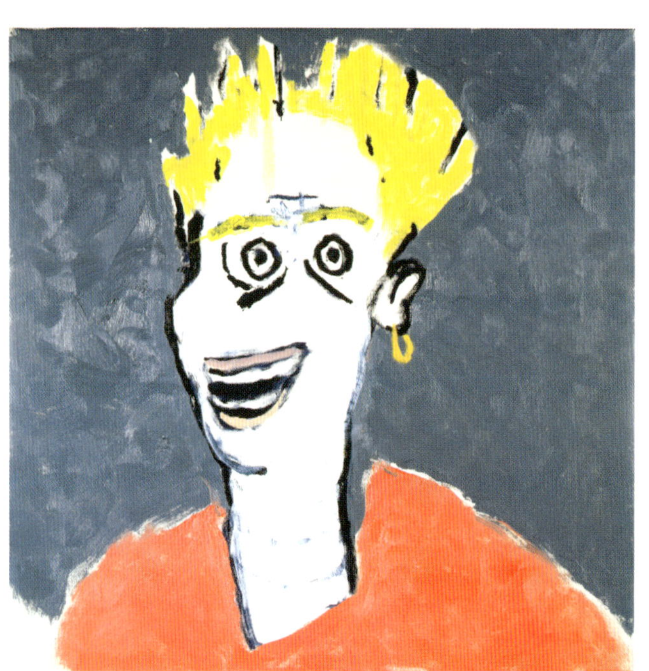

Circulator 1986
Oil on canvas
50 × 50 cm

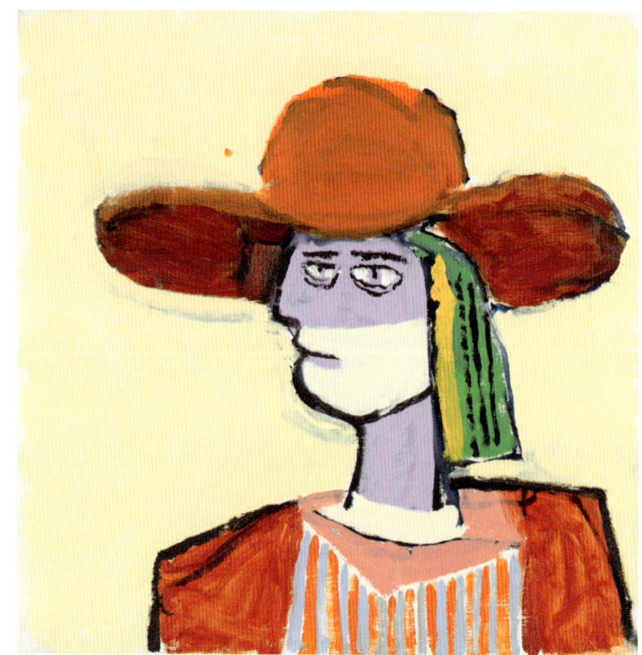

Uffizi 1987
Oil on canvas
50 × 50 cm

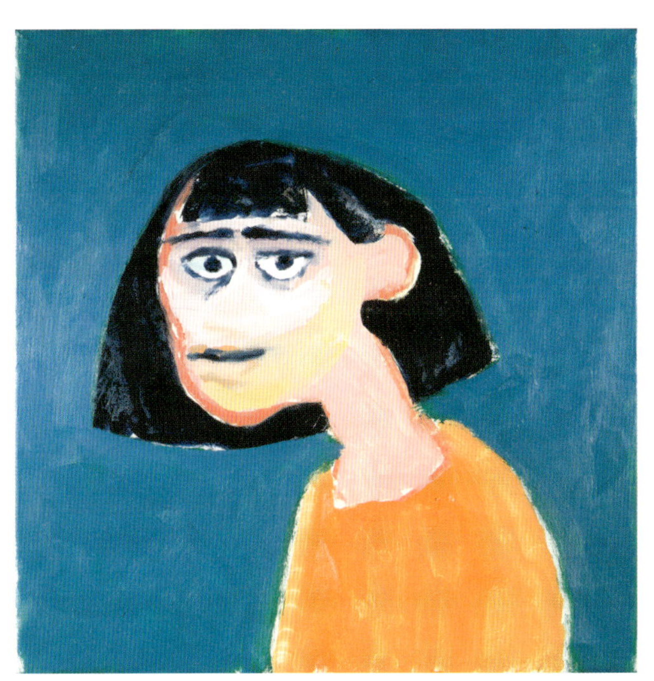

Justine 1986
Oil on canvas
50 × 50 cm

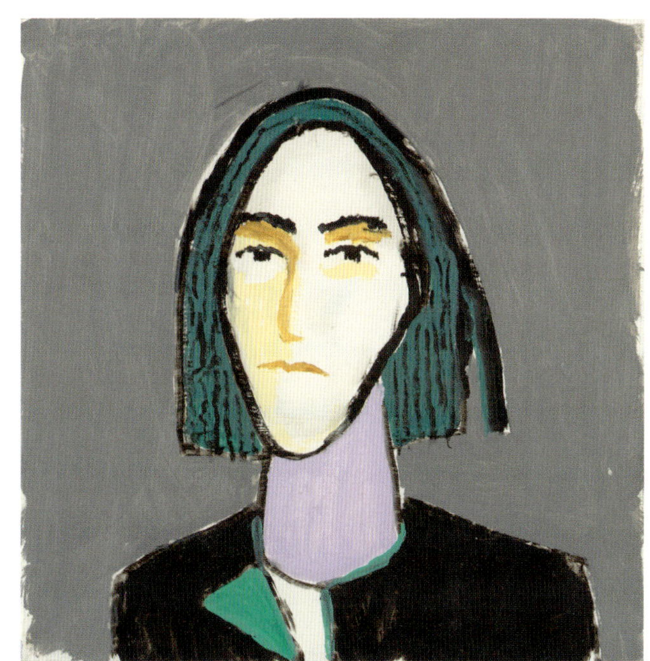

Head 1987
Oil on canvas
50 × 50 cm

Ascot 1987
Oil on canvas
three parts,
each 50 × 50 cm

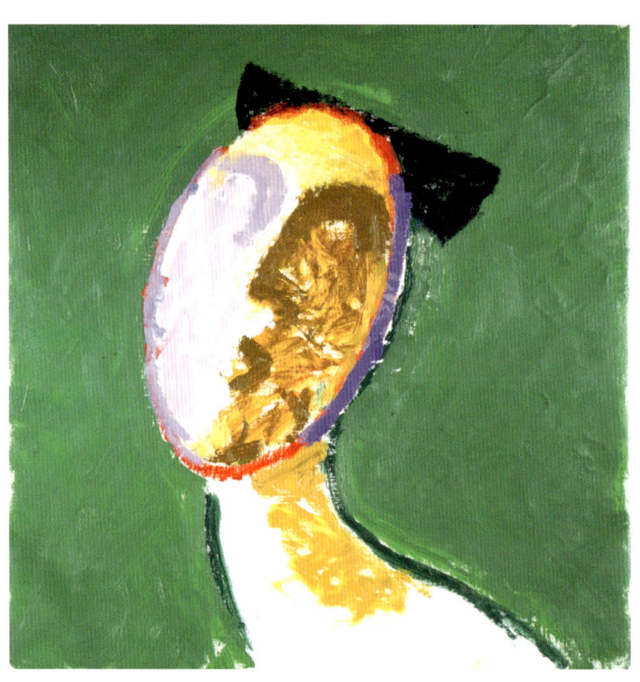

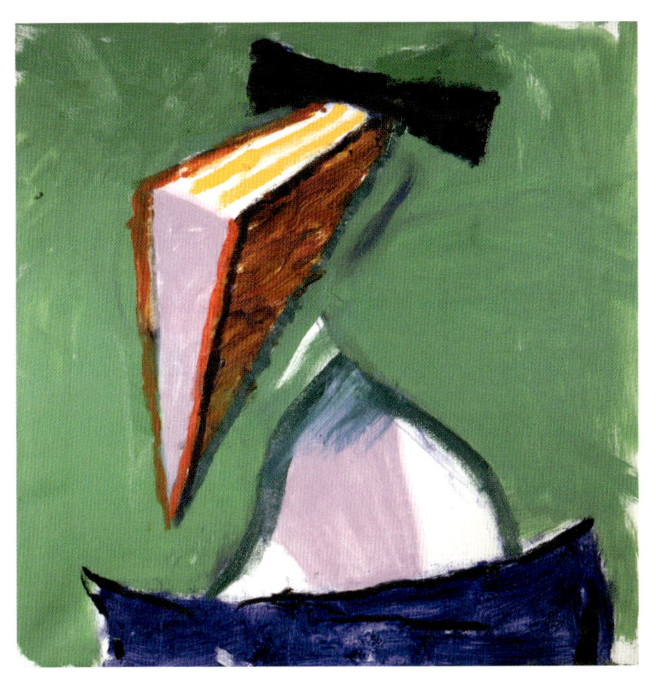

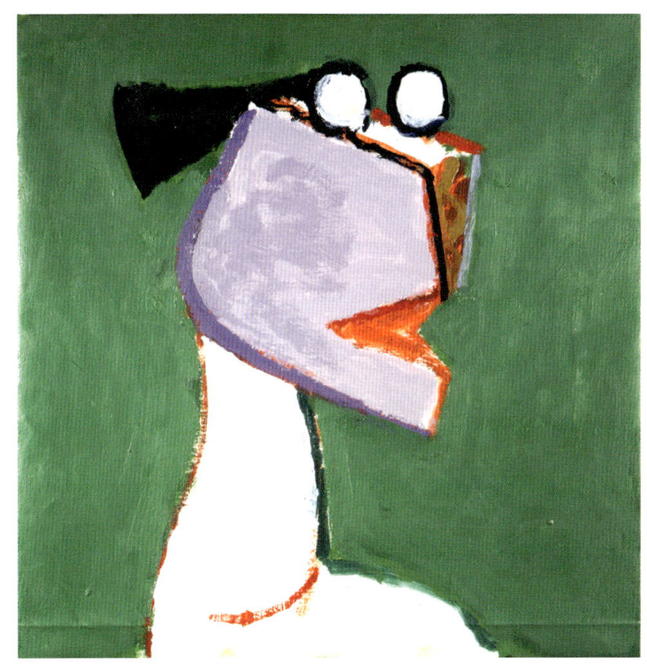

'THE SELF-PORTRAIT AT SEVENTY IS PRETTY CURSORILY DONE. THERE IS NO CAREFUL OVERPAINTING OR ANYTHING LIKE THAT. IT'S ALL ALLA PRIMA. IT'S AS THOUGH YOU CAN SEE STRAIGHT THROUGH THE HEAD. WHAT I RECOGNISED WAS THE LOOK OF A MAN AT THE END OF HIS LIFE: THAT SLIGHTLY HAUNTED EXPRESSION OF "MY GOD, IS THAT ALL THERE IS?"'

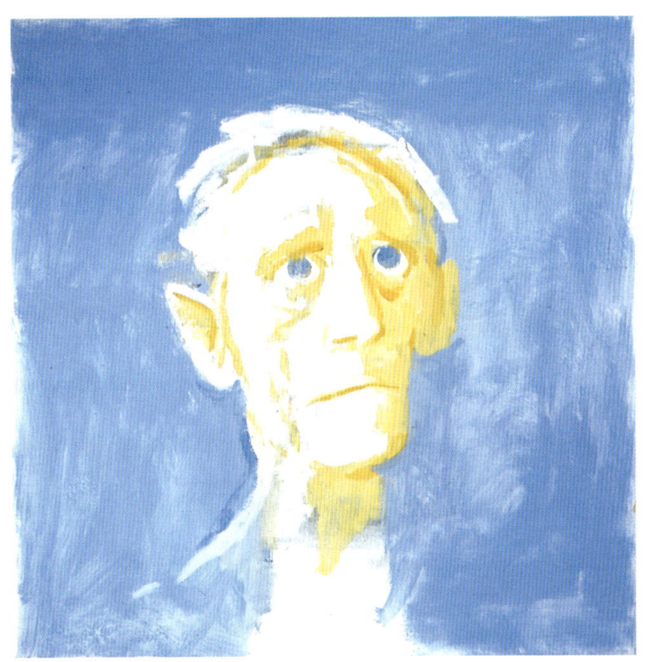

Self-Portrait at Seventy
1987
Oil on canvas
50 × 50 cm
Pallant House Gallery,
Chichester, Wilson Loan
(2006)

EXTRACTS OF A CONVERSATION WITH JOHN McEWEN

The following is taken from a conversation first published in the catalogue of *Victor Willing: A Retrospective Exhibition 1952–85*, Whitechapel Art Gallery, 1986, and republished in *Victor Willing: Selected Writings and Two Conversations with John McEwen*, Karsten Schubert Ltd, London, 1993.

All my life I've tried to recapture the intense pleasure in painting and drawing that I had as a child, when I did battles with people going 'Aaaaarrgh!'

I think it's a means of having a sort of conversation with myself, an attempt to discover myself in a way. I am not painting pictures, I assure you, in order to assert my position in the world or in response to thinking what I'm doing as a career. I don't paint pictures in order to improve the world. I don't do them in a didactic or pedagogical spirit at all. I really am, I must confess, painting very much for myself. We all have an inner reality which only we can know and this is the self that we're inclined to forget about because there isn't much use for it in the world – this better, more real part of ourselves. And there comes a point when you begin to realise that this is the important bit, the bit only you know, and that perhaps you've been neglecting it. Now I think my painting is almost exclusively to do with the self that is normally neglected, and that's a very difficult thing to paint.

...

Can we talk about the individual paintings?

Yes. *Place* was the first picture copied from what I saw in a vision. I did drawings of these when they occurred and then I'd do a painting from the relevant drawing. But I never felt very confident that the drawing did justice to what I'd seen, so if there are discrepancies between the two, it is in the interests of greater truth to the vision. In this painting, I actually saw what appears in the middle and right-hand panels, but the left was added – it's my idea of what a person who inhabits the place might doodle in his spare moments. In the preliminary drawing, I called it *Place of Exile* – the exile referring to myself in Portugal – and that title too was changed for the painting.

Are these geometric notations a reference to your own painting, because geometry comes into your art quite a lot – even in the recent sculpture?

They are the kind of doodles I do in any case, schematic representations of my mood.

Are they intentionally symbolic?

Not intentionally, but unavoidably. I suppose you could say that the circle stands for integration, the square for power, and the ascendant form of the triangle for aspiration.

No sex? I mean something like a triangle seems unavoidably sexual in its symbolism.

Gosh? Well, I didn't mean it that way.

...

You said once that you'd prefer it if the spectator told you what the content of the pictures was, but clearly you have your own ideas!

In general, I should say that they are scenarios – to use a fashionable word – in which something has happened or is about to happen but is not happening at the time depicted. So they have this mood which people recognise, because the people will have fallen into a similar state of expectation or remembrance when they look at the paintings.

Is this true of *Errant*?

The painting was done at Stepney. It was very cold there and the paintings at that time took far longer to paint than they did latterly – and as a result the objects depicted took on a particular significance. Even before I had consigned roles and personalities to the apparently insignificant objects in *Errant*, I was thinking about myself as an infant in Egypt; and gradually, as I built up the painting, so I came to identify my father with the jacket hanging over the screen, my mother with the electric fire, and myself with the chair in between. There's nothing to identify Egypt in the painting, but Egypt was what I had on my mind and the rest developed out of that association.

So why 'Errant'?

I began to associate it with St George and the Dragon. My father's name was George and I think my mother was a bit of a dragon, a fiery creature, and I'm the damsel in distress in the middle.

As I say, no one could possibly see this the way I see it, but I think a sinister mood is communicated. Anyway, people invariably seem to look at it. It's a large painting for a still life.

So it isn't consciously symbolic?

It never is. *Swing*, for instance, recalls when I was a small boy and took great delight in going backwards and forwards on a swing, upside down. What was marvellous about that was the disorientation. You had the impression that the world was swinging, not you. Later, I discovered that the 'hanged man' card in the tarot pack is an upside-down figure, representing chaos. So there seemed a connection. It is chaotic if the whole world is moving.

So in the picture just the clothes are left as witness to the body. Did you paint the picture after the fact of the idea or is your interpretation a later ornamention?

I found myself painting the picture as a result of having a particularly uncomfortable feeling. In *Swing*, a feeling of discomfort began to resolve itself as an upside-down figure. I found myself doing drawings of this figure, and then I was reminded of the experience I had had as a child and then in the process of doing the painting – and this is where reading books comes in – I connected the image with that of the tarot.

So it's nothing to do with winds, deserts, clothes lines?

Nothing.

The supporting posts are placed and painted rather ambiguously, aren't they?

Yes – all the pictures of that time have that characteristic. In *Mud*, though, the daffodil and the tent are the product of a vision. The mud itself was the smooth kind, with objects marooned in it that you see in estuaries. That's what I saw. And then I added the meat. The meat just seemed to go with the feeling I had about the rest of it.

What was that feeling?

It seemed to me that this was a place occupied by someone who was cut off from the normal means of supply. I suppose it reflects a siege mentality. He's got to lay in stocks. Looking at it logically, it doesn't make sense of course, because the meat isn't going to last very long hanging up in the open like that – but we don't think logically – do we? – when we do these things!

Mother is also very much a vision. The drawing is more faithful to what I saw than the painting, which isn't uncommon because I usually prune the paintings as I go along. In the drawing, there is a line of flagpoles with the flags flapping, which emphasises the subject – a woman in a flap at the seaside.

When I first saw this painting, I remember being reminded of one of Henry Moore's sculptures in the 1930s, when he was trying to be a surrealist and composed one of his reclining figures as an arrangement of separate parts.

If we are looking for derivations, then I would think more of earlier work by Picasso, when he made a number of fragmented figures and studies for vast monuments. The picture refers to my actual mother, it's an impression I had of her. She was a beefy sort of woman who probably bashed me about a bit when I was a kid. She had very thick arms and she tended to get emotional about things at times and you'd have to be jolly careful to keep out of the way of these enormous boughs flailing about. So the image I present is of my mother in a rather wild uncontrolled action.

It's not a figure reduced to some sort of minimum?

No, it's just my mother all over the place.

Place with a Red Thing, in the Tate Gallery collection, is a straightforward recording of one of the visions I used to have. In fact, in terms of those visions, it is the most purely illustrative picture I have done. It hardly differs from the drawing I did immediately after the vision was over.

You haven't come to any interpretative conclusions since doing it?

Well, as I wrote to Ronald Alley for the Tate's catalogue, the '*red thing*' seems to be something very much alive in a rather desiccated tomblike place – so much alive that it's actually bleeding.

Did the year working in Cambridge as official artist-in-residence to the University have an effect on your work? To me, the pictures you did there have a great sense of stillness, and they were painted in the peace of that studio in the garden at Newnham. They depict single objects – imposing structures that nevertheless seem precariously on the edge of collapse. In most cases, they are pictures of imagined sculptures really, aren't they?

Yes they are. And I did feel quite calm when I was doing them – much calmer than I had in my visionary period before the AIR exhibitions. But *Tatters*, which is a visionary painting, was done in Cambridge.

So it was done long after the event?

Yes. But I had no visions at home. They were mostly at my windowless studio in Stepney where I was always in artificial light; and partly due to taking ACTH, I was experiencing this very disturbing sleep pattern. But my supposition that the visions were in some way caused by the steroids has been discounted subsequently both by my psychotherapist and, more recently, by my neurologist. And that makes sense, because I took ACTH before and after the four years in which I had the visions. As for the cause of these hallucinations, my neurologist had no explanation; my psychotherapist said it was due to my state of mind and I would have experienced them at that time whether I had been on steroids or not.

...

A number of your images, such as *Griffin*, include this litter at the base.

Yes. In this case, I think the intended suggestion is that the figure is in the process of being constructed.

The floor line is interrupted.

On the left, there is the usual wall-meeting-the-floor line, but on the right-hand side what I saw, in the vision, was another scene through the wall – a number of cups and bowls, rather boring. So I didn't paint it. It may exist in the drawing or I may have painted it out on the canvas. I can't remember.

Judge is not a vision.

No, it isn't. It's one of several pictures of judge images that I've produced. Does it say anything about judges and judgement to you?

Certainly. Balance, apart from anything else.

Yes. *Cythère* wasn't seen though the wall either. Here's a plant burgeoning, with flowers and dead bits of the plant as well – and all taking place within a very rigid architectural framework.

I remember you telling me that the blocks could be seen as a labyrinth and the plant as a metaphor of ecstasy – blooming and dying in the same instant.

I've done a number of paintings inspired by the engravings of Callot. They're not visions. Callot is the supreme artistic witness to the Thirty Years' War of the seventeenth century, and the atmosphere he evokes – of armies devastating a population constantly on the move, of people constantly having to change sides, of a mercenary soldiery and civilians in chaos – greatly impressed me. The story he tells is of this awful situation gnawing away at the heart of Europe. So that's why this one is called *Fusilier*, after Callot. It's the formalised head of a man with a moustache and a smile – pretty far-fetched!

What about the second *Judge*?

A Callot judge – a rather rickety construction of planes and cubes. My recent sculptures derive from the *Judge* paintings. One, rather like this – a pile of planes – is called *Magister*; and the one with a silver crescent surmounting a golden ball is another *Judge*. Another is called *Widow* – not to suggest bereavement, but a woman cut off from her sensual roots. I called them 'Judge' because they suggested power, rigidity, the letter of the law.

But earlier on the thought of sculpture never crossed your mind?

That's right. I hadn't thought of doing sculpture when I did these paintings, though they are very much paintings of 3-D objects.

Is that another face in *Callot: Cavalier*?

No, this is a horse and rider. This big sausage with a toothpick through it is the horse's body. Why it's traversed by this thorn I don't know. The falling ringlets are the horse's tail, and at the top are the cavalier's plumes. The standing figure is a foot soldier, I guess.

The figure in *Callot: Harridan* is meant to be a hairy old hag at the beach. That crescent shape is her dress slung between her thighs; and that little hut in the background reminds me of those changing cubicles that Picasso drew the summer he was nipping off for quick screws there with Marie-Thérèse Walter, while his wife was sunbathing unawares 100 yards down the beach. I wanted something smaller to give distance.

...

Do you think your own physical state has had any effect on the content of your pictures – given that all the post-1970 work has been done after the diagnosis of multiple sclerosis?

I suppose so, but I have never painted a picture to illustrate the way I felt. I think MS made me take a rather more serious view of life than I might otherwise have done at forty. Forty is an age when you expect people to think seriously about things, but I think I might have gone on living a rather vain, egotistical sort of life if I had enjoyed good health. MS did make me more introspective – though I'd always been quite introspective – and less concerned with the notion I had of myself as a person in the world.

...

Picasso seems the artist you are most attuned to. Can you remember that marvellous description you gave me once of your reaction to his work at the famous V&A exhibition of 1945 – about the horse?

Oh yes – being next to a Picasso painting was like being trapped in a stall with a horse. For me, he is without doubt the great artist of our century.

Your *Heads* are particularly Picassoan.

They are certainly the result of looking at Picasso. It's very difficult to do something original. Everything we do seems to be done with some existing artistic form in mind. But when we redo it, it doesn't look the same. Even forgeries are an unconscious witness to the time when they were done. Contemporary eyes can't see it, but later ones can.

What especially appeals to you about Picasso?

Well, as I myself am an artist who has painted very few pictures, the first thing I am in awe of is his Promethean capacity to go on pouring it out. His vitality is superhuman. And he's never afraid of his imagination. I've often recoiled from my imagination, as I was suggesting, which is one explanation of my recourse to geometric forms – they are a way of keeping the imagination at bay.

But you wouldn't prefer to have them censored out?

Oh no – I can't pretend I haven't done them, and they are a valid statement in their way. It's just that we – I – have to try and recover from the fright I give myself when my imagination gets cracking.

So which of your pictures most frightens you?

When I start painting them, the fear is over, but often they have been like an open door one hesitates to go through.

Even when you're not seeing them as visions?

Yes. It's like standing safely here while something rather alarming is going on over there. *Night*, which was a vision, was an alarming glimpse.

What is *Night* about?

In Jungian imagery, the sea represents the unconscious, and so does a basement. If you put a boat in a basement, you're obviously in pretty deep. And then to have a boat which is out of control tells us that this basement is a stormy place.

And there are the objects sinking.

I was thinking about their significance. It's all very insecure. *Place with a Red Thing* was also rather alarming because I think it's a tomb, and to have something growing in a tomb is a rather frightening situation. I find the *aediculae*, the little houses, also unnerving to think about. Perhaps for that reason I never did consider what they implied until [Tate director] Alan Bowness actually asked me. And I said, without hesitation, that they were 'images of self-containment'. And then I said I'd agonised over what to put inside and all I could think of was a bowl – which is another image of self-containment. I had a plan to have them built full scale once, but it never materialised.

They derived from the shelter in *Place*, didn't they? Can you elaborate on this notion of an 'image of self-containment'?

I can imagine a devout monk in his cell feeling that he was bringing his disparate self down to a hard core; and that the smallness and plainness of the cell helps him achieve that.

In your autobiographical essay 'Walking-Wounded', you write that art always comes back to the same problem: 'reality, how to know and how to trap it'.

Truth or morality, it's the same thing.

So you're a moralist?

If we're talking about an inner truth, a truth about ourselves, we have to be sincere and honest; but this pretension immediately makes us vulnerable – not only to other people's doubts, but to our own self-doubt. To explain what we sincerely believe requires care and self-consciousness. And this can easily sound like bullshit. But mine is a moral position – trying to get to the truth.

Do politics intrude? Having been dispossessed by the revolution in Portugal, you've experienced political action as sharply as a man can.

The terrible thing about revolution is that it forces everyone into an extreme position – the middle ground disappears. At the Slade, I was an anarchist, much taken with Kropotkin, now I'm more of a green. Like most people in Portugal, I was delighted with the revolution in April 1974; but I was disconcerted to find myself seen automatically as a man of the Right, because I was middle-class and my wife's family owned a factory. Liberal possibilities disappeared. There were suddenly only two kinds of people: progressives and fascists. To my horror, I was seen as a fascist. Development in art occurs in liberal or laissez-faire regimes, doesn't it? Because we think of modern art as revolutionary, we imagine that revolution favours it. But social turmoil leads to autocracy – one's scores are settled. If one autocracy follows another, similar means are used to flatter the new power. In its essentials, the arts remain unchanged.

Do you really think art has anything to do with politics?

I think the artist's sense of inner necessity overrides external necessities. Politics are an external matter, hence for me an artistic irrelevance. Though, as I have suggested, some regimes make it impossible to take that view. Since the reason society is organised should be to facilitate the arts (what other reason could there be?), these societies are a setback.

Does that inner necessity override learning too? You're very well read, you've looked at a lot, do you feel you could have painted these pictures without any of this accumulated knowledge?

Of course! Once having done it, you think: 'Why didn't I do it twenty years ago, thirty years ago? Why did I waste so much time agonising over it?'

So do books and pictures and all those '-isms' come into it at all for you?

We spend our lives searching for something and we keep on adding to our understanding of what it is. We read something or we hear something or we see something and we bank it. I've got hundreds of books on my shelves, for example, and most of them I've read; but only about half a dozen have really meant anything to me – and that half dozen I seem to have read over and over again. It's as if they contain vital clues to my goal in life, solutions to my quest. I think most people are like this. We go through life in search of something so particular that most of what we learn we reject, because it has nothing to do with what we're looking for. And then occasionally, inspiringly, we come across someone who is looking for the same thing or place that we are. On strolls in Portugal, I would sometimes find myself confronting a view, a spread of landscape, and feeling this was it. This was a special place. Like these *aediculae* are a special place for me, a suitable repository for the self. Both have been places I feel at home in.

What are the books you've most constantly reread?

Nietzsche's *Birth of Tragedy* and, less of a chestnut, Donnington's

Wagner's Ring. There is a description of how Wagner, in a reverie, found himself under water hearing the introduction to Rhinegold – the beginning of the Ring, of the 'poem', and itself an image of the beginning of everything in the gestating unconscious.

What about Bachelard?

Ah, he's another one! There's a passage in which he describes how a row of houses is connected by a subterranean system of passages – a wonderful metaphor for the ways of the subconscious. He often uses buildings as metaphors of thought. They are a persistent part of his mental imagery. This also made sense. I have often had architectural dreams – dreams in which buildings have figured in the most precise detail, particularly with regard to the edges of things – mouldings, door frames, windows – and in the relation of their size to mine. Often they seem rather small.

And yet the buildings in your pictures are very plain.

I've had several in which I've been wandering about in an extremely crowded district of a city with very narrow streets; and on one occasion, property speculators were buying up all the buildings – it appeared that the occupants had run away, leaving great piles of pictures, dreadful things like enormous Victorian photographs, blocking the streets. I was trying to get to some vital point in this chaotic city, but these horrible pictures blocked my path and the streets were a maze. In desperation, I ran into the empty houses and tried to find out where I was from their roofs, but the view from every roof was also blocked on every side by the walls of higher buildings.

That seems a particularly relevant dream, a metaphor of your artistic quest. You've painted reveries or visions, things seen when you were awake, but you've never painted a dream seen in sleep have you?

No, I never have.

Your pictures have a dreamlike quality for me, but would you agree you are much more of an existentialist than a surrealist?

An existentialist, definitely.

You gave me a title for a catalogue introduction I once wrote for you: 'Time is a shallow stage'. Would you still agree with the view that you had then that the illusion of depth in pictures speaks of optimism and control, and flatness of its opposite, for instance? And the way this relates to time. If the subject of your art was to be described in a word that would be 'Time', wouldn't it be fair to say?

I think so, yes. Panofsky pointed out that in the Renaissance, artists introduced perspective, a measurable space, into pictures because time had become measurable. This meant that the notion of future and past time was made believable and practical, which in turn had all sorts of socioeconomic results. Inherited wealth became possible, for instance, and vertical mobility, socially speaking, replaced the brutish battles for kingship. Now, what we've had in the twentieth century is an abrupt reminder of our own imminent disaster. The piecemeal destruction of a whole generation of Europe's fittest young men traumatised our century at its outset, since when we have progressed relentlessly to our present point of apparently no military return. So, to reverse Panofsky's principle, it might be said that the lack of a credible future explains the flatness of modern painting, because we've been forced into thinking principally of the present. I believe in the continuity of life, enough at least to allow myself a shallow space – but there's an emphatic back wall in my paintings – no distant horizons.

So you view the future with some hope, but the times we live in have restricted that hope?

Yes. With regard to time, though, I think it's also worth pointing out that my drawings always have the date on which they were drawn, clearly inscribed. In a manifesto I drew up in my Slade days, I found that one of its injunctions was 'Make a note of the date'. Twenty years later, I always found I did.

Why?

It enforced the notion that my art is not about life or society in general. It is about me – my life, my world. The date just emphasises that this was the way I felt about things at that particular time. Space implies time and time implies events – a drama. Painting since the Renaissance has shown us an instant in time, a moment in the drama, when figures are seen. Time is implied if the image is still, landscape, still life, Vermeer's stationary figures, but when figures are in movement, it is difficult to suggest a sequence of events. I never saw figures in my visions, but they seemed dramatic at the time. I don't know what to make of that.

You are not a religious man in the sense that you believe in life after death, are you?

I do not believe in everlasting life.

So, to take your Panofskian interpretation one step further, do you think it's fair to say that the spatial flatness or shallowness of modern painting also denotes materialism – in other words, the opposite of religious faith?

I think you could draw that deduction from my work, certainly. Religious faith has various aspects – a belief in God, prayer, ritual and ceremony, a moral code, the sense of the sacred, a mystical relationship with nature – you have to accept the lot to be religious. I don't. But as well as that inner reality, I have found myself aware also of those images that have been insistent, that others recognise and which we might call archetypal because they are more than coincidental. A sense of the numinous takes us further than humanist ethics. When we enter caverns measureless to man, we are already treading a path also to religious experience. I have been too timid, in the event, to do more than peep at what might be there. I would like another go.

CHRONOLOGY

1928 Born to George and Irene Willing on 15 January in Alexandria, Egypt, where George is stationed as a professional soldier.

1932 Family returns to the UK, living in various south-western towns, until settling more permanently in Guildford.

1940–5 Attends the Royal Grammar School, Guildford.

1946–8 National Military Service, including in Northern Ireland and Dover.

1948–9 Studies sculpture at the Guildford School of Art under Willi Soukop. A fellow student is Elisabeth Frink.

1949–53 Studies at the Slade School of Art in London. His arrival coincides with William Coldstream's first year as director of the Slade. Fellow students include Craigie Aitchison, Euan Uglow, Michael Andrews, Myles Murphy, and Paula Rego.

1949 Victor is fascinated by a Francis Bacon exhibition and invites him to talk at the Slade. They become friends.

1951 Marries Hazel Whittington, his girlfriend from their teens. They separate in 1956.

1955 Solo exhibition at Hanover Gallery, which is well received.

Meets Samuel Beckett through fellow Slade alumnus and theatre designer Peter Snow. Beckett asks him about a picture that intrigues him, and Vic describes it as about a lone man listening to tape recordings of himself.

1956 Moves to Portugal to be with Paula Rego and their newborn daughter Caroline. They live in her family's *quinta* in Ericeira and set up adjoining studios in a former grape-pressing barn in the grounds.

1959 Second daughter Victoria born.

1961 Son Nicholas born.

1962 Suffers a heart attack while out walking the dog in the grounds of the *quinta*. He is thirty-four.

1957–64 Lives a fairly isolated life in Portugal. He receives welcome visits from artist friends, including Andrew Forge, Peter Snow, and his closest friend from the Slade, Michael Andrews.

1966 Victor's father dies, as does his father-in-law, whose electronics business in Lisbon he subsequently commits to running.

He is diagnosed with multiple sclerosis, the symptoms of which will not be fully manifest for a few years.

1974 The family settles permanently in Camden Town, London. The collapse of the electronics business will eventually lead to the loss of the beloved *quinta* in Ericeira and financial hardship.

1976–80 Returns to painting, renting a studio in east London and creating a series of paintings drawn from 'hallucinations' – visions he is now experiencing and translating onto paper or canvas straight away.

1978 Exhibition at AIR Gallery, London.

1980 Receives the Thorne Scholarship.

1982 Exhibition at the Serpentine Gallery, London.

Becomes artist-in-residence at Corpus Christi College and Kettle's Yard, Cambridge.

1983–8 Continues to work, now at home in Hampstead due to his multiple sclerosis.

1986 A retrospective exhibition at the Whitechapel Art Gallery, curated by then director Nicholas Serota.

1987 Exhibition of his final paintings, *Heads*, at Karsten Schubert, London.

1988 Dies at home on 1 June, with Paula and their children around him. He is sixty.

Solo exhibitions

1955 *Paintings by Victor Willing*, Hanover Gallery, London (6 September – 1 October)

1978 *Paintings by Victor Willing*, AIR Gallery, London (6 – 28 October)

1980 *Paintings by Victor Willing*, House Gallery, London (15 September – 12 October)

1982 *Victor Willing: Drawings and Paintings*, Bernard Jacobson Gallery, London (16 October – 30 December)

Paintings by Victor Willing, Serpentine Gallery, London (23 October – 21 November)

1983 *Victor Willing: Paintings Since 1978*, Kettle's Yard, Cambridge (15 January – 20 February)

Victor Willing: Drawings, Hobson Gallery, Cambridge (15 January – 20 February)

Victor Willing: Paintings, Bernard Jacobson Gallery, New York City (May)

Victor Willing: Paintings, Bernard Jacobson Gallery, Los Angeles (September)

1984 *Victor Willing: Recent Paintings*, Bernard Jacobson Gallery, London (26 April – 29 May)

1985 *Victor Willing: Recent Work*, Bernard Jacobson Gallery, London (22 October – 27 November)

1986 *Victor Willing: A Retrospective Exhibition 1952–85*, Whitechapel Art Gallery, London (6 June – 20 July)

1987 *Victor Willing: Recent Paintings*, Karsten Schubert, London (20 October – 14 November)

2000 *Victor Willing*, Marlborough Fine Arts, London

2008–9 *Victor Willing: Revelations, Discoveries, Communications*, Pallant House Gallery, Chichester

2010 *Victor Willing: A Retrospective*, Casa Das Histórias Paula Rego, Cascais, Portugal (September – January 2011)

2019 *Victor Willing: Visions*, Hastings Contemporary, Hastings (October – January 2020)

Selected group exhibitions

1952 *Nine Young Painters*, Institute of Contemporary Arts, London (October – November)

New Trends in Realist Painting, Institute of Contemporary Arts, London (July – August)

1956 New Burlington Galleries, London

1962 *Arts Council as Patron*, Arts Council Gallery, London (April – May)

1962–5 *New Paintings 1958–1961*, Arts Council of Great Britain, Torbay Art Society, Torquay, and tour

Paintings 1950–1957, Arts Council of Great Britain, Upper Mill Library, Saddleworth, Oldham, and tour

1979 *British Art Show*, Arts Council of Great Britain, Graves Art Gallery, Sheffield, and tour

1980 *Pictures for an Exhibition*, Whitechapel Art Gallery, London (March – May)

Summer Exhibition, Blond Fine Art, London (July – September)

Whitechapel Open, Whitechapel Art Gallery, London (August)

1981 *Summer Exhibition*, Blond Fine Art, London (July – September)

The Subjective Eye, Midland Group Gallery, Nottingham, and tour (October)

1981–2 *Winter Exhibition*, Blond Fine Art, London (December 1981 – January 1982)

1982–6 *Inner Worlds*, Arts Council of Great Britain, E. M. Flint Gallery, Walsall, and tour

1982 *British Drawing, Hayward Annual*, Hayward Gallery, London (July – August)

Summer Show, Bernard Jacobson Gallery, London (August – September)

1984 *British Art Show, Old Allegiances and New Directions*, Arts Council of Great Britain, Mappin Art Gallery, Sheffield, and tour

1984–7 *New Works on Paper*, British Council, Warsaw, Poland, and tour

1985 *Hayward Annual*, Hayward Gallery, London (May – June)

'3 x 14' Mixed Summer Show, Bernard Jacobson Gallery, London (July – September)

1985–6 *Preview 1986*, Bernard Jacobson Gallery, London (December 1985 – January 1986)

1986 *Surprises in Store: Twentieth Century British Painting from the Rugby Collection*, University of Warwick, Coventry (May – June)

2010–18 Various exhibitions at Casa Das Histórias Paula Rego, Cascais, Portugal

Public collections

Arts Council Collection, London, United Kingdom

British Council, London, United Kingdom

Casa Das Histórias Paula Rego, Cascais, Portugal

Gracefield Arts Centre, Dumfries and Galloway, Scotland, United Kingdom

Pallant House Gallery, Chichester, United Kingdom

Royal College of Art, London, United Kingdom

Rugby Art Gallery and Museum, Rugby, United Kingdom

Saatchi Gallery, London, United Kingdom

Tate, London, United Kingdom

UCL Art Museum, London, United Kingdom

Writings by the artist

'Travel by bus: A brief manifesto', December 1954

'Goya', lecture, Royal College of Art, 1954

'Thoughts after a car crash: Note after the death of Jackson Pollock', *Encounter*, October 1956, no. 37, pp. 66–9

'*Exhibition of German Art (1910–30)*, Marlborough Gallery', review, British Broadcasting Corporation, December 1959

'Poets and painters', lecture, Bath Academy of Art, Corsham, 1964

'Morality and the model: Conversation with Michael Andrews', *Art and Literature*, 1964, no. 2, pp. 49–65

'The necessity of the forbidden in drama', series of six lectures at the Slade School of Art, 1965:

1. Initiation and ritual in New Guinea; Greek religious ritual; origins of drama; Nietzsche
2. Tragedy and comedy: Contrasting masks; Lear and the fool; *Commedia dell'Arte*
3. Hamlet and the Ghost; The Grail quest
4. *Marat/Sade*: The Peter Brook production; Artaud and 'The Theatre of Cruelty'
5. Jarry and *Ubu Roi*; Guignol
6. Genet; Beckett; the Abyss

'The floating world' (Symbolism to Surrealism), series of six lectures at the Chelsea School of Art, 1966: Lautréamont, Wagner, Monet, Baudelaire, Mallarmé, Debussy, Rodin, Gauguin, Rimbaud, Redon, Apollinaire, Diaghilev, Stravinsky, Moreau, Matisse, de Chirico, Breton, Ernst, Masson, Picasso, Miró, Bataille; illustrated with slides and tapes of music and poetry

'What kind of art education? An introduction, and conversations with Herbert Read, Professor Misha Black and Richard Hamilton', *Studio International*, London, September 1966, vol. 172, no. 881, pp. 131–9

'The imagiconography of Paula Rego', *Coloquio Artes*, April 1971, vol. 2, pp. 43–50

'Opaque perception: The painting of Euan Uglow', *Art Monthly*, December 1977 – January 1978, no. 13, pp. 15–16

'Now', *Victor Willing: Paintings Since 1978*, exhibition catalogue, Kettle's Yard, Cambridge, October 1982

'Paula Rego', *Paula Rego*, Arnolfini, Bristol, 1983

'Notes on *Place with a Red Thing and Rien*', *Illustrated Catalogue of Acquisitions*, Tate Gallery, London, 1984, pp. 221–2

'Masks', December 1984

'Walking-Wounded', 1985

'Water: Fire', 1985

'Blood', 1986

Writings on the artist

Lawrence Alloway, 'Art news from London', *Artnews*, September 1955, vol. 54, no. 5, p. 56, illustrated: *Man at a Table*

'Mr Willing's first one man show, a gifted painter', *The Times*, 9 September 1955

John Russell, *Sunday Times*, 11 September 1955

Alan Clutton-Brock, 'Round the London galleries', *Listener*, 15 September 1955, vol. LIV, no. 1385, p. 430, illustrated: *Man with a Kitten* (now destroyed)

Helmut Wohl, 'Victor Willing: Paintings', *Art Monthly*, December 1977 – January 1978, no. 20, pp. 15–16, illustrated: *Green Drape* (drawing)

John McEwen, 'Figurative', *Spectator*, 21 October 1978, vol. 241, no. 7842, p. 29

James Heard, 'Barbara Delaney and Victor Willing', *Arts Review*, 27 October 1978, vol. XXX, no. 21, p. 582

Michael Shepherd, 'Well met', *Sunday Telegraph*, 6 April 1980

William Packer, 'Whitechapel Open', *Financial Times*, 12 August 1980

Sarah Kent, 'Visual Arts', *Time Out*, 15–21 August 1980, no. 539, p. 35

Sarah Kent, 'Visual Arts', *Time Out*, 19–25 September 1980, no. 544, p. 75

John McEwen, 'Dreamlike', *Spectator*, 20 September 1980, vol. 245, no. 7941, p. 26

Sarah Wittekind, 'Up Front', *Observer*, 21 September 1980

Peter Davies, 'Victor Willing', *Arts Review*, 26 September 1980, vol. XXXII, no. 19, pp. 419–20

John McEwen, *Art Monthly*, October 1980, no. 40, pp. 17–18, illustrated: *Place with a Red Thing*

Fenella Crichton, 'The Gene Pool', *Art and Artists*, October 1981, no. 181, p. 30, illustrated: *Mother*

Matthew Collings, 'Summer Show at Blond', *Artscribe*, October 1981, no. 31, p. 54

Sarah Kent, 'Visual Arts', *Time Out*, 1–7 January 1982

John McEwen, 'Drawback', *Spectator*, 24 July 1982, vol. 249, no. 8037, p. 26

John McEwen, 'The Hayward Annual', *Art Monthly*, September 1982, no. 59, p. 2

Max Wykes-Joyce, 'Contemporary Choice and Victor Willing', *Arts Review*, 5 October 1982, vol. XXXIV, no. 23, p. 580

John McEwen, 'Singular', *Spectator*, 6 October 1982, vol. 249, no. 8052, p. 33

Sarah Kent, 'Visual Arts', *Time Out*, 5–11 November 1982, no. 637, p. 82, illustrated: *Plants*

Waldemar Januszczak, 'Serpentine Gallery', *Guardian*, 5 November 1982

Michael Shepherd, 'Breaking the Rules', *What's On in London*, 12 November 1982

John McEwen, 'Time as a shallow stage', *Victor Willing: Paintings Since 1978*, exhibition catalogue, Kettle's Yard, Cambridge, 1982

John McEwen, 'Victor Willing', *Spectator*, 29 January 1983, vol. 250, no. 8064, p. 26

John McEwen, 'Report from London: Art in the Year of the Falklands', *Art in America*, February 1983, p. 21

Alexandra Anderson, 'Victor Willing', *Harpers and Queen*, February 1983, p. 135

Sarah Jones, 'Victor Willing', *Arts Review*, 4 February 1983, vol. XXXV, no. 2, pp. 51–2

Sarah Wilson, 'Victor Willing', *Artscribe*, March – April 1983, no. 40, pp. 51–2, illustrated: *Tatters*

Lewis Biggs, 'Victor Willing, Paintings since 1978', *Aspects*, Spring 1983, no. 22, illustrated: *Night*

Alexander Moffat, 'Retrieving the Image', *British Art Show*, catalogue, Arts Council of Great Britain, 1984, p. 125

Sarah Kent, 'Visual Arts', *Time Out*, 17–23 May 1984, no. 717, p. 95

'Youth Allowed to Shine or Scowl', *The Times*, 27 November 1984

Lynne Cooke, 'Victor Willing', *Art of Our Time: The Saatchi Collection*, vol. 4, Lund Humphries, London, 1984

Alistair Hicks, *Spectator*, 2 March 1985

Nigel Greenwood, 'A Journey through contemporary art with Nigel Greenwood', *Hayward Annual*, catalogue, Arts Council of Great Britain, 1985, pp. 20–1, illustrated: *22. 9.84* (drawing)

Waldemar Januszczak, 'The Annual Argument', *Guardian*, 15 May 1985

William Feaver, 'One Man Annual', *Observer*, 19 May 1985

William Packer, 'Hayward's One Man Show', *Financial Times*, 21 May 1985

Richard Cork, 'Remote Regions', *Listener*, 30 May 1985, vol. 113, no. 2911, p. 37

Peter Fuller, 'The Hayward Annual', *Artscribe*, July – August 1985, no. 53, pp. 54–6

Nena Dimitrijevic, 'London, Hayward Annual', *Flash Art*, Summer 1985

Alistair Hicks, 'Round the Galleries', *The Times*, 19 November 1985, p. 10, illustrated: *Head VI*

Lynne Cooke, 'Victor Willing', *Flash Art*, February – March 1986, no. 126, p. 55, illustrated: *Head VI*

Fiona Bradley (ed.), *Victor Willing*, Tate Publishing, London, 2000, with contributions from Lynne Cooke, John McEwen, John Mills, Paula Rego, and Nicholas Serota

Victor Willing: A Retrospective Catalogue, Casa Das Histórias Paula Rego, Cascais, 2010, with contributions from Helmut Wohl (curator), António d'Orey Capucho, Helena de Freitas, and John McEwen

ACKNOWLEDGMENTS

Victor Willing: Visions is an exhibition organized by Hastings Contemporary and The Estate of Victor Willing

With thanks to Nick, Victoria, and Cas Willing, Paula Rego, June and Mel Andrews, John Mills, and John McEwen.

Hastings Contemporary
Rock-a-Nore Road
Hastings Old Town
TN34 3DW
www.hastingscontemporary.org

Hastings Contemporary brings a dynamic programme of contemporary and modern art to the South East. The gallery presents a broad range of works by historically important and internationally renowned artists and emerging practitioners, as well as exploring the rich cultural history of artists from the region and further afield in the UK.

Registered Charity No. 1150383

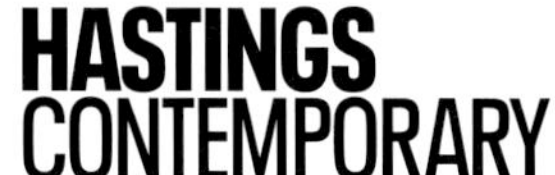

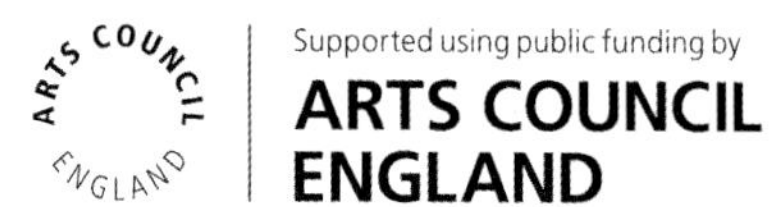

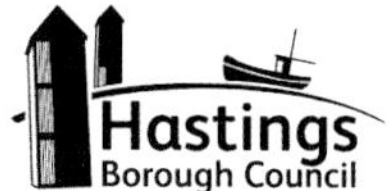